# Multinational Firms, Cooperation and Competition in the World Economy

# Multinational Firms, Cooperation and Competition in the World Economy

Peter J. Buckley

First published in Great Britain 2000 by
**MACMILLAN PRESS LTD**
Houndmills, Basingstoke, Hampshire RG21 6XS and London
Companies and representatives throughout the world

A catalogue record for this book is available from the British Library.

ISBN 0-333-75977-X

---

First published in the United States of America 2000 by
**ST. MARTIN'S PRESS, LLC,**
Scholarly and Reference Division,
175 Fifth Avenue, New York, N.Y. 10010

ISBN 0-312-22900-3

Library of Congress Cataloging-in-Publication Data
Multinational firms, cooperation and competition in the world economy / [editor] Peter J. Buckley
p. cm.
Includes bibliographical references and index.
ISBN 0-312-22900-3 (cloth)
1. International business enterprises. 2. Investments, Foreign. 3. International trade. I. Buckley, Peter J., 1949–
HD2755.5 .M83444 2000
338.8′8—dc21 99-054659

---



Please see the Preface and Acknowledgements for full details of original publication.



This book is printed on paper suitable for recycling and made from fully managed and sustained forest sources.

Printed in Great Britain by
Antony Rowe Ltd, Chippenham, Wiltshire

For Alice (again!)

# Contents

*Foreword by V. N. Balasubramanyam* ix
*Preface and Acknowledgements* xii
*Notes on the Contributors* xiii

1 Introduction 1

**PART I THEORY OF THE MULTINATIONAL ENTERPRISE**

2 Models of the Multinational Enterprise 9
*with Mark C. Casson*

3 The Investment Development Path: The Case of Portugal 44
*with Francisco B. Castro*

**PART II FOREIGN DIRECT INVESTMENT AND FOREIGN MARKET SERVICING STRATEGY**

4 Analyzing Foreign Market Entry Strategies: Extending the Internalization Approach 61
*with Mark C. Casson*

5 Atlantic Foreign Direct Investment Flows 94
*with Jeremy Clegg*

6 Transfer Pricing and Economic Functions Analysis: The Japanese Paradigm 123
*with Jane Frecknall-Hughes*

7 Foreign Direct Investment in Japan: Theoretical Explanation and Evidence from European Direct Investors 144

**PART III INTERNATIONAL COOPERATION: JOINT VENTURES AND ALLIANCES**

8 Measures of Performance in UK International Alliances 157
*with Keith W. Glaister*

9 Management–Performance Relationships in UK Joint Ventures 201
*with Keith W. Glaister*

10 The Use of Native Categories in Management Research 235
*with Malcolm Chapman*

11 The Management of Cooperative Strategies in R&D and Innovation Programmes 269
*with Malcolm Chapman*

12 Cross-Border Governance in Multinational Enterprises 289

*People Index* 305
*Subject Index* 309

# Foreword

Peter Buckley describes himself (Chapter 10 in this book) as 'English, English-speaking, male, white, middle class (at least by adoption) and well educated (at least by some measures)'. He is English by birth, but also ebullient, irrepressible and outspoken; English-speaking, but also at home in the lingua of cultural anthropologists, sociologists and management speak; middle class, by conventional standards, but indisputably an upper-class Brahmin among scholars of his subject (by acclaim); well educated, yes, not on some but most measures including the rigorous standards of the professional economist. Peter is one of the rare breed of economists who is at home among both the professional economists and management specialists. He cannot be dismissed as an economist far removed from the real world preoccupied with mathematical models and futile econometric exercises or as a positivist – the usual opprobrium heaped on economists in business schools. The one feature which runs through Peter's copious work on the multinational enterprise and foreign direct investment is his ability to build bridges between his chosen discipline and other areas of inquiry, be it sociology, history or his new-found love – social anthropology. This he does with an expert eye for intellectual insights other disciplines can offer, with none of the disdain economists are supposed to entertain for other related disciplines and with candour and good grace when it comes to acknowledging the limitations of economics.

This collection of Peter Buckley's essays, several written with colleagues from other disciplines and with fellow economists, is a testimony to his ability to extend the analytical tool-kit of the economist to embrace methods of analysis developed by other social science disciplines. The agenda Peter outlines for this endeavour is ambitious. It would be all too easy to reject the framework of economics grounded in assumptions of rationality and profit maximization in favour of observation, interpretation, case studies and narration. It would also be tempting to assert that each and every phenomenon, be it technology transfer, the joint-venture process or foreign direct investment in Japan, can be analysed with the traditional tools of the economist such as transaction cost economics. Peter Buckley rejects both of these easy options in favour of the much more challenging one. It is to borrow from other disciplines and integrate the insights they offer with the traditional rigorous framework of economics, and analyse and explain a wide variety of issues associated with the multinational enterprise. And, even when he chooses to operate within the confines of his chosen discipline, he is intent on extending the analysis in new directions.

The essay on the theory of the multinational enterprise (co-authored with Mark Casson) provides a splendid example of his attempt to incorporate uncertainty generated by volatility in international markets in analysing flexible and novel strategies of international market penetration adopted by multinational enterprises.

Each of the essays in the book attests to Peter's powers of analysis and exposition, his ability to forge successful joint ventures with colleagues from economics and other disciplines and his keen eye for evolving issues in need of investigation. The essay which I savoured and read with growing admiration for my former pupil is the one with the intriguing title 'The Use of Native Categories in Management Research', co-authored with Malcolm Chapman, a social anthropologist. This cannot have been an easy essay to write for either of the two authors, nor is it an easy read. The message of the essay, though, is worth pondering. It is that it is essential to understand concepts and phenomena such as alliances, partnerships, trust and understanding as perceived and understood by people who belong to a category (native category) such as managers, and not as defined in advance by researchers and management consultants. The essay attempts to reconcile this sort of a paradigm of the anthropologist with that of transaction cost economics.

The essays in the volume provide a blend of theoretical rigour and incisive analysis of variety of issues and recent developments in the global economy. They are informative and often entertaining, but they are also provocative and controversial, as is to be expected from Peter Buckley.

V. N. BALASUBRAMANYAM
*Professor of Development Economics*
*Lancaster University*

# Preface and Acknowledgements

I would like to thank my co-authors for their help and encouragement – and for permission to print our joint work here.

The authors and publishers are grateful for permission to reproduce copyright material as follows: Chapter 2 first appeared in *Journal of International Business Studies*, 29, 1, 1998; Chapter 3 in *Transnational Corporations*, 7, 1, 1998; Chapter 4 in *Journal of International Business Studies*, 29, 3, 1998; Chapter 5 in Gavin Boyd (ed.), *The Struggle for World Markets* published by Edward Elgar, Cheltenham, in 1998; Chapter 6 in *Applied Economics*, 30, 5, 1998; Chapter 7 in Noritake Kobayashi (ed.), *Management: A Global Perspective*, published by the Japan Times (Tokyo) in 1997; Chapter 8 in *Organization Studies*, 19, 1, 1998; Chapter 9 in *International Business Review*, 7, 3, 1998; Chapter 10 in *British Journal of Management*, 8, 4, 1998; Chapter 11 in *International Journal of the Economics of Business*, 5, 3, 1998; and Chapter 12 in Kevin Keasey, Steve Thompson and Mike Wright (eds), *Corporate Governance: Economic, Management and Financial Issues*, Oxford University Press, 1997.

I would also like to thank Sheila Fordham, the Secretary of CIBUL, for her help and forbearance.

# Notes on the Contributors

**Mark Casson** is Professor of Economics, University of Reading.

**Francisco Barros Castro** is Lecturer at Faculdade de Economia do Porto and Researcher in the Centre for International Business, University of Leeds (CIBUL)

**Malcolm Chapman** is Senior Lecturer in International Business, Centre for International Business, University of Leeds (CIBUL).

**Jeremy Clegg** is Jean Monnet Senior Lecturer in European Integration and International Business Management, Centre for International Business, University of Leeds (CIBUL).

**Jane Frecknall-Hughes** is Lecturer in Accounting, Leeds University Business School.

**Keith Glaister** is Professor of International Strategic Management, Leeds University Business School.

# 1 Introduction

In the rapidly developing world economy, it is vital to update the analytical basis of our knowledge. This book is a contribution to that endeavour. It contains eleven articles published in 1997 and 1998 written by myself and six co-authors.

This is the seventh book in my series of 'greatest hits', as Bob Pearce calls them, although the first was a joint effort with my long-term collaborator, Mark Casson.[1] In that time both the multinational enterprise (MNE) and the world economy in which it operates have developed greatly. Much of this volume tracks the developments towards a 'global economy' and the analytical progress necessary to understand globalization. The volume is organized under three headings – the theory of the multinational enterprise, foreign direct investment (FDI) and foreign market servicing strategy and international cooperation in joint ventures and alliances.

## THEORY OF THE MULTINATIONAL ENTERPRISE

Chapter 2, co-authored with Mark Casson, attempts to update our analytical model of the multinational enterprise. Since Buckley and Casson (1976), the 'internalization view' of multinational enterprises has become a standard means of explaining the growth of such firms, by reference to the market alternative. Chapter 2 examines the concept of flexibility as a key element of a modern approach to strategy in MNEs. The argument of this chapter is that the volatility in the world economy is increasing and the more rapid transmission of shocks means that costs are imposed on firms which are slow to react to the resultant changes in markets and in cost conditions. The search for flexibility places a premium on certain types of location and ownership decisions. Flexibility implies that foreign ventures be treated as 'real options' where the value of the option resides in its ability to be used or reversed. Thus firms envisage a sequence of strategic moves and avoid being 'locked-in' prematurely to any given choice. This has important implications for the interaction between strategic moves and knowledge acquisition. The 'knowledge content' of decisions, feeding back to improved subsequent decisions is an increasingly important component of strategy. Flexibility may imply an increased attention being paid to joint ventures and alliances but also (as the long example on pp. 36–40 shows) to 'hub and spoke' operations across regional markets.

Chapter 3 is a revisiting of the investment development path (IDP) for the case of Portugal, co-authored by Francisco Barros Castro. The IDP was developed at Reading in the mid-1970s by John Dunning, Bob Pearce and myself (see note 1 to Chapter 3, p. 56). John Dunning went on to refine and develop it and it reappeared in my work in the late 1990s in the Portuguese context. This chapter suggests a reformulation of the model and the IDP is assessed with regard to the light that it sheds on competitiveness. Care is needed to apply it in a time period when political and economic changes (such as EFTA and EU membership) are profound.

## FOREIGN DIRECT INVESTMENT AND FOREIGN MARKET SERVICING STRATEGY

The explanation of foreign direct investment and its choice from among the potential modes of servicing a foreign market has been a parallel line of enquiry to the theory of the MNE for over 20 years. The choice of internalized (FDI) versus market (licensing) mode of doing business abroad is a key empirical issue in international business. Chapter 4 (again, co-authored with Mark Casson) is an attempt to revisit the key issues in a rigorous, theoretical fashion.

Chapter 5 relates the theory of foreign direct investment to trans-Atlantic flows. These flows, in the context of deepening integration on both sides of the Atlantic, through the European Union and NAFTA, provide an interesting case study and a springboard for future research with my CIBUL colleague, Jeremy Clegg. There is much research remaining to be done on the location strategies of multinationals with expanding regional blocs. There are signs of 'hub and spoke' operations of the kind envisaged in Chapter 2, already emerging in NAFTA and the EU.

The internal operational decisions of multinational firms are of great importance for the world economy, especially when it is recalled that around 50 per cent of world trade is internal to multinational firms. This internal trade takes place at 'transfer prices' set by the firm rather than at market prices. Chapter 6 is the second in a series of articles on the transfer pricing strategy of multinational firms (with Jane Frecknall-Hughes). This piece examines the difficulties of tax authorities facing prices which reflect intangible asset services and group-wide decision-making. It highlights a problem when transactions-based valuations are used in these circumstances.

Japan is the subject of Chapter 7, which examines the low level of FDI into Japan from a theoretical perspective. It suggests that internalization theory is capable of explaining this phenomenon when the barriers to inward FDI in Japan are taken into account. These barriers include difficulties in internalizing intermediate goods markets, cultural barriers, intensive levels of competition, 'process issues' (including barriers to takeover) and the relative competitive weaknesses of incoming firms.

## INTERNATIONAL COOPERATION: JOINT VENTURES AND ALLIANCES

Chapters 8 and 9 examine international joint ventures and alliances from an empirical point of view. These papers, co-authored with Keith Glaister, focus on measures of performance, partner selection criteria and management issues in UK joint ventures. Joint ventures and alliances allow a focus on relatively unconventional variables in international business theorizing (see also Chapter 4) and enable the analyst to highlight management and process issues within the firm.

The next two chapters of this section are co-authored by Malcolm Chapman and are derived from our ESRC-funded project 'The Management of Cooperative Strategies'. Chapter 10 examines the key notion of 'native categories' in management research – attempting to conceptualize the world in the way in which the key actors (managers, in this case) see it, rather than imposing pre-existing researcher categories on their discourse. Chapter 11 considers the issue of cooperative strategies in research and development and innovation generally. It examines the choice of 'in-house' versus external contract R&D and finds this choice to be a complex one, where uncertainty looms large. Repeated transactions, as a key mode of building trust, are found to be of great importance and strong relationships between managers in different companies assumed much more importance than specific assets and 'up front' asset costs.

The final chapter examines issues of governance in multinational enterprises. The incidence of internal transactions costs (agency costs) and cultural issues are found to be important determinants of governance structures in multinational firms. A sequence of solutions to problems of governance costs have been attempted by managers in multinational firms including divisionalization, matrix structures, strategic business units, alliances and joint ventures. International elements complicate governance costs as they arise from the increased resource costs of managing complex internal markets and higher communication costs.

## CONCLUSION

It is right that, theoretically and in research method, international business should be a broad church. The study of the multinational firm should feed back to the theory of the firm in general, in the way that international economics has often played a pioneering role in introducing new concepts into the main body of economics. Notions of cultural distance, commitment, trust and management processes are beginning to become accepted as determinants of the firm's behaviour. As cooperative behaviour becomes more widely acknowledged as a key element in business activities, so the innovations of international business theory need wider recognition.

The issue of knowledge management is currently one of the hottest topics in management research. Again, international business theory has much to offer, as it was the value of internationally transferred knowledge which theorists, long ago in the 1950s and 1960s, saw as giving crucial competitive advantages to multinational firms. The importance of firms' ability to combine knowledge across nations, cultures and technologies is again at the forefront of research and this development again illustrates the centrality of the international dimension of business activities.

## Note

1. They are:

   Peter J. Buckley and Mark Casson (1985) *The Economic Theory of the Multinational Enterprise*, Macmillan.
   Peter J. Buckley (1989) *The Multinational Enterprise: Theory and Applications*, Macmillan.
   Peter J. Buckley (1992) *Studies in International Business*, Macmillan.
   Peter J. Buckley (1995) *Foreign Direct Investment and Multinational Enterprises*, Macmillan.
   Peter J. Buckley (1998) *International Business: Economics and Anthropology, Theory and Method*, Macmillan.
   Peter J. Buckley (1998) *International Strategic Management and Government Policy*, Macmillan.

# Part I

# Theory of the Multinational Enterprise

# 2 Models of the Multinational Enterprise*

Peter J. Buckley and Mark C. Casson

**Flexibility is identified as the hallmark of recent modelling of the multinational enterprise. The focus on flexibility is a response to the rationalization and restructuring of international business, which has occurred since the end of the 'golden age' of Western economic growth. Flexibility has been sought in factor markets, intermediate product markets and markets for final products. It has been sought by both governments and firms. Flexible firms are attracted to locations with flexible host governments. This contrasts the modern research agenda based on flexibility with the more traditional research agenda which predominates in the literature reviewed by Caves (1996).**

## INTRODUCTION

The appearance of a major work of survey and synthesis, which goes into successive editions (Caves, 1996), is a clear sign that a subject has reached maturity. Maturity can sometimes indicate stagnation, however, and so the question naturally arises as to whether stagnation has set in to international business research. Caves' second edition is an encyclopaedic work, but it is very much like the first edition in its general structure. Only the details have been modified in the light of recent research.

This chapter argues that any impression of stagnation is misleading. Rather than quibble over a number of minor details of Caves' exposition, this chapter makes a single substantive

* First published in *Journal of International Business Studies*, 29, 1 (1998).

point. It identifies a new research agenda for modelling multinational enterprises (MNEs) which is not fully reflected in Caves' work. This agenda has emerged over the last ten years. It is difficult to recognize because its various components have not yet coalesced. It is nevertheless unfortunate that Caves has failed to emphasize its significance in his recent revision of his book.

## MODELS OF MULTINATIONAL ENTERPRISES

The new agenda emphasizes dynamic issues. It highlights the uncertainty that is generated by volatility in the international business environment. To cope with volatility, corporate strategies have to be flexible, and flexibility can be achieved by several means. New dimensions of corporate strategy therefore have to be recognized. Efficient information processing is crucial to cope with the resultant increase in the complexity of decision-making. This has important implications for the organizational structure of the MNE, and for the motivation of its managerial employees. The new agenda spells out these implications in a rigorous fashion.

The traditional agenda of Caves takes a more static view of international business. It focuses on:

- the nature of firm-specific competitive advantage;
- the choice of location of production; and
- the determination of the boundaries of the firm.

The classic application of the traditional agenda is to the foreign market entry decision. This agenda recognizes change, but interprets it as a sequence of independent one-off events, rather than as a continuous systemic process. Thus, entry into any given market is analyzed independently of entry into others, and each entry strategy tends to be evaluated in terms of its immediate effects rather than in terms of the new opportunities to which it may ultimately lead. The market entry issue will remain important; it has, indeed, received new impetus from the recent wave of foreign direct investment (FDI) into Central and Eastern European markets (Hood and Young, 1994). But the models of market entry developed in the 1970s remain too static to address the crucial issues of the 1990s, because they fail to take proper account of volatility.

This does not mean that static analysis is obsolete. Static analysis is much simpler than dynamic analysis, and for this reason the traditional static approach is a natural preliminary to the new dynamic one. A dynamic model always contains a static model as a special case, and the properties of this special case provide important clues as to whether the dynamic model is logically sound.

The new dynamic agenda focuses on:

- uncertainty and market volatility
- flexibility and the value of real options;
- cooperation through joint ventures and business networks;
- entrepreneurship, managerial competence and corporate culture; and
- organizational change, including the mandating of subsidiaries and the 'empowerment' of employees.

The stimulus for the new agenda was the end of the 'golden age' of Western economic growth, which came abruptly with the oil price shock of 1973–74 (Marglin and Schor, 1990). Lags in recognizing and interpreting the symptoms of this change caused its impact on academic literature to be delayed. The event marks a watershed in the post-war growth of Western MNEs. The intensification of international competition in the late 1970s had dramatic adverse effects on corporate profitability in the West. The focus of corporate strategy switched from entering new foreign markets to defending existing ones. International operations were restructured to drive down costs and improve supply responsiveness. Flexibility became the key to international competitiveness in the turbulent 1980s.

Flexibility is the *leitmotif* of the new agenda. It may be defined as the ability to reallocate resources quickly and smoothly in response to change. The significance of flexibility is greater, the greater is the amplitude and frequency of change in the environment. As far as MNEs are concerned, the impact of change is captured by the volatility induced in the profit stream. The volatility of profit that would occur if the firm made no response to change summarizes the impact on the firm of volatility in its environment.

Low volatility characterized the economic environment during most of the 'golden age'. The economic literature reviewed by Caves remains dominated by the experiences of this age. Selecting the most appropriate mode of entry into a foreign market remains the focus of attention. The international rationalization of production receives surprisingly little attention. While flexibility has been the focus of some of the most original research of the last decade, there is little sense of this in Caves' work.

Following a brief review of economic methodology, the chapter examines the factors underlying the end of the 'golden age'. With the aid of theory and the benefit of hindsight, it is shown how international business factors stimulated productivity growth in Asia and eventually undermined the competitiveness of the West. It is argued that the entry of new multinational producers, and a general commitment to continuous innovation, has increased volatility in global markets. It is shown that survival and prosperity in a volatile environment depend upon flexible response. This applies to nation states, to industrial regions and to individual firms. Flexible firms need to locate in flexible regions of nation states with flexible economic policies. In this way the forces of flexibility are continuously restructuring the world economy. To understand these forces properly, the traditional 'tool kit' of international business theory, as deployed in Caves, needs to be supplemented with new techniques. The article concludes by setting out the kind of economic modelling that is appropriate for building a new dynamic theory with flexibility at its core.

## METHODOLOGY: MODELS VERSUS FRAMEWORKS

The economic theory of international business attempts to answer practical questions in a rigorous way. This means making assumptions explicit – in particular, specifying the strategies available to each firm, and spelling out their details. Strict assumptions are used in order to simplify the analysis as much as possible. Simplicity provides logical transparency, and ensures that the results can be easily understood. This is the methodology employed by Caves, and adopted in this chapter.

Economists invoke the principle of rational action to predict the circumstances under which firms will choose a given strategy. The assumption of rationality is not a piece of misguided psychology, but a response to the practical need for simplicity (Buckley and Casson, 1993). When the firm's objective is profit maximization, the choice of strategy is driven by the firm's structure of revenues and costs. This is determined by the firm's environment. The identification of the key characteristics of this environment enables the firm's behavior to be modelled in a very parsimonious way. The predictions of the model emerge jointly from the profit maximization hypothesis, and the restrictions imposed by the modeller on the structure of revenues and costs. Predictive failure of the model is addressed by re-examining these restrictions and not by discarding the maximization principle that is at the core of the theory (Buckley, 1988).

This method can be contrasted with an alternative approach in international business which leaves the assumptions implicit and derives propositions from a discursive literature review. This dispenses with formal analysis and relies on synthesis. Unfortunately, a synthesis is no better than the analytical components from which it is built. The more complex the synthesis, the more important it is that each component is sound. The logic of rational action provides just the check on analytical consistency which is required.

The variables entering into the theory do not have to be of a strictly economic nature. The criterion for inclusion is that they are analyzed from a rational action point of view (Buckley and Chapman, 1996). A good illustration here is the analysis of international joint ventures (IJVs), where economic factors, such as market size, are supplemented by technological, legal, cultural and psychological factors to generate a satisfactory model (Geringer and Hebert, 1989).

The development of an economic model is often stimulated by the desire to explain certain 'stylized facts'. The traditional agenda, for example, sought to explain the predominance of US MNEs in high technology manufacturing industries during the 'golden age'. The new agenda seeks to explain the rise of IJVs after the end of the 'golden age'. Economic models offer a simple, yet rigorous, explanation of facts, which other approaches explain in more complicated and more heuristic terms. If economic models did no more than rationalize what everyone already knows, then their value would be limited, however. Fortunately, the way in which economic models are constructed means that they do not merely explain the facts which they were designed to deal with, but they also provide new predictions. It is their ability to draw attention to phenomena that have not been noticed and to integrate the explanation of these phenomena with explanations of already known phenomena, that is a true measure of their success.

It is instructive to contrast the methods of economics with those of strategic management (Porter, 1991) and development studies (Lall and Streeten, 1977). Porter contrasts 'models' and 'frameworks'. He sees the traditional method of economics as model-building which 'abstracts the complexity of competition to isolate a few key variables whose interactions are examined in depth' (Porter, 1991, p. 97). 'The applicability of any model's findings are almost inevitably restricted to a small subgroup of firms or industries whose characteristics fit the model's assumptions' (p. 98). Porter identifies the progress of strategic management with its ability to construct frameworks. 'Instead of models, however, the approach was to build frameworks. A framework, such as the competitive forces approach to analyzing industry structure, encompasses many variables and seeks to capture much of the complexity of actual competition' (p. 98). Frameworks are analogous to expert systems which are tailored to particular industries or companies. 'My own frameworks embody the notion of optimization, but no equilibrium in the normal sense of the word. Instead, there is a continually evolving environment in which a perpetual competitive interaction between rivals takes place. In addition, all the interactions among the many variables in the frameworks cannot be rigorously drawn.'

In contrast to Porter's support for frameworks rather than models, Krugman attributes the failure of development studies precisely to its rejection of rigorous models. Despite having identified important themes which are key to successful modelling of development issues – 'emphasis on strategic complementarity in investment decisions and on the problem of coordination failure' – development economists failed to explain them to academic colleagues and policy-makers in a coherent way (Krugman, 1995, p. 28).

According to Krugman, 'mainstream economic theory rests on two observations: obvious opportunities for gain are rarely left unexplored and things add up' (1995, p. 74). This formulation is similar to, but subtly different from, the two key principles put forward by Buckley and Casson (1993) – optimization and equilibrium. There is a difference between optimization and being self-interested. Buckley and Casson's formulation allows for objectives which are beyond self-interest or 'opportunities for gain'. These may include following ethical injunctions and pursuing altruistic sentiments. Similarly, the truism 'things add up' is valid only *ex post*, where it is true by definition. Things add up *ex ante* only in situations of equilibrium – and equilibrium may not always hold. Krugman's justification for this method is that 'what we do when we construct an economic model is to try to use these two principles to cut through the complexities of a situation. And the remarkable thing is how often that succeeds . . . the basic principles of economics tell us that there is an unexpected order in the outcome, which is quite independent of the details' (1995, p. 75).

A significant strength of Porter's framework is that it postulates continuous incremental change. Its weakness is that it does not analyse the strategic response to change in a rigorous way. The new agenda in economic modelling, being more dynamic than the old, addresses the point about continuous change head-on. Because of its economic logic, rigour is guaranteed. It is therefore not only a natural successor to the traditional agenda, but also a necessary refinement of Porter's work as well.

It could be argued, of course, that the insights of the new agenda should be simply grafted onto the old agenda, rather than developed in a distinct, but complementary, way. But forcing dynamic considerations into an essentially static context results in loss of simplicity (Buckley, 1983). Complex typologies must be developed to distinguish all of the special cases that arise – a process that can clearly be traced in the evolution of Dunning's eclectic theory in response to the growth of IJVs and 'resource-seeking' investment (Dunning,

1977, 1993). Once the complexity of the model approaches the complexity of the phenomena that it attempts to analyse, it ceases to function as a model, and becomes simply a description of the situation instead.

## THE END OF THE 'GOLDEN AGE'

During the 'golden age' of Western economic growth, trade was liberalized through GATT and through customs unions, such as the EEC and EFTA. US mass production technology was transferred through the internal markets of MNEs. Key European industries were transformed. Cheaper motor vehicles created a more mobile society. Female labour force participation increased. Cheaper consumer durables combined with higher incomes raised aspirations to historically unprecedented levels. Mass consumer demand fuelled demand for branded products, such as convenience foods. The glamour of U.S affluence made US marketing and advertising skills easy to transfer abroad.

The 'golden age' terminated suddenly with the oil price shock of 1973. Imports of manufactured goods from Japan and the newly industrializing countries (NICs) of South-East Asia quickly began to replace domestic production in Western markets – including motor vehicles, which had been one of the 'engines' of Western growth up to that point. The West woke up to the fact that for some time Asian firms had been systematically absorbing Western technologies, and adapting them to local conditions. The full consequences of international technology transfer and trade liberalization were finally being felt.

Traditional international business theory can easily explain how technology transfer to Asia was effected. However, the mechanisms were somewhat more varied than those emphasized by Caves. Technology transfer was effected on government initiative, as well as on the initiative of Western multinationals (Fransman, 1995). Licensing agreements and joint ventures were widely used. The domestic partner was often a 'national champion'. Once it had mastered the technology, the champion diffused it to other firms. Diffusion to other large firms was effected through social networking, factory visits and collaborative research. Diffusion to smaller firms was effected through subcontracting arrangements in which substantial training could be involved. Small firms could also play a direct role in pirating technologies that were easy to copy. 'Reverse engineering' was important too. Product designs were easier to imitate than technologies because patent protection was weaker, and 'me too' designs proliferated as a result.

The price advantage of Asian products stemmed from a number of factors. The weakness of trades unions (often as a direct consequence of political measures) maintained wages at competitive market-clearing levels (Mirza, 1986). The limited scope of social security gave a strong incentive to work. Government expenditure was concentrated on infrastructure investment, such as roads, ports, airports and telecommunications, which reduced the costs of intermediate inputs, such as transport. Investment in large container terminals cut the cost of shipping to Western markets, for example. Improved domestic communications facilitated 'just in time' production, which economized on inventory costs. Mass production was initiated from the outset to exploit economies of scale to the full. Temporary protection of the domestic market helped to build up demand quickly, and exporting commenced at the outset. A strong desire to save ensured that domestic demand did not crowd out export demand in the long run.

The contrast with the West is clear. During the 'golden age', Western public expenditure was focussed on fighting the 'Cold War' and on building a 'Great Society' or 'Welfare State'. Military expenditures and transfer payments to the poor crowded out productivity-enhancing investment. Rising taxes, it is alleged, discouraged work and risk-taking. The concept of a 'corporate economy' (Marris, 1979) institutionalized collective bargaining and legitimated union strike-threat power. Wage inflation and 'featherbedding' increased costs – particularly the costs of intermediate inputs like transport, which were supplied by highly unionized industries.

A similar set of factors explains why technology transfer succeeded in Asia, but failed in Africa. (The Latin American experience lies somewhere between these two extremes.) The deficiencies of European governments were mirrored in their former colonies in Africa. Industrial strategy was based on state-of-the-art technology applied to mega-projects rather than on the diffusion and incremental improvement of established techniques (Ergas, 1987). Competition for status between neighbouring nations encouraged lavish public expenditure, financed by foreign borrowing, which could not be repaid when projects failed. Foreign borrowing was also used to finance wars, as well as conspicuous consumption by the political elite. Corruption raised transaction costs. Inward-looking protectionist policies distorted domestic prices and inhibited agricultural development. Industry, though protected, failed to reap economies of scale because of the low growth of the domestic market. When Western MNEs retrenched in the 1970s, they therefore retreated from Africa in order to concentrate on defending their markets at home.

The lessons for international business theory are fairly clear. It is not sufficient to focus exclusively on the choice of mode when analyzing technology transfer. As Dunning (1997) has emphasized, full account must be taken of location factors, such as the structure of the host economy, the policies of the host government and the nature of local business culture, in explaining the comparative success and failure of FDI.

## FLEXIBILITY

Competition from Asia was a visible symbol of a less apparent, but more fundamental change in the business environment, namely, a persistent increase in the amount of volatility with which firms have to contend. Volatility has become much greater since the end of the 'golden age'. There are several reasons for this.

The international diffusion of modern production technology has increased the number of industrial powers, and hence increased the number of countries in which political and social disturbances can impact significantly on global supplies of manufactured products. The liberalization of trade and capital markets means that the 'ripple' effects of shocks travel farther and wider than before (Casson, 1995, chap. 4). Ripples are transmitted more quickly too: news travels almost instantaneously, thanks to modern telecommunications. Thus speculative bubbles in stock markets spread quickly around the world. Following the breakdown of the Bretton Woods system, exchange rate fluctuations have created a new dimension of financial volatility too.

As a result, any given national market is now affected by a much wider range of disturbances than ever before. Every national subsidiary of a MNE experiences a multiplicity of shocks from around the world. It is no longer the case that a national subsidiary has to respond to shocks originating in its national market alone. The shocks come from new sources of import competition and new competitive threats in export markets too. While most shocks reveal themselves to firms as competitive threats, new opportunities for cooperation may sometimes be presented as well. The awareness of this sustained increase in volatility has led to a search for more flexible forms of organization.

Increased volatility is not the only reason for greater interest in flexibility. Contemporary culture is very much opposed to building organizations around a single source of monopoly power. The nation state, for example, is under threat from advocates of regional government. The traditional role of the state, to supply defence, can in principle be effected through multilateral defence treaties in which politically independent regions club together for this specific purpose. The demise of the Soviet bloc, and the subsequent political realignment between its member states, may be seen as an example of this kind of cultural change at work. This distrust of monopoly power may be linked to an increase in other forms of distrust, as suggested below.

The aversion to internal monopoly is apparent amongst MNEs as well. This movement began in the early 1980s when the powerful central research laboratories of high-technology MNEs were either closed down, shifted to the divisions, or forced to operate as suppliers to 'internal customers' in competition with outside bodies, such as universities (Casson, Pearce and Singh, 1991). Headquarters' bureaucracies came under attack shortly afterwards, as 'de-layering' got under way. The favoured form of firm has become a federal structure of operating divisions drawing on a common source of internal expertise, but where each division belonging to the federation is free to out-source expertise if it so desires. As with any trend, there has been a tendency for certain advocates to take it to extremes. Just as the 'golden age' was rife with suggestions that oligopolies of hierarchical MNEs would come to dominate world markets, so the 1990s have spawned visions of the 'network firm' and the 'virtual firm'. A factor common to these visions is a 'fuzzy' boundary of the firm, where the firm fades into the market through joint ventures with declining proportional equity stakes. These arguments for fuzzy boundaries are, unfortunately, often based on equally fuzzy reasoning. Fuzzy boundaries can be configured in many different ways. The new research agenda outlined in this article places arguments for fuzzy boundaries on a rigorous basis, and predicts the specific form that fuzziness will take in each particular case.

It is evident that the search for flexibility has a number of important implications for:

- the external environment of the firm;
- the boundaries of the firm; and
- the internal organization of the firm

These issues will now be considered in turn.

## EXTERNAL FLEXIBILITY: THE NATIONAL COMPETITIVENESS ISSUE

Initial Western reaction to de-industrialization and the plight of the 'rust-belt' heavy industries was concern over competitiveness. There continues to be considerable debate, however, over what competitiveness really means (Buckley, Pass and Prescott, 1988). Some economists argue, using the Ricardian concept of comparative advantage, that loss of manufacturing competitiveness is a natural consequence of economic maturity (Krugman, 1996). The strength of Western economies no longer lies in manufacturing, but in services. Thanks to jet travel, television broadcasting and other technological developments, an increasing number of services, such as tourism and media entertainment, are readily exportable. Consumer demand for services is income-elastic, moreover, so the long-term prospects for the service sector are good. Furthermore, manufacturing is increasingly capital-intensive, whereas many service industries are inherently labour intensive, because they are more difficult to automate. To regain competitiveness, therefore, labour must be shifted out of manufacturing and into services. To eliminate frictional and structural unemployment, this process must be expedited by measures to promote labour market flexibility.

According to this view. Asian countries, being at an earlier stage of industrial development, have exploited labour market flexibility to switch labour out of agriculture and into industry. First-generation workers who have just left the land are often very hard-working, and so, despite their inexperience, this gives a productivity boost to nascent industry. If flexibility can be sustained, then workers can be switched from one industry to another – from textiles to semiconductors, for example – as competition increases from other countries following up the ladder of development. It is in this way that Japan has stayed ahead of competition from the Republic of Korea and Taiwan (China). Such has been the speed of Asian development that several economies, including Singapore, Hong Kong and Japan, have already completed the manufacturing phase, and have become major service economies in their own right.

An alternative view of competitiveness emphasizes the firm-specific nature of competitive advantage. There are wide differences in productivity between firms in the same industry, it is claimed. Theories of comparative advantage, framed in terms of a representative firm, ignore this (Thurow, 1992). Some firms have major competitive advantages, and others have none at all. The competitive advantages of leading Western firms have been eroded by internal failings, it is alleged. It is not that Western workers have lost comparative advantage in manufacturing, but that Western firms have lost the ability to manage instead.

The distinction between firm-specific competitive advantage and nation-specific comparative advantages is essentially a question of the period of analysis. Firm-specific competitive advantage is essentially a short-run concept. Firm-specific advantages cannot be taken as given in the long run because they continually obsolesce and have to be regularly renewed (Buckley and Casson, 1976). A nation with a comparative advantage in entrepreneurship will be able to renew firm-specific advantages through sustained innovation, but a nation without such comparative advantage will not. An explanation of loss of competitiveness that emphasizes loss of firm-specific advantages is equivalent, from a long-run perspective, to an argument that local comparative advantage in entrepreneurship has been lost. Countries that systematically generate firms with specific advantages are those that have a nation-specific comparative advantage in entrepreneurship.

From this perspective, it is plausible to argue that the West has lost comparative advantage in both manufacturing and entrepreneurship. The first is an unavoidable consequence of economic maturity, but the second is an avoidable consequence of institutional failure and inappropriate business culture. The conflict between the nation-specific view and the firm-specific view is actually a disagreement about whether nation-specific comparitive advantage has declined more in manufacturing than in entrepreneurship, or less. Those who adhere to the firm-specific view, which probably includes the majority of international business scholars, implicitly believe that entrepreneurial decline is the major problem, and that cultural and institutional changes are required to put it right. The increased volatility of the world economy, and the consequent increase in demand for flexibility, has put Western entrepreneurial failures under the spotlight.

## RESTORING COMPETITIVENESS

Western governments have attempted to restore labour market flexibility through legislation. In the United Kingdom, for example, the legal privileges of trades unions (such as secondary picketing) have been reduced, and minimum wage laws relaxed. Qualifications for the receipt of unemployment benefit have been tightened up. Firms have responded in a predictable way. Greater use is made of temporary labour to accommodate peaks and troughs in demand. Full-time workers are expected to work more flexible hours. Work has been subcontracted out to avoid statutory national insurance premiums. The rise in labour-only subcontracting has brought back the 'putting out' system, which was characteristic of the eighteenth-century 'commercial revolution'.

Privatization has been used to promote greater flexibility in the supply of intermediate products to industry. The United Kingdom has privatized 'strategic' heavy industries (steel), public transport (railways and airlines), and utilities (telecommunications, electricity, gas and water). Privatization allows peripheral activities to be sold off, and complementary activities to be combined, thereby facilitating significant changes in the scope of the firm. Newly privatized enterprises can acquire other newly privatized enterprises, or enter into joint venture agreements with them. For the first time in the post-war period, large-scale involvement by MNEs is now possible in most of the utility industries.

Steps have also been taken to improve entrepreneurship. Business education has been expanded, top rates of income tax have been reduced to encourage risk-taking, and successful business people have been encouraged to play a more active role in public life in order to raise the status of entrepreneurs. Politicians have increasing promoted the values of competitive individualism, and downgraded the values of organic solidarity, which characterized the 'Welfare State' (Casson, 1990).

Links between universities and business have been strengthened in order to improve the coordination of product development and basic research. This may not directly benefit the nation as much as it might have been expected, however. Products researched in one country can be produced in another country, and even exported back to the country where they were researched to compete with local products there. The decentralization of R&D within large MNEs (Pearce and Singh, 1992) creates internal markets where this kind of transfer can be easily effected. Thus a US MNE could use a wholly owned research laboratory in the United Kingdom to tap into government-funded research in order to develop a product to be made in the United States for export to the United Kingdom. The profits from the product innovation will also accrue to the United States – an effect that has been stressed, in a somewhat different context, by Reich (1990).

Government measures to improve competitiveness seem to have been reasonably successful over the past decade. However, it should not be forgotten that the reason why some MNEs continue to produce in Europe for the European market has more to do with the common external tariff of the European Community, and the threat that it might increase, than with the location advantages of Europe *per se*. Thus, tariff considerations and substantial job-creation subsidies have played a major role in the attraction of Asian motor vehicle manufacturers to the United Kingdom. Similarly, one of the advantages to foreign firms of producing in the United States is that it is easier to adapt product designs to the market using a local production base.

The fact that Asian firms can successfully produce in the West behind a tariff wall suggests that they possess firm-specific advantages of the type generated by sustained entrepreneurship. One of these advantages appears to lie in *internal* labour market flexibility. There is a tendency in the West to see labour market flexibility as something external to the firm. It is reflected simply in low wage rates. There is less emphasis on firm-specific training, and workers are less versatile than in Asian firms. This is apparent on the shop-floor. On-the-job training is weaker, and attention to quality is lower as a result. Machine down-time is greater because workers cannot fix minor repairs, or help each other out when re-tooling a production line.

In general, Asian firms appear to have taken flexibility more seriously as a production issue. Not only have they invested more in labour versatility, but they have also invested more in equipment for flexible manufacturing systems too. This is reflected not only in their Asian plants, but also in their operations in the West as well.

## FLEXIBLE BOUNDARIES OF THE FIRM: NETWORKS AND JOINT VENTURES

The typical US MNE of the 'golden age' was a vertically, as well as horizontally, integrated firm. In consequence, each division of the firm was locked into linkages with other divisions of the same firm. As Asian competition intensified, there was growing recognition of the costs of integration of this kind.

Commitment to a particular source of supply or demand is relatively low-cost in a high-growth scenario, since it is unlikely that any investment will need to be reversed. It is much more costly in a low-growth scenario, where production may need to be switched to a cheaper source of supply, or sales diverted away from a depressed market. The desire for flexibility therefore discourages vertical integration – whether it is backward integration into production, or forward integration into distribution. It is better to subcontract production and to franchise sales instead. The subcontracting of production is similar in principle to the 'putting out' arrangement described above, but differs in the sense that the subcontractor is now a firm rather than just a single worker.

Dis-integration was also encouraged by a low-trust atmosphere that developed in many firms. Fear of internal monopoly became rife, as explained above. Production managers faced with falling demand wished that they did not have to sell all their output through a single sales manager. Sales managers resented the fact that they had to obtain all their supplies from the same small set of plants. Each manager doubted the competence of the others, and ascribed loss of corporate competitiveness to selfishness and inefficiency elsewhere in the firm. Divisions aspired to be spun off so that they could deal with other business units instead. On the other hand, managers were wary of the risks that would be involved if they severed their links with other divisions altogether.

A natural way to restore confidence is to allow each division to deal with external business units, as well as internal ones. In terms of internalization theory, internal markets become 'open' rather than 'closed' (Casson, 1990, p. 37). This provides divisional managers with an opportunity to bypass weak or incompetent sections of the company. It also provides a competitive discipline on internal transfer prices, preventing their manipulation for internal political ends, and bringing them more into line with external prices. There are other advantages too. Opening up internal markets severs the link between the capacities operated at adjacent stages of production. The resulting opportunity to supply other firms facilitates the exploitation of scale economics because it permits the capacity of any individual plant to exceed internal demand. Conversely, it encourages the firm to buy in supplies from other firms that have installed capacity in excess of their own needs.

The alignment of internal prices with external prices increases the objectivity of profit measurement at the divisional level. This allows divisional managers to be rewarded by profit-related pay based on divisional profit rather than firm-wide profit. Management may even buy out part of the company. Alternatively, the firm may restructure by buying in a part of an independent firm. The net effect is the same in both cases. The firm becomes the hub of a network of interlocking joint ventures (Buckley and Casson, 1988, 1996). Each joint venture partner is responsible for the day-to-day management of the venture. The headquarters of the firm coordinates the links between the ventures. Internal trade is diverted away from the weaker ventures towards the stronger ones, thereby providing price and profit signals to which the weaker partners need to respond. Unlike a pure external market situation, the partners are able to draw upon expertise at headquarters, which can in turn tap into expertise in other parts of the group.

A network does not have to be built around a single firm, of course. A network may consist of a group of independent firms instead. Sometimes these firms are neighbours, as in the regional industrial clusters described by Best (1990), Porter (1990) and Rugman, D'Cruz and Verbeke (1995). Industrial districts, such as 'Toyota city', have been hailed as an Asian innovation in flexible management, although the practice has been common in Europe for centuries (Marshall, 1919). As tariffs and transport costs have fallen, networks have become more international. This is demonstrated by the dramatic growth in intermediate product trade under long-term contracts. For example, an international trading company may operate a network of independent suppliers in different countries, substituting different sources of supply in response to both short-term exchange rate movements and long-term shifts in comparative advantage.

Flexibility is also needed in R&D. A firm cannot afford to become over-committed to the refinement of any one technology in case innovation elsewhere should render the entire technology obsolete. As technology has diffused in the post-war period, the range of countries with the competence to innovate has significantly increased. The pace of innovation has consequently risen, and the threat of rapid obsolescence is therefore higher as a result. The natural response for firms is to diversify their research portfolios. But the costs of maintaining a range of R&D projects are prohibitive, given the enormous fixed costs involved. The costs of basic R&D have escalated because of the increased range of specialist skills involved, while the costs of applied R&D have risen because of the need to develop global products which meet increasing stringent consumer protection laws. Joint ventures are an appropriate solution once again. By establishing a network of joint ventures covering alternative technological trajectories, the firm can spread its costs whilst retaining a measure of proprietary control over new technologies.

The advantage of joint ventures is further reinforced by technological convergence, for example, the integration of computers, telecommunications and photography. This favors the creation of networks of joint ventures based on complementary technologies, rather than on the substitute technologies described above (Cantwell, 1995).

Joint ventures are important because they afford a number of real options (Trigeorgis, 1996) which can be taken up or dropped depending upon how the project turns out. The early phase of a joint venture provides important information which could not be obtained through investigation before the venture began. It affords an opportunity later on to buy more fully into a successful venture – an opportunity which is not available to those who have not taken any stake. It therefore provides greater flexibility than does either outright ownership or an alternative involving no equity stake.

## FLEXIBILITY AND INTERNAL ORGANIZATION

In a very volatile environment the level of uncertainty is likely to be high. Uncertainty can be reduced, however, by collecting information. Flexibility was defined above in terms of the ability to respond to change. The costs of response tend to be smaller when the period of adjustment is long. One way of 'buying time' to adjust is to forecast change. While no one can foresee the future perfectly, information on the present and the recent past may well improve forecasts by diagnosing underlying long-term trends. Collecting, storing and analyzing information therefore enhances flexibility because, by improving forecasts, it reduces the costs of change.

Another way of buying time is to recognize change as early as possible. In this respect, continuous monitoring of the business environment is better than intermittent monitoring because the potential lag before a change is recognized is eliminated. Continuous monitoring is more expensive than intermittent monitoring, though, because more management time is tied up.

Investments in better forecasts and speedier recognition highlight the trade-off between information cost and adjustment cost. This trade-off is particularly crucial when volatility is high. High volatility implies that more information should be collected to improve flexibility, which in turn implies that more managers need to be employed. This is reverse of the usual recommendation to downsize management in order to reduce overhead costs.

To improve flexibility whilst downsizing management, the trade-off between information cost and adjustment cost must be improved. There are two main ways of doing this. The first is to reduce the cost of information processing through new information technology (IT). The second is to reduce adjustment costs by building flexibility into plant and equipment, both through its design and its location. A combination of IT investment and flexible plant can reconcile greater flexibility with lower management overheads in the manner to which many MNEs aspire.

The information required for strategic decision-making is likely to be distributed throughout the organization. It is no longer reasonable to assume that all the key information can be handled by a single chief executive, or even by the entire headquarters management team. It is difficult to know in advance where the really crucial information is likely to be found. Every manager therefore needs to have the competence to process information effectively. Managers need to be able to recognize the significance of strategic information that they acquire by chance, and to have the power of access to senior executives in order to pass it on. In other words, ordinary managers need to become internal entrepreneurs.

Few entrepreneurs have sufficient information to make a good decision without consulting other people, however. In a traditional hierarchical firm, the right to consult is the prerogative of top management. If ordinary managers are to have the power to initiate consultation, and act upon the results, then channels of communication within the firm need to be increased. Horizontal communication, as well as vertical communication, must be easy, so that lower-level managers can readily consult with their peers.

A natural response is to 'flatten' the organization and encourage managers to 'network' with each other. This improves the trade-off between local responsiveness and strategic cohesion (Bartlett and Ghoshal, 1987; Hedlund, 1993). Unfortunately, though, there has been some confusion over whether flatter organizations remain hierarchies at all. However, as Casson (1994) shows, the efficient managerial processing of information normally requires a hierarchical structure of some kind. The key point is that the more diverse are the sources of volatility, the greater are the advantages of widespread consultation. The less predictable is the principal source of volatility on any given occasion, the greater is the incentive to allow consultation to be initiated anywhere in the organization. In practice this means that an increased demand for flexibility is best accommodated by flattening the organization, whilst maintaining basic elements of hierarchy.

## THE COSTS OF FLEXIBILITY: ENGINEERING TRUST

If flexibility were costless, then all organizations could build in unlimited flexibility at the outset. In practice, the greater is flexibility, the higher transactions costs become. For example, the flexibility to switch between different sources of supply and demand (described above) means that relations with customers and suppliers become more transitory than before. Cheating becomes more likely, because the prospect of further transactions between the same two parties is more remote. Direct appeals to the other party's loyalty lose their credibility too.

The same effect occurs when internal entrepreneurship is promoted. Internal entrepreneurs are given more discretion to act upon information that they have collected for themselves, and this increases their opportunity to cheat.

Giving managers a direct stake in the business activities they help to build is one solution. The firm incubates new business units in which particular managers, or groups of managers, have equity stakes. An alternative approach is to appeal to the integrity of managers instead. They are treated well, and in return are expected to be open and honest about what they know.

It is one of the ironies of the 1970s that at a time when personal integrity needed to be high in order to support more flexible organization, it had been allowed to fall very low. The decline of traditional religion, the intellectual cynicism created by two world wars, and the rise of mass consumerism have all been blamed for this state of affairs. Communitarians argue correctly that moral values like integrity are most efficiently engineered at the societal level, through family, church and school. But when these institutions fail, they must be engineered to support specific economic relations instead (Fukuyama, 1996). Firms must engineer these values amongst their employees at their own expense instead (Kotter, 1996). Greater flexibility therefore implies greater costs in promoting a corporate culture that reinforces moral values.

## INTERACTION OF FIRM FLEXIBILITY AND LOCATION FLEXIBILITY

The desire for flexibility may encourage the firm to produce the same product in several locations so that it can switch production between them as circumstances change. Multiple internal sourcing may therefore be pursued even where some sacrifice of economies of scale is involved. DeMeza and Van der Ploeg (1987), Capel (1992) and Kogut and Kulatilaka (1994) have all emphasized that firms can switch production between alternative locations in response to real exchange rate shocks. The basic idea is that MNEs can combine their superior information on foreign cost conditions with their ability, as owners of plants, to plan rather than negotiate output levels, to switch production more quickly than can independent firms.

This strategy requires, however, that the firm should commit in advance to the locations where it believes it will wish to produce. If it is difficult to foresee where the best locations may lie, then flexibility may be enhanced by subcontracting arrangements instead. Speed of response may be slower, but the range of potential locations is greater. Where short-run volatility predominates, multinational integration may well enhance the value of the firm (Allen and Pantzalis, 1996), but long-run volatility may favour the dis-integration of the firm instead.

If a firm is seeking flexibility at one stage of production, then it will experience a derived demand for flexibility at adjacent stages of production. This flexibility is conferred by ease of transport to and from all the locations employed at the adjacent stage. Some locations are inherently more flexible in this respect than others, because they are at nodal points on transport networks. They therefore have low transport costs to a wide range of different destinations. For example, if production is dispersed, then warehousing of finished product should be at an appropriate hub. Greater demand for flexibility concentrates demand for warehousing at such hubs – for example, Singapore (for South-East Asia) and Lille (for North-West Europe).

An MNE that is seeking flexibility in its sources of supply will wish to choose a location where government policy is *laissez faire*, so that there are no import restrictions. It may be seeking flexibility in the range of products it produces too. This encourages it to seek out locations with a versatile labour force. Flexibility is also conferred by supplier networks that operate with a high degree of trust. Local production needs to be embedded in an impartial legal system and in strong social networks to ensure that trust is high. An 'invisible infrastructure' of mediating institutions, or equivalently, a large endowment of 'social capital', is therefore a feature of the locations that MNEs committed to flexibility are likely to seek out. Flexibility is not just an element of corporate strategy, but a component of location advantage too. Such location advantage depends crucially on the nature of local institutions and local culture.

## FLEXIBILITY AND FIRM-SPECIFIC COMPETITIVE ADVANTAGE

Flexibility also has implications for firm-specific competitive advantage. Skill in recruiting imaginative employees becomes a competitive advantage when internal entrepreneurship is required. Charismatic leadership by the chief executive may promote loyalty and integrity amongst key staff. A tradition of informal and consultative management will facilitate the sharing of information amongst employees. One way of expressing this is in terms of the 'capabilities' or 'competencies' of managers, or the human resources controlled by the firm (Richardson, 1960; Loasby, 1991). In a volatile environment where flexibility is crucial, the key resources of the firm are those that promote internal entrepreneurship. The firm consists not of a single autocratic entrepreneur, but a team of entrepreneurs (Wu, 1988) coordinated by a leader who promotes high-trust communication between them.

It is worth noting that the need for flexibility does not necessarily support the idea of a 'learning organization'. To be more exact, flexibility has important implications for what people in a learning organization actually need to learn. According to Nelson and Winter (1982), learning supports the refinement of existing routines. This is misleading. It suggests that the firm operates in a basically stable environment, and merely learns how to do even better what it already does very well. In a volatile environment, however, much of what has been 'learned' from past experience quickly obsolesces. The truly durable knowledge that needs to be learned in a volatile environment consists of techniques for handling volatility. These techniques include forgetting transitory information about past conditions which are unlikely to recur. But while 'unlearning' or 'forgetting' is important, it is often difficult to do. The difficulty of 'unlearning' helps to explain why so many 'downsizing' and 'de-layering' exercises have identified middle-aged middle managers as targets for redundancy or early retirement. Such people are believed to find it too hard to forget. The 'knowledge' they acquired as junior managers was very relevant during the 'golden age', but has since become obsolete. Some managers have proved sufficiently flexible to be 'retrained'. but others have not. Those who were too inflexible to benefit from retraining have been required to leave because their 'knowledge' had become a liability instead of an asset in the more volatile situation of today.

## NEW TECHNIQUES OF ANALYSIS

The key to modelling volatility is to postulate a steady stream of shocks impinging at random on the international business environment. There are exogenous shocks, which are autonomous, and endogenous shocks, which are induced as a consequence of the exogenous ones. The need for simplicity means that many shocks have to be treated as exogenous, even though they are in fact endogenous. The formation of customs unions, the reduction of international shipping costs through containerization, and the breakdown of the Soviet system may all be treated as exogenous random shocks impinging on the global economy. These shocks influence the relative rise and decline of individual nations. This emphasis on the modelling of shocks means that probability theory has a significant role to play in the new research agenda (Dixit and Pindyck, 1994). In particular, the probabilistic foundations of stochastic processes assume particular significance. There is a close link between the collection of information and the refinement of probability measurement, and another link between optimal forecasting and the concept of a 'martingale' (Dempster and Pliska, 1997). These ideas are most extensively developed in the field of financial options, but they can be applied to 'real options' too (Mello, Parsons and Triantis, 1995).

Managers of MNEs perceive the growth and decline of individual national economies as the result of random shocks. Increased volatility in the international economy means that there is greater uncertainty than before about the future growth of any particular economy. For example, there is currently considerable uncertainty about the growth prospects of Thailand and other South-East Asian economies. Theories of rational choice under uncertainty (Hirshleifer and Riley, 1992) are therefore central in analyzing corporate behaviour in volatile environments.

Uncertainty can be reduced by gathering information, as noted earlier. Information improves the quality of decision-making, but the returns to information diminish at the margin as with any other resource. Efficient search is normally conducted sequentially, and stops when the expected value of the next item of information is just equal to its expected cost of collection. The cheapest information is usually obtained second-hand through communication with other people. It can also be obtained as a by-product of other activity. The organization of a firm may be understood as a rational response to the challenge of collecting the right sort of information in the most appropriate way. This is the major insight of the economic theory of teams (Marschak and Radner, 1972). The organization effects a division of labour in information processing, and assigns particular managers to particular roles according to where their personal comparative advantage lies. Some are good observers, others are good communicators, whilst the most entrepreneurial types make the best decision-makers. They are all slotted into appropriate niches in the organization.

The timing of decisions is absolutely crucial in a volatile environment. The right decision may be of little use if it is taken at the wrong time (Rivoli and Salorio, 1996). Committing resources too early to a growing market, for example, means that costs are incurred before adequate revenues can be generated, while deferring until too late means that the market may be permanently lost to competitors (Buckley and Casson, 1981). An important reason for deferring investment is that new information may become available later which would lead to a better decision. This is the central point in the theory of options (Trigeorgis, 1996). Investment is often irreversible, in the sense that the resources committed are illiquid, and cannot be fully recovered later through divestment. Deferring a decision on an irreversible investment reduces the risk that the investment may go ahead on a mistaken assessment of the situation (Campa, 1994). The more volatile the environment, the more likely it is to change, and hence the greater the advantage of waiting until all imminent changes have occurred.

It would be wrong to infer, however, that investment is always discouraged by volatility. Investment often leads to the discovery of new information. Suppose, for example, that there are two foreign markets, one of which is known to be similar to the other. Investing in the smaller market involves a smaller commitment than investing in the larger one. A by-product of investment in the smaller market is information about the larger market. This information reduces the risk of investing in the larger one. It therefore pays to invest first in the smaller market, even though the prospects are worse than in the larger one, because the experience gained can be used to improve the later, more important, decision. This idea is central to the Scandinavian model of the internationalization of the firm (Johanson and Vahlne, 1977).

In general, the growth of MNEs may be understood as a sequence of investments undertaken in a volatile environment, where each investment feeds back information which can be used to improve the quality of subsequent decisions. In this sense, the expansion of the firm is a path-dependent process (Kogut and Zander, 1993). Most expositions of path-dependency assume, however, that the choice of path is essentially myopic, in the sense that decision-makers make no attempt to anticipate the kind of information that will get fed back at each stage. This need not be the case, though. An entrepreneurial firm may be able to anticipate how the information that it will obtain in the future depends on the decision that it currently has to make. In this case its managers can exploit the logical structure of this learning process to expand in a optimal manner. The sequence of industries into which the firm diversifies, and the sequence of the countries in which it invests, represents a rational dynamic strategy of growth.

Similarly, strategic divestment in response to competition may also be seen as a consequence of a rational dynamic strategy. In a volatile environment a rational firm will anticipate the possibility of competition by investing in a manner that takes subsequent divestment options into account. It will make only those investments that it is either unlikely to want to divest, or which will be easy to divest because the sunk costs involved are relatively low. The typical investment will involve assets that have several alternative uses, and are easy to sell off to other firms. Since assets of this kind are easy to obtain in the first place, through acquisition, the theory suggests that acquisitions and divestment of highly 'liquid' or 'non-specific', assets are likely to play a major role in flexible investment strategies. This is one reason why acquisitions and divestments became more common at the same time that IJVs became more common too. Both are implications of the strategic pursuit of flexibility in a volatile environment.

The pursuit of sophisticated strategies of this kind requires a great deal of information to be shared within the organization. It is crucial that this information is communicated in an honest manner. Integrity is often assured by repeated interaction, as explained by the theory of non-cooperative games (Kreps, 1990). Alternatively, integrity can be assured by cultural engineering (Casson, 1991). Cultural engineering within a firm can be effected in two main ways. One is by selecting people who have already been subjected to appropriate cultural influences. This explains why many firms recruit selectively from certain communities, educational institutions and ethnic groups. Cultural homogeneity not only improves internal communication, but standardizes employees on a uniform set of moral values. The alternative is for the firm to recruit people purely on the basis of competence, and standardize the morals through active dissemination of a corporate culture. The first strategy allows the firm to 'free ride' on cultural engineering by other institutions, and reduces the demands on the chief executive's leadership role. The second strategy allows the firm to recruit more widely, and to tailor the moral system to its specific requirements. MNEs will tend to favour the latter strategy because they need to recruit a range of different nationalities, and to combine the expertise of members of very different professional groups.

## AN EXAMPLE

What does a scholar pursuing the new research agenda actually *do*? How does the formal specification of a dynamic model differ from that of a static one, and how exactly does a dynamic model differ from a 'framework' of the Porter type? A full answer can only be obtained from the literature cited above, but a simple example may clarify the position.

Consider the problem of modelling market entry from a dynamic, rather than a static, point of view (Chi and McGuire, 1996). The most important new point to take into account is that the foreign market can decline as well as grow. Divestment or withdrawal must be considered as serious strategies. Clearly, these strategies do not apply until the market has been entered, but once it has been entered they may need to be used. Static models assume that the market will be constant, while very simple dynamic models, such as Buckley and Casson (1981), only suppose that the market will grow. In a volatile environment a market may grow to begin with, attracting investment, but then go into decline, requiring divestment instead. Such explicit recognition of adverse scenarios is a characteristic of the new research agenda.

Switching between strategies is costly, and the costs depend on both the strategy the firm is switching from, and the strategy the firm is switching to. In some cases, switching costs decompose neatly into a cost of exit from the old strategy and a cost of setting up the new strategy. Detailed modelling of such costs is a key element of the new research agenda.

To preserve flexibility, it is important for the firm to choose at the outset strategies whose exit costs are low. This tends to favor exporting over host-country production, and licensing over internalization. In other words, it reveals FDI as a high-risk strategy.

Switching decisions can be mistaken, however, because the information upon which they are based is poor. Expected switching costs are reduced by avoiding unnecessary switches. Different strategies afford different opportunities for capturing information from the host environment and feeding it back to inform subsequent switching decisions. The new agenda involves explicit modelling of how the strategy chosen at one stage affects the information available at following stages.

Foreign direct investment offers better opportunities for information capture than either licensing or exporting, since ownership of assets confers ownership of information too. This means, for example, that if volatility caused the market to unexpectedly grow, then the foreign investor would recognize this quickly. Since it often cheaper to expand existing capacity than to build from scratch, the foreign investor also faces lower costs of capacity expansion than does an exporter who decides to switch to foreign production at this stage. While exporting continues to confer more flexibility in response to market decline, therefore, FDI confers more flexibility in respect of market growth.

Is it possible to find a strategy with a better combination of characteristics than either exporting, licensing or FDI? An IJV may provide the answer (Kogut, 1991). Investing in a 50:50 partnership with a host-country producer lays off some of the risks associated with wholly owned FDI. At the same time, information capture remains reasonably good. There is an option to expand capacity if there is unexpected market growth, and a further option to increase commitment by buying the partner out. There is also an easy option to withdraw by selling out to the partner. The partner provides a ready market for divested assets that an ordinary direct investor lacks. There is a down-side, of course – an obvious problem is that the partners may themselves become a source of volatility. This is why trust is such an important element in an IJV. In this way the emphasis on risk management within the new research agenda leads to the emergence of new 'compromise strategies', which would be dominated by more conventional strategies were it not for the 'option value' they possess within a volatile environment.

IJV options can only be exercised once, of course, unless the investor switches back to an IJV arrangement at a later date, when they can be exercised all over again. This explains IJV instability as a rational response to the role that IJVs fulfil. An IJV in which the options are never exercised is probably inferior to a wholly owned investment, while an IJV in which the options are exercised at the first available opportunity does not last for very long. When IJVs are chosen because of their option value, it is normally inefficient both to switch out right away, or to never switch at all. The optimal timing of a switch is one at which uncertainty about future market growth is dispelled for a reasonable period of time. This implies that the duration of IJVs is, on average, fairly short, and relatively variable. The new research agenda provides a simple means of deriving such hypotheses about the period of time for which a given strategy will be pursued.

The globalization of markets has been a major factor in the growth of volatility, as explained above. A feature of many global markets is the use of regional production and distribution hubs, where several neighbouring countries are serviced from the same location. The regional hub, like the IJV, can be understood as a strategy that offers superior flexibility. Just as an IJV offers a compromise ownership strategy, a regional hub offers a compromise location strategy. Because the hub is nearer to each market than is the home location, it reduces transport costs, and offers better information capture too. Yet, because it is close to several markets, it avoids exclusive commitment to any one. If one market declines, production can be switched to other markets instead. Provided the shocks affecting the national markets are independent (or less than perfectly correlated, at any rate) the hub provides gains from diversification. These are real gains that only the firm can achieve, as opposed to the financial gains from unrelated product diversification, which have proved disappointing in the past because they are best exploited through the diversification of individual share portfolios instead.

The two strategies of IJV and hub can be combined. Since one is an ownership strategy and the other a location strategy they can, if desired, be combined directly in an IJV production hub. Closer examination the issues suggests that this is not normally the best approach, however. The model suggests that a combination of a wholly owned production hub supplying IJV distribution facilities in each national market is a better solution. A hub facility is too critical to global strategy to allow a partner to become involved, because the damage they could do is far too great. Even with a wholly owned hub facility, the combination still affords considerable flexibility to divest or withdraw from any single market. The advantage of the combination is that when divesting, the distribution facility can be sold to the partner, while the production capacity can be diverted to markets elsewhere. These options for divestment are combined with useful options for expansion too.

This example illustrates the crucial role that the concepts of flexibility and volatility play in analyzing foreign market entry in the modern global economy. Without these concepts it is impossible to fully understand the rationale for IJVs and production hubs. It is also impossible to understand why these strategies have emerged at this particular historical juncture and not before.

While some of the insights of this model can certainly be expressed in terms of a framework, a framework is too crude to analyse the interplay of the different factors in a completely rigorous way. The concepts of adjustment costs and exit costs can already be found in the strategy literature, for example, but even this simple example above is sufficient to show that the interplay of present entry and future exit cannot be properly understood without the aid of a fully specified model. This does not mean that the strategy literature is flawed. The new dynamic agenda is perfectly compatible with much of the existing strategy literature, but it goes beyond it by developing and refining the insights in a way that the strategy framework is unable to do.

## CONCLUSION

There are many other subjects in international business to which the new agenda can be applied, and many other new techniques which can be used. Enough has been said to indicate the promise that the new agenda holds for future research. The key to success in international business theory is to avoid becoming overwhelmed by the complexity of the issues. New issues, centred on flexibility, call for theory to refocus on the new insights described above. The use of economic methodology means that these new issues can be addressed in a simple and elegant way. The traditional agenda has plenty of life left in it yet. But it is not the only agenda. As Arpan (1997) has noted, international business research must change if it is to retain its relevance and its basic simplicity. The new agenda sets out the way in which this can be done.

### Acknowledgements

The authors are grateful to Jose Paulo Esperanca, Mohammed Azzim Gulamhussen and Filipe Ravara for suggestions regarding the application of real options theory to joint ventures. Useful comments were received from Sarianna Lundan, an anonymous referee, and the editor of the special issue of *Journal of International Business Studies*.

### References

Allen, Linda and Christos Pantzalis (1996) 'Valuation of the operating flexibility of multinational corporations', *Journal of International Business Studies*, 27, 4, 633–53.

Arpan, Jeffrey S. (1997) 'Palabras del Presidente', *AIB Newsletter*, 3, 3, 2.

Bartlett, Christopher A. and Sumantra Ghoshal (1987) 'Managing across borders: New strategic requirements', *Sloan Management Review*, Summer, 6–17.

Best, Michael H. (1990) *The new competition: Institutions of industrial restructuring*. Oxford: Polity Press.

Buckley, Peter J. (1983) 'New theories of international business: Some unresolved issues', in Mark C. Casson (ed.), *The growth of international business*. London: Allen and Unwin, 34–50.

——(1988) 'The limits of explanation: Testing the internalization theory of the multinational enterprise', *Journal of International Business Studies*, 19, 2, 1–16.

——and Mark C. Casson (1976) *The future of the multinational enterprise*. London: Macmillan.

——(1981) 'The Optimal timing of a foreign direct investment', *Economic Journal*, 91, 75–87.

——(1988) 'A theory of co-operation in international business', in Farok J. Contractor and Peter Lorange (eds), *Co-operative strategies in international business*. Lexington, MA: Lexington Books, 31–53.

——(1993) 'Economics as an imperialist social science', *Human Relations*, 46, 9, 1035–52.

——(1996) 'An economic model of international joint venture strategy', *Journal of International Business Studies*, 27, 5, 849–76.

——and Martin J. Carter (1996) 'The economics of business process design: Motivation, information and coordination within the firm', *International Journal of the Economics of Business*, 3, 1, 5–25.

——and Malcolm Chapman (1996) 'Economics and social anthropology – Reconciling differences', *Human Relations*, 49, 9, 1123–50.

——Pass L. Christopher and Kate Prescott (1988) 'Measures of international competitiveness: a critical survey', *Journal of Marketing Management*, 4, 2, 175–200.

Campa, Jose Manuel (1994) 'Multinational investment under uncertainty in the chemical processing industries', *Journal of International Business Studies*, 25, 3, 557–78.

Cantwell, John (1995) 'Multinational enterprises and innovatory activities: Towards a new evolutionary approach', in J. Molero (ed.), *Technological innovation, multinational corporations and the new international competitiveness*. Chur: Harwood Academic Publishers, 21–57.

Capel, Jeanette (1992) 'How to service a foreign market under uncertainty: A real option approach', *European Journal of Political Economy*, 8, 455–75.

Casson, Mark C. (1990) *Enterprise and competitiveness*. Oxford: Clarendon Press.

——(1991) *Economics of business culture*. Oxford: Clarendon Press.

——(1994) 'Why are firms hierarchical?', *International Journal of the Economics of Business*, 1, 1, 3–40.

——(1995) *Organization of international business*. Aldershot: Edward Elgar.

——Robert D. Pearce and Satwinder Singh (1991) 'A review of recent trends', in Mark C. Casson, (ed.), *Global research strategy and international competitiveness*. Oxford: Blackwell, 250–71.

Caves, Richard E. (1996) *Multinational enterprise and economic analysis*. Cambridge: Cambridge University Press. Second Edition.

Chi, Tailan and Donald J. McGuire (1996) 'Collaborative ventures and value of learning: Integrating the transaction cost and strategic option perspectives on the choice of market entry modes', *Journal of International Business Studies*, 27, 2, 285–307.

DeMeza, David and Frederick van der Ploeg (1987) 'Production flexibility as a motive for multinationality', *Journal of Industrial Economics*, 35, 3, 343–51.

Dempster, Michael A. H. and Stanley R. Pliska (eds) (1997) *Mathematics of derivative decurities*. Cambridge: Cambridge University Press.

Dixit, Avrinash and Robert S. Pindyck (1994) *Investments under uncertainty*. Princeton, NJ: Princeton University Press.

Dunning, John H. (1977) 'Trade, location of economic activity and the multinational enterprise: The search for an eclectic approach', in B. Ohlin, P. O. Hessleborn and P. M. Wijkman (eds), *The international location of economic activity*. London: Macmillan.

—— (1993) *Multinational enterprises in the global economy*. Wokingham, Berks: Addison-Wesley.

—— (1997) *Alliance capitalism and global business*. London: Routledge.

Ergas, Henry (1987) 'Does technology policy matter?', in B. R. Guile and H. Brooks (eds), *Technology and global industry*. Washington, DC: National Academy Press, 191–245.

Fransman, Martin (1995) *Japan's computer and communications industry*, Oxford: Oxford University Press.

Fukuyama, Francis (1996) *Trust*. Harmondsworth: Penguin.

Geringer, J. Michael and Louis Hébert (1989) 'Control and performance of international joint ventures', *Journal of International Business Studies*, 20, 2, 235–54.

Hedlund, Gunnar (1993) 'Assumptions of hierarchy and heterarchy: An application to the multinational corporation', in S. Ghoshal and E. Westney (eds), *Organization theory and the multinational corporation*. London: Macmillan, 211–36.

Hirshleifer, Jack and John G. Riley (1992) *The analytics of uncertainty and information*. Cambridge: Cambridge University Press.

Hood, Neil and Stephen Young (1994) 'The internationalization of business and the challenge of East European business', in P. J. Buckley and P. N. Ghauri (eds), *The economics of change in East and Central Europe*. London: Academic Press, 320–42.

Johanson, Jan and Jan-Erik Vahlne (1977) 'The internationalization process of the firm – A model of knowledge development and increasing foreign market commitments', *Journal of International Business Studies*, 8, 1, 23–32.

Kogut, Bruce (1991) 'Joint ventures and the option to expand and acquire', *Management Science*, 37, 1, 19–33.

—— and Nalin Kulatilaka (1994) 'Operating flexibility, global manufacturing, and the option value of a multinational network', *Management Science*, 40, 1, 123–39.

—— and Udo Zander (1993) 'Knowledge of the firm and the evolutionary theory of the multinational corporation', *Journal of International Business Studies*, 24, 4, 625–45.

Kotter, John (1996) *Leading change*. Cambridge, MA: Harvard Business School Press.
Kreps, David M. (1990) *Game theory and economic modelling*. Oxford: Oxford University Press.
Krugman, Paul (1995) *Development, geography and economic theory*. Cambridge, MA: MIT Press.
——(1996) 'The myth of Asia's miracle', in Paul Krugman, *Pop internationalism*. Cambridge, MA: MIT Press.
Lall, Sanjaya and Paul Streeten (1977) *Foreign investment, transnationals and developing countries*. London: Macmillan.
Loasby, Brian J. (1991) *Equilibrium and evolution*. Manchester: Manchester University Press.
Marglin, Stephen A. and Juliet B. Schor (1990) *The golden age of capitalism: Reinterpreting the post-war experience*. Oxford: Clarendon Press.
Marris, Robin L. (1979) *The theory and future of the corporate economy and society*. Amsterdam: North-Holland.
Marschak, Jacob and Roy Radner (1972) *Economic theory of teams*. New Haven, CN: Yale University Press.
Marshall, Alfred (1919) *Industry and trade*. London: Macmillan.
Mello, Antonio S., John E. Parsons, and Alexander J. Triantis (1995) 'An integrated model of multinational flexibility and hedging policies', *Journal of International Economics*, 39 (August): 27–51.
Mirza, Hafiz (1986) *Multinationals and the growth of the Singapore economy*. London: Croom Helm.
Nelson, Richard and Sidney G. Winter (1982) *An evolutionary theory of economic change*. Cambridge, MA: Harvard University Press.
Pearce, Robert D. and Satwinder Singh (1992) *Globalising research and development*. London: Macmillan.
Porter, Michael E. (1990) *The competitive advantage of nations*. London: Macmillan.
——(1991) 'Towards a dynamic theory of strategy', *Strategic Management Journal*, 12 (Special Issue): 95–117.
Reich, Robert B. (1990) 'Who is us?', *Harvard Business Review*. 68(1): 53–65.
Richardson, George B. (1960) *Information and investment*. Oxford: Oxford University Press.
Rivoli, Pietra and Eugene Salorio (1996) 'Foreign direct investment under uncertainty', *Journal of International Business Studies*, 27, 2, 335–54.
Rugman, Alan M., Joseph R. D'Cruz and Alain Verbeke (1995) 'Internalisation and de-internalisation: Will business networks replace multinationals?', in G. Boyd (ed.), *Competitive and cooperative macromanagement: The challenge of structural interdependence*. Aldershot: Edward Elgar, 107–28.
Thurow, Lester C. (1992) *Head to head: the coming economic battle among Japan, Europe and America*. New York: Morrow.
Trigeorgis, Lenos (1996) *Real Options*. Cambridge, MA. MIT Press.
Wu, Shih-yen (1988) *Production, entrepreneurship and profits*. Oxford: Blackwell.

# 3 The Investment Development Path: The Case of Portugal*

Peter J. Buckley and
Francisco B. Castro

**The Investment Development Path (IDP), which relates net foreign direct investment (FDI) to per capita income is developed for Portugal. A novel form of the relationship is proposed, based on empirical evidence for 1943–1996. This modification is supported by an analysis of Portuguese conditions which suggest that not only is government policy a major influence on the IDP, but so also are external political events, such as Portugal's accession to the EEC, EU integration and the fall of the Berlin wall which brought Central and Eastern European countries to the fore as location competitors for inward investment.**

## INTRODUCTION

The idea of an Investment Development Cycle, or Path, was introduced by Dunning (1981a) as a dynamic approach within the OLI paradigm.[1] The Investment Development Path suggests an association between a country's level of development (proxied by GDP per capita) and its international investment position (net FDI stock, that is, outward minus inward direct investment stocks). The basic hypothesis is that, as the country develops, the conditions facing domestic and foreign companies change, which affects the flows of inward and outward FDI. However, inward and outward FDI affect the economic structure as well – there is a dynamic interaction between the two. The IDP also acknowledges that governments can

---

* First published in *Transnational Corporations*, 7, 1 (1998).

influence the country's conditions by creating public goods on which competitiveness can be based (Buckley and Casson, 1998) and, consequently, FDI flows and domestic firms' ownership advantages (Dunning, 1988), a notion new to the mainstream theory of FDI.

According to the theory of the IDP, countries evolve through five stages of development (Dunning, 1981a, 1981b, 1986; Tolentino, 1987; Dunning and Narula, 1996a). *Stage 1* is associated with pre-industrialization. Inward and outward FDI flows are almost non-existent due to very small domestic markets, inadequate infrastructure, a poorly educated labour force and undeveloped commercial and legal frameworks. The development of some location specific advantages (e.g. basic infrastructure, eventually as the result of government policies) will give access to *Stage 2*. This corresponds to increasing inward direct investment, mostly targeting the emergent domestic market in consumer goods and infrastructure, but to low outward investment because of the very low ownership advantages of domestic firms. Consequently, net stocks of outward investment will become increasingly negative, as inward FDI stocks rise faster than GDP.

*Stage 3* is associated with decreasing growth rates of inward FDI. This is eventually overtaken by outward direct investment, and net FDI stock will for the first time start to increase despite remaining negative for some time. Behind this change are domestic firms' growing ownership advantages, which also become more firm-specific and less country-specific. Stronger domestic firms will be more competitive in the domestic market, while engaging in resource-seeking investment in less developed countries and in market- and strategic asset-seeking investment in more developed countries.

The deepening of these trends will eventually turn countries into net outward investors (*Stage 4*). Location advantages become almost entirely based on created assets, and the firms' ownership advantages that result from managing and coordinating geographically dispersed assets (Ot-advantages) become far more important than those based on the home country's specific characteristics (Oa advantages). Intra industry production is a consequence of the growing similarity in the O-advantages of countries at this stage, and it generally follows prior growth in intra-industry trade. In part, it results from increasing propensity by MNEs to internalize trade and production (Dunning and Narula, 1996a, p. 7).

Finally, Dunning (1986, pp. 30–1) and Dunning and Narula (1996a, pp. 7–9) postulate the existence of a fifth stage of the IDP, which corresponds to today's situation in the leading developed countries. Despite permanent high stocks of both inward and outward FDI, the net outward investment (NOI) position of stage 5 countries will revolve around zero, alternating between positive and negative balances according to the short-term evolution of exchange rates and economic cycles. 'Beyond a certain point in the IDP, the absolute size of GNP is no longer a reliable guide of a country's competitiveness; neither, indeed, is its NOI [net FDI stock] position' (Dunning and Narula, 1996a, p. 11).

Dunning and Narula (1996a) suggest, however, that the shape and position of the IDP varies widely across individual countries due to specific economic structures (market size, natural resources availability), the type of FDI undertaken, and government policies. This raises the question of whether the concept of an individual country's IDP is of any use, or even if individual countries do follow at all a pattern similar to the one suggested in the theory and supported by cross-section tests (Dunning, 1981a; Tolentino, 1987; Narula, 1996).

Although the theory and some existing studies (e.g. those in Dunning and Narula, 1996b) seem to support the notion of an IDP for individual countries and even industries inside countries, empirical tests are rare. The unavailability of long series of FDI stocks, in particular, make this a difficult task, that probably explains researchers' apparent reluctance to test the hypothesis. On the other hand, the interactions between the large number of variables that affect inward FDI, outward FDI and GDP growth are unlikely to allow secure conclusions using only secondary data.

## TESTING THE PORTUGUESE IDP

The present test of the Portuguese IDP uses a recently available new data set on FDI flows into and out of the country to see if Portugal's direct investment is following a path similar to the one described above. The data available does not permit an analysis disaggregated by industry or country of origin/destination. However, we aim to provide a first step towards a more integrated evaluation of the Portuguese IDP.

## The Data

As far as we know, no estimations exist of inward or outward stocks of FDI for Portugal apart from those based on past flows. In fact, even the data on flows was largely unreliable and figures for different periods could not be easily put together to build a coherent long series (Taveira, 1984). However, as part of a major exercise to review Portugal's long-term macroeconomic data, the Bank of Portugal recently published updated figures of the FDI flows between 1965 and 1993 (Banco de Portugal, 1997). This data is now consistent with the more recent information on FDI produced by that institution (Banco de Portugal, 'FDI by Economic Activity – Major Investing Countries', unpublished), so the series does run between 1965 and 1996.[2]

A further step was to estimate FDI flows before 1965. The Bank of Portugal keeps a record of medium and long-term capital flows since 1943, but until 1963 only the aggregated values were collected and published (Salgado de Matos, 1973). It was possible, however, to obtain estimates of FDI flows between 1943 and 1964 which were both fairly reliable and coherent with the new figures. This was done by computing the relation between the new values of FDI (as in Banco de Portugal, 1997) and the old values for medium and long-run capital movements (Salgado de Matos, 1973, p. 111) between 1965 and 1974.[3] This value (20.0 per cent for inward capital movements, 8.2 per cent for outward capital movements) was then used as an estimate of the percentage of medium and long-term capital movements that corresponded to direct investments between 1943 and 1965.[4]

Equipped with this new series of inward and outward FDI flows, longer and more reliable than any other existing before, new estimates of foreign capital stocks were produced. Narula (1996, pp. 40–42) raises several criticisms of the use of FDI flows to estimate stocks. Apparently, the sum-of-flows method underestimates both inward and outward investment

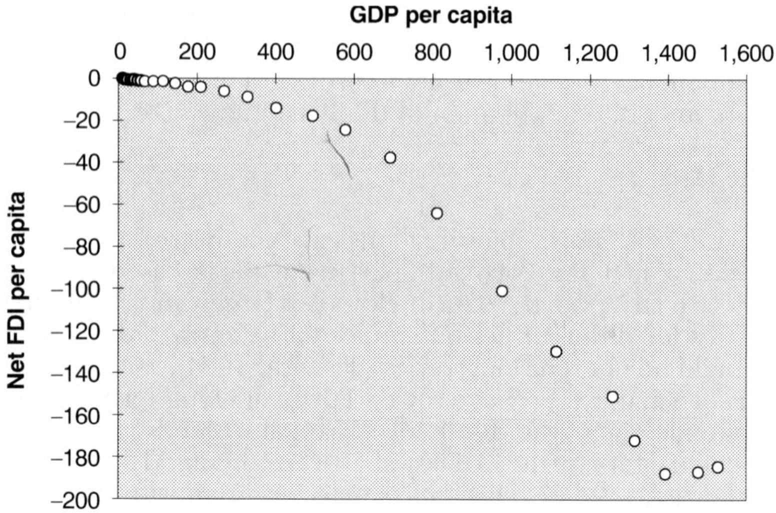


*Figure* 3.1 GDP per capita versus Net FDI per capita Portugal, 1965–1996

*Source*: Authors' calculations based on Bank of Portugal and INE data (thousand PTE).

stocks, in particular for industrialized countries. But Narula (1996, p. 41) uses only five-year flows in his comparison with stocks. Our main point in estimating the FDI flows since 1943 was precisely to obtain a workable estimate of FDI stocks at the point from which flows are more reliable (1965). We expect this to improve the quality of our estimates of FDI stocks, even keeping in mind the shortcomings of the sum-of-flows method.

Banco de Portugal (1997) also offers revised GDP and Population figures for the same period (1965–1993). For 1994 to 1996, estimations were used based on growth rates implicit in Nominal GDP (Banco de Portugal, *Relatório e Contas*) and other sources' Population estimates (INE, 1997).[5] A plot of the values obtained is presented in Figure 3.1.

## The Function

Dunning (1981a, 1981b, 1986), Tolentino (1987, 1993) and Narula (1996) used a quadratic function to describe the IDP curve. The observation of Figure 3.1, however, suggests that it might not be the best fit. We decided to test two alternative models:

$$\text{Model A}: \quad NFIpc = \alpha + \beta_1 GDPpc + \beta_2 GDPpc^2 + \mu$$

$$\text{Model B}: \quad NFIpc = \alpha + \beta_1 GDPpc^3 + \beta_2 GDPpc^5 + \mu$$

where: *NFIpc* = Net Foreign Investment Stock per capita (Outward FDI per capita – Inward FDI per capita); *GDPpc* = Gross Domestic Product per capita.

Although the choice of Model B was partially based on the observation of Figure 3.1, there is strong theoretical support for this rather unfriendly expression. Implicit in the quadratic function is the assumption that inward FDI is the engine of growth – Net Outward Investment per capita decreases sharply in the early stages of the Investment Development Path (reflecting high inward FDI and low or nil outward FDI), while GDP per capita has a slow start. But this is not in line with the IDP rationale.

Dunning and Narula (1996, p. 2) suggest that in the first stage of the IDP both inward and outward FDI will be very low. It is argued that governments must intervene, 'providing basic infrastructure and the upgrading of human capital via education and training' (p. 3). In other words, before the country can attract significant inward direct investment it must develop its Location-advantages, including improving the levels of GDP per capita.[6] Consequently, what must be expected in the first stage is a faster increase in GDP per capita than NOI per capita. Only in the second stage the growth rate of NOI per capita should be expected to be higher than GDP per capita (Dunning and Narula, 1996a, p. 4).

This evolution can be fully appropriated by Model B. Having an inflection point previously to the turning point (a minimum in our case), it represents a function where the dependent variable grows very slowly at the early stages. Only at a second stage it grows faster than the independent variable, but soon slowing down and eventually reaching a minimum – the U-turn that corresponds to the transition between Stages 2 and 3 when the country becomes a net investor.

## Estimation

The statistical software SPSS (version 7.0) was used for OLS estimation of the models described above. The results are presented in Table 3.1.

Both estimates seem to give quite a good fit, but the quadratic function in Model A has, in fact, the wrong curvature. If the trend of the last two years continues, the goodness of the fit will erode, which suggests that Model A is not a good description of the Portuguese IDP.

Model B, on the other hand, performs better by any standard and, as expected, provides very strong results – all the parameters estimated are highly significant (very strong t-tests), as seems to happen with the overall model (F-test significant at 1 per cent), and the Durbin-Watson statistic does not seem to be a major problem. Fitted and real values can be compared in Figure 3.2.

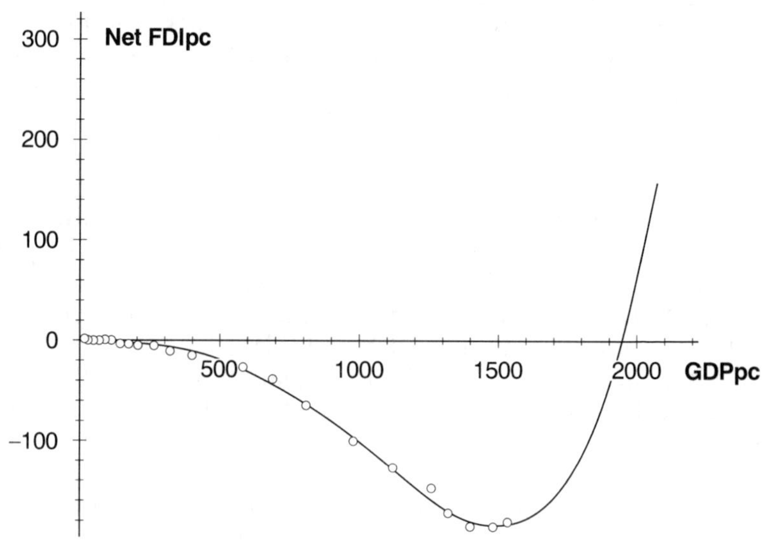


*Figure* 3.2 Estimation of the investment development path for Portugal (Model B)
*Source*: Authors' calculations (thousand PTE).

*Table 3.1* Estimation of the Portuguese IDP

| | | | | | | |
|---|---|---|---|---|---|---|
| | *Dependent variable: net FDI per capita* | | | | | |
| **Model A** | *R* | *R square* | *Adjusted R sqr* | *F* | *F (sig.)* | *DW* |
| | 0.993556 | 0.987147 | 0.986261 | 1113.675 | 0.000 | .641 |
| | | *Unstandardised coefficients* | | *Standardised coefficients beta* | *t* | *Sig.* |
| | | *β* | *Std. error* | | | |
| | (Constant) | 0.98873555 | 2.155410737 | | 0.45872 | 0.64985 |
| | GDPpc | −0.015531435 | 0.01098474 | −0.12047 | −1.41391 | 0.16803 |
| | GDPpc2 | −7.95595E-05 | 7.73498E-06 | −0.87637 | −10.28567 | 0.00000 |
| | *Dependent variable: net FDI per capita* | | | | | |
| **Model B** | *R* | *R square* | *Adjusted R sqr* | *F* | *F (sig.)* | *DW* |
| | 0.999205 | 0.998411 | 0.998301 | 9108.059 | 0.000 | 1.670 |
| | | *Unstandardised coefficients* | | *Standardised coefficients Beta* | *t* | *Sig.* |
| | | *β* | *Std. error* | | | |
| | (Constant) | −1.622025855 | 0.575861318 | | −2.81670 | 0.00864 |
| | GDPpc3 | −1.37645E-07 | 2.48157E-09 | −2.15163 | −55.46699 | 0.00000 |
| | GDPpc5 | 3.67821E-14 | 1.18787E-15 | 1.20115 | 30.96463 | 0.00000 |

*Source:* Authors' calculations.

**Comments**

The regression provided above seems to support the claims that international investment follows a more or less predictable path, accompanying and influencing economic growth. It suggests that Portugal entered Stage 2 of the IDP in the early 1980s, when GDP per capita reached around 150–200 thousand Escudos (approximately US$3,000 at the time). The positive net increases of the country's foreign investment stock in 1995 and 1996 (despite still being largely negative) also hints that Portugal is now in Stage 3.

This aggregate analysis must be taken with care, nevertheless. Despite what has been said, the classification of Portugal as a Stage 1 country during the second half of the 1960s and the 1970s is to difficult to support. Between 1965 and 1980 inward FDI averaged 0.5 per cent of the GDP and net FDI flows (minus) 0.4 per cent. Despite not being an outstanding value, it is by no means negligible. It also explains why it seemed that Portugal was already approaching Stage 3 both in 1975 and in 1988 (Narula, 1996, pp. 47–48).

In fact it must be accepted that the transition from Stage 1 to Stage 2 happened years ago, in the early 1960s, after Portugal joined EFTA as a founding member. EFTA membership, and not the level of GDP per capita or other economic characteristics of the country, seems to have been the element that triggered inflows of FDI (Salgado de Matos, 1973). The dictatorial regime that lasted until 1974 and the political and economic instability that followed probably deterred bigger inflows of foreign investment. Between 1965 and 1975 they remained rather stable around 0.4/0.5 per cent of the GDP, dropping to 0.3 per cent between 1976 and 1979. Outward FDI flows, on the other hand, remained very low throughout all this period, averaging just 0.1 per cent of the GDP between 1965 and 1980.

This picture changed dramatically after 1980, at least for inward FDI. As expected (Dunning, 1988; Dunning and Narula, 1996a), government policies played a significant role. Not only did the government mount a major effort to stabilize the economy and to upgrade Portugal's infrastructure and other domestic assets, but in particular it sought to attract inward foreign investment (Taveira, 1984, p. 192). Economic integra-

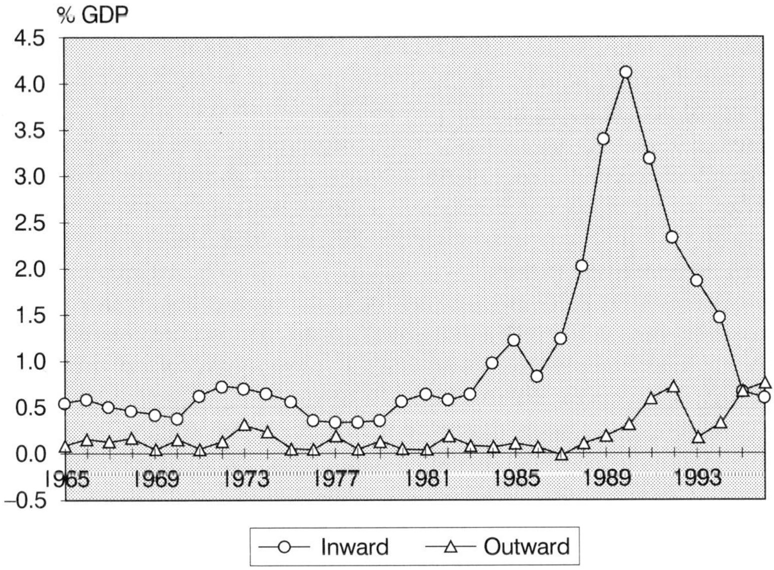


*Figure* 3.3 FDI flows in Portugal, 1965–1996 (% GDP)
*Sources*: Banco de Portugal (1997), *Séries Longas para a Economia Portuguesa*. Banco de Portugal (several), 'FDI by Economic Activity'.

tion again played a substantial role. By the beginning of the 1980s it was already clear that Portugal was soon to join EEC. It did so in 1986, and this was followed by a dramatic increase in the stock of inward direct investment. Like in the 1960s, however, the new international conditions were accompanied by substantial changes in domestic macroeconomic and industrial policies, which makes it difficult, if not impossible, to distinguish between the two.

On the other hand, outward flows, that averaged less than 0.1 per cent during the 1980s (even lower than in the previous two decades), registered a sudden increase in the 1990s.[7] This is very likely to correspond to the effect described by Dunning and Narula (1996a, p. 15): as a medium-income and reasonably fast-growing industrializing nation, Portugal is expected to engage in strategic asset seeking investment at an early stage of development. The EU's Internal Market Programme can only increase this pressure. This claim receives clear support from the fact that most of that foreign investment was directed towards other EU countries, in particular the most developed (Banco de Portugal).

But there is also growing evidence that several Portuguese firms are investing abroad to exploit their specific O-advantages. In particular, those investing in Central and Eastern Europe are probably taking advantage of the acquired knowledge of how to do business in fast-growing markets in the fringe of the European core, and probably also of technologies and firm structures well adapted to low/medium income countries strongly and increasingly integrated with the European Union. Again, this exploitation of O-advantages by firms from middle-income countries in less developed markets totally complies with the IDP theory.

A last but not insignificant comment on the specific shape of the Portuguese IDP concerns the effect of a major drop in inward FDI in the 1990s. After reaching 4.1 per cent of GDP in 1990, it plunged to a mere 0.6 per cent in 1996. Despite the increase in outward FDI, this reduction was the key element behind the U-turn in the Portuguese IDP curve. The reasons behind this fall are not yet clear, although it is feared that the political changes in Central and Eastern Europe might play some role – suddenly Portugal was no longer the lowest labour cost location among the European democracies.

However, from this combination of events it resulted that in 1995 and 1996 inward FDI flows were lower than outward flows for the first time in the country's recent history. The consequent increase in net outward stocks in those years – the last in our analysis – is clearly influencing our estimations. But from the information available on the Portuguese economy and individual industries it is not clear if the upturn shown in Figure 3.2 will be sustained in the future.

## CONCLUSION

The present analysis seems to give some support to the Investment Development Path theory, although the IDP cannot be described by the traditional quadratic function. The evidence is that Portugal did follow a pattern very much like the one predicted in the IDP theory. More importantly, the transformations that took place in the Portuguese economy can be reasonably well explained by the interaction between government policies, creating public goods which firms in Portugal can internalize, indigenous resources, and the evolution of FDI inward and outward stocks.

But this study of the Portuguese IDP also highlights some of the weaknesses of the paradigm. First of all, it is quite clear that the IDP cannot be used as a prediction mechanism. Data for 1975 and 1988 both suggested that Portugal was approaching Stage 3 of the IDP (Narula, 1996), but it is now clear that it was not the case in either of these years, the former in particular. The unpredictability of economic and non-economic variables is probably the reasons for this limitation. Second, the IDP curve taken straightforwardly can be misleading. We have shown that it seemed that Portugal entered Stage 2 only in the early 1980s, which was proven to be a miscalculation of some 20 years. A more careful analysis of the individual elements behind the IDP is obviously necessary. Finally, non-economic factors – EFTA and EEC membership, the 1974 revolution, the political changes in Eastern Europe – can be more important for the evolution of inward and outward FDI than the economic determinants usually discussed in the IDP theory. That is, despite the relevance of interaction between domestic economic variables and FDI flows and stocks, politics will always play a substantial role. It can be argued, as in Dunning and Narula (1996a), that this 'politics' is simply one of the elements that will make each individual IDP idiosyncratic, like the possession of natural resources, but it must be admitted that this undermines the relevance of the paradigm.

Despite these shortcomings, it must be acknowledged that, as a dynamic analysis, the IDP is a major contribution to the theory of international investment. It can largely explain the role of the Portuguese government in the evolution of the country competitiveness, as it predicts fairly well the direction of the Portuguese outward direct investment. It also highlights the relevance of the two-way relationship between inward flows and the upgrading of the country's L-advantages (location), on the one hand, and with the development of domestic firms' O-advantages on the other hand. Undoubtedly, further research on the lines presented here is needed to fully address the potential of the theory.

## Acknowledgements

The authors would like to thank Paulo Sousa (Faculdade de Economia do Porto) and two anonymous referees for their comments on an earlier version of the paper.

## Notes

1. Dunning (1991: p. 134, footnote 13; 1981a: p. 30, footnote) refers to the genesis of the Investment Development Cycle. It was first presented in 1975 by him and Peter Buckley at a conference of the UK Chapter of the Academy of International Business, and again in 1978 with Peter Buckley and Robert Pearce in a similar conference.
2. We must thank Dr António Agostinho, from the Department of Statistics and Economic Studies of the Bank of Portugal, for making the data available to us.
3. The data available permitted to use a longer period, but the figures suggest that the changes brought about by the revolution in 1974 changed considerably the proportion of FDI in total capital movements.
4. A similar method was used by Salgado de Matos (1973) and Taveira (1984), but with a different data set.
5. We used estimates based on implicit growth rates instead of the figures published in those sources because the latter were not consistent with the 1965–1993 series in Banco de Portugal (1997).
6. Even if not a policy target in itself, GDP growth will inevitably be a consequence of such policies.
7. 1993 and 1994 registered serious slowdowns in outward FDI flows, but this probably simply reflects the difficult economic conditions at home – GDP real growth rates of –0.2% and 0.5%, respectively.

## References

Banco de Portugal (1997) *Séries Longas para a Economia Portuguesa – Pós II Guerra Mundial* (Volume I – Séries Estatísticas). Lisboa.

——(several) *Relatório e Contas*.

——(several) 'FDI by Economic Activity – Major Investing Countries' (unpublished).

Buckley, Peter J. and Mark Casson (1998) 'Models of MNEs', *Journal of International Business Studies*, forthcoming.

Dunning, John H. (1981a) 'Explaining the International Direct Investment Position of Countries: Towards a dynamic and development approach', *Weltwirtschaftliches Archiv*, 117, 30–64.

——(1981b) 'Explaining Outward Direct Investment of Developing Countries: In support of the eclectic theory of international production', in K. Kumar and M. McLeod (eds), *Multinationals from Developing Countries*, 1–22. Lexington.

——(1986) 'The Investment Development Cycle and Third World Multinationals', in Khushi M. Khan (ed.), *Multinationals of the South*, 15–47. Frances Pinter.
——(1988) 'The Eclectic Paradigm of International Production: A restatement and some possible extensions', *Journal of International Business Studies*, 30, 1–31.
——(1993) *Multinational Enterprises and the Global Economy*. Addison-Wesley.
——and Rajneesh Narula (1996a) 'The Investment Development Path Revisited: Some emerging issues', in John H. Dunning and Rajneesh Narula (eds), *Foreign Direct Investment and Governments*, 1–41. Routledge.
——and Rajneesh Narula (eds) (1996b) *Foreign Direct Investment and Governments*. Routledge.
INE (Instituto Nacional de Estatística) (1997) 'Estimativas de População', in *Demografia e Census, Temas Estatísticos*. Infoline (28.10.97). [http://infoline.ine.pt/infoline/tema02/sb0201/info0201.htm]
Narula, Rajneesh (1996) *Multinational Investment and Economic Structure: Globalisation and Competitiveness*. Routledge.
Salgado de Matos, Luís (1973) *Investmentos Estrangeiros em Portugal*. Lisboa: Scara Nova.
Taveira, Elisa Ferreira (1984) 'Foreign Direct Investment in Portugal' (Unpublished PhD Thesis, University of Reading).
Tolentino, Paz Estrella E. (1987) 'The Global Shift in International Production: The growth of multinationals from the developing countries: The Philippines' (Unpublished PhD Thesis, University of Reading).
——(1993) *Technological Innovation and Third World Multinationals*. Routledge.

# Part II

# Foreign Direct Investment and Foreign Market Servicing Strategy

# 4 Analyzing Foreign Market Entry Strategies: Extending the Internalization Approach*

Peter J. Buckley and Mark C. Casson

**A new fully integrated analysis of the foreign market entry decision is presented, encompassing the choice between exporting, licensing, joint venturing and wholly owned foreign investment. The choice between acquisition and greenfield investment is examined, and so too are options based on subcontracting and franchising. The model extends the insights of internalization theory, and draws on concepts from the economics of industrial organization. A special feature of the model is the distinction between investment in production facilities and investment in distribution facilities – an important practical distinction that has been overlooked in much of the international business literature. The strength of competition from indigenous rivals is emphasized as a determinant of entry strategy into both production and distribution.**

Empirical studies of foreign direct investment (FDI) have become much more ambitious in scope over the last 30 years. In the 1960s, the main focus of the Hymer-Kindleberger theory (Hymer, 1976, Kindleberger, 1969) and the product cycle theory (Vernon 1966) was exporting versus FDI. In the 1970s the internalization approach identified licensing, franchising and subcontracting as other strategic options. The resurgence of mergers and acquisitions in the 1980s – often

* First published in *Journal of International Business Studies*, 29, 3 (1998).

as a 'quick fix' route to globalization – highlighted the choice between greenfield ventures and acquisitions. At the same time, the growing participation of US firms in international joint ventures (IJVs) drew attention to the role of cooperative arrangements.

In the 1990s, the role of FDI in 'transitional' or 'emerging' economies (East and Central Europe, China, Vietnam, etc.) has brought back into focus some of the classic issues of the 1960s: The 'costs of doing business abroad', and the importance of 'psychic distance'. It has renewed interest in the general questions as to why some modes of entry offer lower costs than others, and why certain circumstances seem to favour certain modes over others.

Linking all these issues together generates a high degree of complexity. Although the eclectic theory has been regularly revised and updated to accommodate the changing foci of applied research, it is too much of a 'paradigm' or 'framework' and too little of a 'model' to provide detailed advice on research design and hypothesis testing (Dunning, 1980). Complexity appears to have created a degree of confusion amongst scholars, which only a formal modelling exercise can dispel.

The model presented below has three distinctive features. First, it is based on a detailed schematic analysis that encompasses all the major market entry strategies. In existing literature, most strategies are appraised as alternatives to exporting, or as alternatives to greenfield FDI. It is unusual to see a direct comparison between, say, licensing and joint ventures, or between franchising and subcontracting. The present model permits any strategy to be compared with any other strategy. It is therefore particularly useful when the leading strategies in contention do not include either exporting or conventional FDI.

The second feature of the model is that it distinguishes clearly between production and distribution. Historically, a large proportion of initial FDI relates to foreign warehousing and distribution facilities. Production facilities only come later, if at all. The distinction is obvious in empirical work, but it has not been properly reflected in theory up until now. The result has been some confusion as to how theory should be applied to situations in which investment in distribution has a prominent role.

Finally, the model takes account of the strategic interaction between the foreign entrant and its leading host-country rival after entry has taken place. Following recent developments in industrial organization theory (as summarized, for example, in Tirole, 1988), it is assumed that the entrant can foresee the reaction of its rival, and take this into account at the time of entry. It is argued that this theoretical refinement is of the utmost practical importance in explaining the choice between greenfield investment and acquisition as entry modes.

The model concentrates on FDI for market access reasons, and excludes resource-orientated FDI and offshore production.

## HISTORICAL DEVELOPMENT OF THE THEORY

Much of the early literature on foreign market entry concerned the choice between exporting and FDI (for previous overviews, see Root, 1987; Young, *et al.* 1989; Buckley and Ghauri, 1993). The cost-based view of this decision suggested that the firm must possess a 'compensating advantage' in order to overcome the 'costs of foreignness' (Hymer, 1976; Kindleberger, 1969). This led to the identification of technological and marketing skills as the key elements in successful foreign entry (Hirsh, 1976; Horst, 1972). This tradition of firm-specific advantages (Caves, 1971; Rugman, 1981) connects with the literature on core competences arising from the Penrosian tradition (Penrose, 1959; Prahalad and Hamel, 1990). Sequential modes of internationalization were introduced by Vernon's 'Product Cycle Hypothesis' (1966), in which firms go through an exporting phase before switching first to market-seeking FDI, and then to cost-orientated FDI. Technology and marketing factors combine to explain standardization, which drives location decisions.

### Internalization

Buckley and Casson (1976) envisaged the firm as an internalized bundle of resources which can be allocated between product groups, and between national markets. Their focus on market based versus firm-based solutions highlighted the strategic significance of licensing in market entry. Entry involves two interdependent decisions – on location and mode of control. Exporting is domestically located and administratively controlled, foreign licensing is foreign located and contractually controlled, and FDI is foreign located and administratively controlled. This model was formalized by Buckley and Casson (1981), and empirically tested by Buckley and Pearce, (1979), Contractor (1984) and others.

### Stages Models of Entry

The Scandinavian 'stages' models of entry suggest a sequential pattern of entry into successive foreign markets, coupled with a progressive deepening of commitment to each market. Increasing commitment is particularly important in the thinking of the Uppsala School (Johanson and Wiedersheim-Paul, 1975; Johanson and Vahlne, 1977). Closely associated with stages models is the notion of 'psychic distance', which attempts to conceptualise and, to some degree, measure the cultural distance between countries and markets (Hallen and Wiedersheim-Paul, 1979). For a more recent view see Casson, 1994.

### Non-Production Activities

In explaining foreign market servicing policies, the role of non-production activities must be made explicit. The location of research activities is widely debated, especially in relation to spatial agglomeration (Kogut and Zander, 1993). There is also an extensive literature on the entry aspects of marketing and distribution (Davidson and McFetridge, 1985), much of it in a transactions cost framework (Anderson and Coughlan, 1987; Anderson and Gatignon, 1986; Hill, Hwang and Kim, 1990; Kim and Hwang, 1992; and Agarwal and Ramaswani, 1992).

### Mergers and Acquisitions versus Greenfield Ventures

Stopford and Wells (1972) examined takeovers versus acquisitions as part of the their analysis of the organization of the multinational firm. The predominance of entry via takeovers in most advanced economies has stimulated a number of good empirical studies (Dubin, 1975; Wilson, 1980; Zejan, 1990; Hennart and Park, 1993), which have drawn on both the internalization perspective and the strategy literature (Yip, 1982). Particular attention has been paid to the costs of adaptation and cultural integration that are encountered in the case of mergers. The theoretical issues have recently been surveyed by Svensson (1996) and Meyer (1997).

## Joint Ventures Versus Wholly Owned Subsidiaries

The recent literature on IJVs is immense, and has spawned some innovative developments in international business theory and much insightful empirical work based on extensive data sets (Contractor and Lorange, 1988; Beamish and Killing, 1997). Buckley and Casson (1988, 1996) summarize the conditions conducive to IJVs as: (i) the possession of complementary assets; (ii) opportunities for collusion, and (iii) barriers to full integration – economic, financial, legal or political (see also Beamish, 1985; Beamish and Banks, 1987; Kogut, 1988; Hennart, 1988; and Contractor, 1990).

The IJV literature has focused particularly on partner selection, management strategy and the measurement of performance. Partner selection is examined by Beamish (1987), who relates selection to performance, Harrigan (1988b), who examines partner asymmetries, and Geringer (1991). Kogut and Singh (1987, 1988) relate partner selection to entry method. Management strategy in IJVs is analysed by Killing (1983) and Harrigan (1988), whilst Gomes-Casseres (1991) relates strategy to ownership preferences.

The performance of IJVs is the subject of much debate. It cannot be assumed that joint venture termination indicates failure – an IJV may end precisely because it has achieved its objectives. Similarly, the restructuring of joint ventures and alliances may indicate the exploitation of the flexibility of the organizational form, rather than a response to under-performance see Franko (1971), Gomes-Casseres (1987), Kogut (1988, 1989), and Blodgett (1992). Other analyses of IJV performance include Geringer and Hebert (1991), Inkpen and Birkinshaw (1994) and Woodcock, Beamish and Makino (1994). Nitsch, Beamish and Makino (1996) relate entry mode to performance, and Gulati (1995) examines the role of repeated ties between partners as contributing to success – an interesting attempt to encompass 'cultural' variables.

**Cultural Factors**

The relationship between (national) culture and entry strategy is explicitly examined (using a reductionist version of Hofstede's (1980) cultural classification) by Kogut and Singh (1988) (see also Shane, 1994). Cultural barriers are utilized in an examination of foreign market entry by Bakema, Bell and Pennings (1996), and a 'cultural learning process' is invoked by Benito and Gripsrud (1994) to help explain the expansion of FDI.

**Market Structure and Entry Strategy**

It is one of the contributions of this chapter to introduce market structure issues into the modelling of entry decisions. The relationship between entry behaviour and market structure was emphasized in Knickerbocker's (1973) study of oligopolistic reaction, which set up a crude game-theoretic structure for competitive entry into key national markets. Flowers (1976) and Graham (1978) emphasized 'exchange of threats' in their respective studies of European and Canadian investment in the United States, and two-way investment between the United States and Europe. Yu and Ito (1988) more recently examined oligopolistic reaction and FDI in the US tyre and textiles industry. Graham (1992) laments the lack of attention to competitive structure in the international business literature, where the entrant is effectively a monopolist (Buckley and Casson, 1981). Indeed, Casson's (1985) study of cartelization versus multinationalization is one of the few economic models of multinational industrial organization available.

**Summary**

Location costs, internalization factors, financial variables, cultural factors, such as trust and psychic distance, market structure and competitive strategy, adaptation costs (to the local environment), and the cost of doing business abroad are all identified in the literature as playing a role in determining firms' foreign market entry decisions. The model which follows includes all these variables, and analyzes their interactions in a systematic way.

## THE MODEL

The model applies the economic theory of FDI presented in Buckley and Casson (1976, 1981), Buckley (1983), Casson (1991) and Buckley and Casson (1996) to the set of issues identified in the literature review above. Although the model involves a number of apparently restrictive assumptions, these assumptions can, if necessary, be relaxed, at the cost of introducing additional complications into the analysis. The assumptions are not so much restrictions upon the relevance of the model as indicators of key contextual issues on which every researcher into foreign market entry must pass judgement before their analysis begins. If some of the assumptions seem unfamiliar then it is because few researchers have actually made their assumptions sufficiently explicit in the past.

### The Entrant

1. A firm based in a home country is seeking to sell for the first time in a foreign market. The emphasis on first-time entry makes it important to distinguish between the one-off set-up costs of an entry mode, and the recurrent costs of subsequent operation in that mode. It is assumed, unless otherwise stated, that recurrent operations take place in a stable environment.
2. Foreign market demand for the product is infinitely elastic at a price $p_1$, up to a certain volume at which it becomes totally inelastic. For example, each customer may desire just one unit of the product, which they value at $p_1$, and when everyone has bought that unit no more can be sold however far the price is dropped. The volume at which demand becomes inelastic is determined by the size of the foreign market, $x$.
3. The focus of the model on market entry makes it appropriate to distinguish between production activity ($P$) and

distribution activity (*D*). Distribution links production to final demand. It comprises warehousing, transport, and possibly retailing too. Distribution must be carried out entirely in the foreign market, but production may be located at either home or abroad.

4. The entrant's production draws upon proprietary technology generated by research and development activity (*R*). Effective distribution depends upon marketing activity (*M*). Marketing involves investigating customers' needs, and maintaining the reputation of the product by giving customers the service they require.
5. The entrant has no foreign activity *M* at the time of entry, and consequently lacks market knowledge. This knowledge can be acquired through experience (learning from mistakes) at the time of entry, incurring a once-and-for-all cost of entry, *m*. The knowledge can be obtained in other ways as well, as described below. One of the keys to successful entry strategy is to acquire *M* in the most appropriate way.
6. The flow of technology from *R* to *P* defines the first of three 'intermediate products' in the model. The second is the flow of marketing expertise from *M* to *D*. The third is the physical flow of wholesale product from the factory or production unit *P* to the distribution facility *D*. (The internal flow of information between *R* and *M* is not discussed as it is a fixed cost, which is the same for every form of market entry considered in the model.)
7. Production at home means that the product must be exported. Exporting incurs transport costs and tariffs that foreign production avoids. On the other hand, foreign production incurs additional costs of communicating the technology, e.g., training foreign workers. Foreign production may also result in the loss of economies of scale. Exporting increases the utilization of the domestic plant, and allows it to be extended at low marginal cost. All of these factors are summarized in the net additional cost of home production, *z*, which is equal to transport costs and tariffs *less* savings on account of training costs and economies of scale.
8. The firm may enter the foreign market either by owning and controlling

- $P$ and $D$;
- $P$ only;
- $D$ only; or
- Neither $P$ nor $D$.

In the second case, it uses an independent distribution facility, which is franchised to handle the product. In the third case, it either exports from its home production facility, or subcontracts to an independent local facility. In the final case, the firm licenses an independent local firm to both produce and distribute the product. Because there is only one host-country rival (see 14 below), the possibility that the firm could subcontract to one firm and franchise another is ignored.

9. The transaction cost of operating an external market is normally greater than that of an internal one. The availability of alternative incentive structures in an internal market reduces the costs of haggling and default (Hennart, 1982). Indeed, it is assumed in the present model that the transaction cost of obtaining marketing expertise from an external consultant, rather than from the firm's own $M$ activity, is prohibitive. The entrant can tap into an established $M$ activity only by franchising the local rival, forming a joint venture with the rival, or acquiring its distribution facility.
10. The cost of external transfer of technology is also high, but acceptably so. One of the main problems in transferring technology is to monitor the output of the production process to make sure that the contract is being complied with. This is easier to do under a subcontracting agreement, where the product is 'bought back', than under a licensing agreement, where it is not. The transactions costs of a subcontracting agreement exceed the internal costs of technology transfer by $t_1$, whilst the costs of licensing exceed internal costs by $t_2 \geq t_1$.
11. When the ownership of $P$ differs from that of $D$ then the flow of intermediate products between them is effected through an external market. When compared to the alternative of vertical integration of $P$ and $D$, this incurs additional transaction costs, $t_3$.

12. Entry of any type can be effected by either greenfield investment or acquisition. Under greenfield investment the firm uses its funds to pay for the construction of a new facility. Under acquisition it uses its funds to purchase the facility second-hand as a going concern instead. This is done by acquiring the equity in the firm which previously owned the facility.
13. An effective internal market requires a high degree of trust within the organization. This trust is not available immediately after an acquisition. It costs $q_1$ to build trust in technology transfer when a $P$ facility is newly acquired. It costs $q_2$ to build trust in the transfer of marketing expertise when a $D$ facility is newly acquired, and $q_3$ to build trust in the transfer of intermediate product when either $P$ or $D$ (but not both) is newly acquired.

**The Host Country Rival**

14. The firm faces a single local rival who previously monopolized the foreign market. At the time of entry, this rival operates as a fully integrated firm. It has the expertise, conferred by an activity $M$, which the entrant lacks. However, the local rival has higher costs because of inferior technology, on account of having no activity $R$.
15. It is assumed that in all bargaining (for example, over an acquisition) the local rival plays an essentially passive role. The rival does not bargain for a share of the entrant's profits, but simply ensures that it receives full opportunity earnings for the resources it surrenders to the entrant firm. The rival realizes that the entrant has a superior technology, and believes that when confronted with such a competitor its best strategy is to exit the industry by selling to the entrant those resources it wishes to buy, and redeploying the others to their best alternative use.
16. If the entrant uses the rival's production facility, then a cost of adaptation is incurred. This is because the entrant uses a different technology from the rival, and equipment must be modified accordingly. This applies regardless of whether the entrant acquires the facility outright, or

merely licenses, or subcontracts to the rival firm. However, the rival may have local production expertise, which the entrant lacks, providing savings to offset against the adaptation cost. The net cost of adaptation may therefore be negative. A negative adaptation cost, in this context, signifies that the cost of adapting the entrant's technology to local conditions using a greenfield plant is higher than the cost of adapting an existing local plant to the entrant's technology.

17. By contrast, use of a rival's *D* facility incurs no adaptation cost. This is because warehouses are normally more versatile than production plants. Use of the rival's *D* facility always brings with it the marketing expertise associated with *M*.

18. The rival's *P* and *D* facilities are the only existing facilities that can meet the needs of the market. Other local firms cannot enter the market, and the rival firm itself cannot invest in additional facilities. Under these conditions, acquisition of either a *P* or *D* facility gives the entrant monopoly power: Acquisition of a *D* facility gives the entrant a monopoly of final sales, whilst acquisition of a *P* facility gives the entrant a monopoly of supplies to *D*. Greenfield investment, however, confers no monopoly power because it eliminates no rival facility: greenfield investment in *D* creates duopoly in the sourcing of final demand, whilst greenfield investment in *P* creates duopoly in the sourcing of *D*.

19. When the rival retains ownership of both its *P* and *D* facilities, then it remains a potential competitor. Although it may have switched some of its facilities out of the industry, it can, in principle, re-enter by switching them back again. If it has contracted out its *P* facility under a subcontracting arrangement, or contracted out its *D* facility under a franchising arrangement, then it can, in principle, re-enter competition when the agreements expire. Under a subcontracting arrangement, the entrant and the rival remain potential competitors in the final product market, since each has its own distribution facility. Any attempt by the entrant to charge the full monopoly price would encourage the rival to switch to producing its own output instead. The entrant must persuade the rival

not to compete by reducing its price to a 'limit price' $p_2 < p_1$, at which it just pays the rival to keep its distribution facility out of the industry. Under a franchising arrangement, the local rival retains the option of switching back to supplying its distribution facility from its own production plant. To discourage this, the entrant must set an intermediate output price, which is equivalent (after deduction of distribution costs) to the same limit price $p_2$. The final customers pay the monopoly price, since the franchisee is the sole distributor, but the difference between the monopoly price and the limit price accrues to the franchisee. In either case, therefore, the persistence of rivalry costs the entrant $s = (p_1 - p_2)x$ in lost sales revenue.

20. Matters are slightly different in the case of a licensing agreement. It is assumed that licensing is a long-term agreement, as opposed to short-term agreements like subcontracting and franchising. A licence, it is supposed, involves either an outright purchase of the right to use the technology, or a long-term agreement for the whole of the period over which patent protection is likely to extend. The licence agreement therefore confers effective monopoly power on the local licensee, but at the same time allows the entrant to appropriate all the monopoly rents by negotiating suitable terms for the licence agreement.
21. Apart from licensing, the only way to avoid the competitive threat is acquisition. Acquisition of either the rival's *P* or *D* facility will do. It is assumed that the costs at which these facilities can be acquired are equivalent to the cost of new construction under a greenfield strategy (although acquisition incurs additional conversion costs, as explained above).

## Joint Ventures

22. Joint ventures are owned 50:50 by the two firms. Either the *P* or *D* plant, or both, can be jointly owned. It is assumed that when an IJV is undertaken, the partner is always the local rival. If both *P* and *D* are jointly owned, then they are both part of the same IJV, and so the

market in intermediate output is internalized within the IJV. The IJV does not involve new facilities; it is assumed to be a 'buy in' by the entrant to the local firm. This means that IJV production incurs the costs of adaptation described above. Greenfield IJVs can easily be included in the model, although its complexity increases considerably as a result. Because the local rival contributes its facilities to the IJV, the IJV enjoys monopoly power in the same way that an acquisition does.

23. When an IJV is linked to one of the entrant's wholly owned activities, the relevant intermediate product market is only partially internalized. It is assumed, however, that once the appropriate degree of trust has been built up, the market can operate as though it was fully internal. The relevant costs of building trust are $j_1$ for technology transfer, $j_2$ for marketing expertise, and $j_3$ for intermediate output flow.

24. Where both entrant and rival possess *P* facilities with which to source an IJV *D* facility, they employ the IJV to maintain a monopoly price, but compete to supply it. The competition from the rival's *P* facility forces the entrant to supply the IJV at a limit price, and so allows the rival to obtain half the monopoly rent through its share in the IJV, even though it does not actually supply the IJV itself. If both entrant and rival possess *D* facilities able to draw upon an IJV *P* facility, then they can maintain a monopoly price by competing for a franchise to handle all the output. This forces the entrant to bid up the price for IJV output such that the profits are again shared with the rival through its stake in the IJV.

25. Learning costs $m$, adaptation costs $a$ and trust-building costs $j_i, q_i (i = 1, 2, 3)$ are once-and-for-all set-up costs that are financed by borrowing at the given interest rate $r$. By contrast, the home location cost premium $z$ and the transaction costs $t_i$ $(i = 1, 2, 3)$ are recurrent costs incurred each period.

## Defining the Strategy Set

The basic approach is to determine the set of all possible market entry strategies, to measure the profitability of each, and to identify the most profitable strategy. The dimensions of the strategy set are defined by the following issues:

1. where production is located;
2. whether production is owned by the entrant;
3. whether distribution is owned by the entrant;
4. whether ownership is outright, or shared through an IJV; and
5. whether ownership is obtained through greenfield investment or acquisition.

The first four issues determine twelve main strategies of market entry. These twelve strategies are listed on the left-hand side of Table 4.1, and summarized schematically in Figure 4.1. Six of these strategies have different variants generated by the fifth issue. These variants are indicated on the right-hand side of the table. The figure distinguishes linkages involving the flow of information from *R* to *P* and *M* to *D*, and linkages involving the flow of physical product from *P* to *D*, and from *D* to final demand. Location is distinguished by the columns, and ownership by the rows. Ownership by the entrant is also identified by shading; facilities owned by the local rival are shown as clear. The strategies associated with each particular linkage are indicated by the numbers 1–12 in the figure.

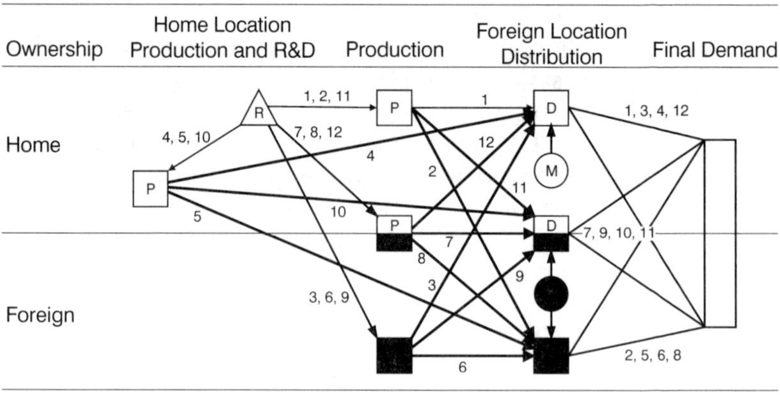


*Figure* 4.1 Twelve entry strategies and their variants

*Table* 4.1 Twelve entry strategies and their variants

| *Ref.* | *Type* | *Description* | *Variants* |
|---|---|---|---|
| 1. | Normal FDI | Entrant owns foreign production and distribution facilities. | 1.1 Both facilities are greenfield<br>1.2 Both facilities are acquired.<br>1.3 Production is greenfield and distribution is acquired.<br>1.4 Distribution is greenfield and production is acquired. |
| 2. | FDI in production | Entrant owns foreign production, but uses independent distribution facilities. | 2.1 Production is greenfield.<br>2.2 Production is acquired. |
| 3. | Subcontracting | Entrant owns foreign distribution, but uses independent production facilities. | 3.1 Distribution is greenfield.<br>3.2 Distribution is acquired. |
| 4. | FDI in distribution | Entrant exports to own distribution facility. | 4.1 Distribution is greenfield.<br>4.2 Distribution is acquired. |
| 5. | Exporting/franchising | Entrant exports to independent distribution facility. | |
| 6. | Licensing | Entrant transfers technology to independent integrated firm. | |

*Table* 4.1 (*contd.*)

| *Ref.* | *Type* | *Description* | *Variants* |
|---|---|---|---|
| 7. | Integrated JV | Entrant jointly owns an integrated set of production and distribution facilities. | |
| 8. | JV in production | Entrant jointly owns foreign production, but uses an independent distribution facility. | |
| 9. | JV in distribution | Entrant jointly owns foreign distribution, but subcontracts production to an independent facility. | |
| 10. | JV exporting | Entrant exports to a jointly owned distribution facility. | |
| 11. | FDI/JV combination | Entrant owns foreign production and jointly owns foreign distribution. | 11.1 Production is greenfield.<br>11.2 Production is acquired. |
| 12. | JV/FDI combination | Entrant owns foreign distribution and jointly owns foreign production. | 12.1 Distribution is greenfield.<br>12.2 Distribution is acquired. |

**Deriving the Profit Equations**

A profit equation for each variant of each entry strategy can be derived by applying the assumptions given above to the schematic illustrations in Figure 4.1. Certain elements of cost and revenue are common to all the profit equations, and it simplifies matters to net these out. This generates a set of summary profit equations in which profitability is expressed in terms of deviations from a profit norm. An appropriate norm is the profit generated by pursuing strategy 1 under ideal conditions, in which the firm is already acquainted with the local market, and there is no indigenous rival. The profit norm is the revenue generated by sales at the monopoly price $p_1$, less the cost of greenfield foreign production, *less* the cost of greenfield foreign distribution, *less* the cost of internal technology transfer to a greenfield foreign plant, *less* the cost of internal transfer of goods from production to distribution.

If the actual profits of each strategy are compared with this norm, then every strategy incurs some additional cost. The relevant cost expressions are given in Table 4.2. The subscripts applied to the cost symbol $c$ refer to the strategies and their variants listed in Table 4.1. The variables on the right-hand side have already been explained when introducing the assumptions of the model. Set-up costs are multiplied by the rate of interest to convert a once-and-for-all cost into a continuous equivalent.

To see how the profit equations are derived, consider strategy 2. This involves FDI in production, with sales being handled by the rival firm. There are two variants of this strategy, depending upon whether the production plant is acquired or not. The only international transfer of resources under this strategy involves technology, which moves across the column boundary from $R$ to $P$. The transfer is internalized because no change of ownership is involved. Change of ownership only occurs where the flow of intermediate output from $P$ to $D$ crosses the row boundary. From $D$ the product is distributed to the entire foreign market, as indicated by the flow fanning out from $D$.

The advantages of this particular strategy are two-fold. It internalizes the transfer of technology within the entrant firm, and it internalizes the transfer of marketing expertise within

*Table* 4.2 Costs of alternative strategies compared with the profit norm

| | | | | | | | |
|---|---|---|---|---|---|---|---|
| $c_{1.1} =$ | | | | | | $+s$ | $+rm$ |
| $c_{1.2} =$ | | $rq_1$ | $+rq_2$ | | $+ra$ | | |
| $c_{1.3} =$ | | | $rq_2$ | $+rq_3$ | | | |
| $c_{1.4} =$ | | $rq_1$ | | $+rq_3$ | $+ra$ | | $+rm$ |
| $c_{2.1} =$ | | | | $t_3$ | | $+s$ | |
| $c_{2.2} =$ | | $rq_1$ | | $+t_3$ | $+ra$ | | |
| $c_{3.1} =$ | | $t_1$ | | $+t_3$ | $+ra$ | $+s$ | $+rm$ |
| $c_{3.2} =$ | | $t_1$ | $+rq_2$ | $+t_3$ | $+ra$ | | |
| $c_{4.1} =$ | $z$ | | | | | $+s$ | $+rm$ |
| $c_{4.2} =$ | $z$ | | $+rq_2$ | $+rq^3$ | | | |
| $c_5 =$ | $z$ | | | $+t_3$ | | $+s$ | |
| $c_6 =$ | | $t_2$ | | | $+ra$ | | |
| $c_7 =$ | | $rj_1$ | $+rj_2$ | | $+ra$ | | |
| $c_8 =$ | | $rj_1$ | | $+rj_3$ | $+ra$ | | |
| $c_9 =$ | | $t_1$ | $+rj_2$ | $+rj^3$ | $+ra$ | | |
| $c_{10} =$ | $z$ | | $+rj_2$ | $+rj_3$ | | $+s/2$ | |
| $c_{11.1} =$ | | | $+rj_2$ | $+rj_3$ | | $+s/2$ | |
| $c_{11.2} =$ | | $rq_1$ | $+rj_2$ | $+rj^3$ | $+ra$ | | |
| $c_{12.1} =$ | | $rj_1$ | | $+rj_3$ | $+ra$ | $+s/2$ | $+rm$ |
| $c_{12.2} =$ | | $rj_1$ | $+rj_2$ | $+rj^3$ | $+ra$ | | |

the local firm. This can only be achieved, however, by externalizing the flow of intermediate output, which generates the transaction cost premium term $t_3$, which appears in the expressions for both $c_{2.1}$ and $c_{2.2}$. This is, in fact, the only term that is common to both expressions. The remaining terms are all accounted for by the difference between greenfield and acquisition methods of FDI. The greenfield strategy avoids the cost $a$ of adapting an existing plant to the needs of a new technology. Thus the term $ra$, which appears in the expression for $c_{2.2}$, does not appear in the expression for $c_{2.1}$. The greenfield strategy also means that the internal transfer of technology is not bedevilled by a lack of trust, which arises when the production facility is acquired instead. The cost of building trust in internal technology transfer, $rq_1$, therefore appears in $c_{2.2}$, but not in $c_{2.1}$.

The compensating advantage of the acquisition strategy is that it does not add to overall capacity in the foreign country.

Indeed, because the entrant faces a single local rival, acquisition of the rival's production facility effectively prevents the rival from entering into competition with the entrant firm. Given that under strategy 2 the local firm retains control of distribution, it can threaten to source distribution from its own production plant instead of from the entrant's plant. Although the entrant may be able to constrain this threat in the short term by signing an exclusive franchise contract with its local rival, in the long run this contract will expire, and the threat will reappear. Only acquisition of one of the rival's facilities can eliminate this threat altogether. This means that the greenfield strategy incurs a loss of revenues compared to the acquisition strategy.

**Dominance Relations**

Theory predicts that the strategy with the lowest cost will be chosen. Which strategy is chosen depends on the relative magnitude of the different variables on the right-hand side of Table 4.2. The easiest way to understand the general properties of the solution is first to eliminate any strategies that are clearly dominated by others, and then to compare the remaining ones in terms of the major trade-offs involved.

Whether strategies are dominated or not depends upon what restrictions are imposed upon the right-hand-side variables. So far, the only restrictions implied by the assumptions are $m, r, s, j_i, q_i, t_i > 0 (i = 1, 2, 3)$ and $t_2 \geq t_1$. In particular, the variables $a$ and $z$ are unrestricted in sign. Under these conditions, only two of the strategies are dominated, namely the bottom two in the table:

$$c_{12.1} > c_8; \; c_{12.2} > c_8$$

These strategies involve a production IJV and a wholly owned sales subsidiary. They are inferior to a production IJV combined with the franchising of sales. This shows that if the entrant is to partner the IJV in production, then there is no point in buying back the product to distribute it afterwards.

Once additional restrictions are imposed, further dominance relations emerge. For example, if the net cost of home production is positive, $z > 0$, then all the export strategies are dominated by equivalent strategies involving greenfield foreign production:

$$c_{4.1} > c_{1.1};\ c_{4.2} > c_{1.3};\ c_5 > c_{2.1}:\ c_{10} > c_{11.1}$$

This illustrates the important point that location effects are independent of internalization effects in models of this kind.

If the net cost of technological adaptation of existing production facilities is positive, $a > 0$, then it follows that:

$$c_{3.1} > c_{1.1}$$

This means that the strategy of investing only in a greenfield distribution facility is inefficient compared to the strategy of investing in a greenfield production facility as well. Put simply, subcontracting production is not a good idea when the net cost of adapting existing plant to the new technology is positive.

So far, no use has been made of restrictions on transactions costs. Suppose now that external market costs exceed the costs of building trust in internal markets after acquisition. In the context of production, this means that $t_1 > rq_1$ from whence it follows that:

$$c_{3.2} > c_{2.2}$$
$$c_9 > c_{11.2}$$

The first inequality shows that subcontracting production in conjunction with the acquisition of a distribution facility is more costly than franchising distribution in conjunction with the acquisition of a production facility. The second inequality shows that subcontracting production in conjunction with a jointly owned distribution facility is more costly than acquiring a production facility in conjunction with a jointly owned distribution facility. These results underline the fact that high transaction costs in technology markets, combined with easy trust-building post-acquisition, discourage subcontracting and favour acquisition instead.

The process of elimination through dominance can be continued by postulating that the cost of building trust is lower after an acquisition than it is within a joint venture:

$q_i j_i (i=1,2,3)$. Not surprisingly, this eliminates several IJV strategies – though not all:

$$c_7 > c_{1.2};\ c_{11.1} > c_{1.3};\ c_{11.2} > c_{1.3}$$

It is inefficient to combine an IJV distribution facility with a production facility that is either wholly or jointly owned. Obviously, if the cost of building trust were thought to be lower in a IJV then the inequalities would be the other way round, and the three acquisitions-based strategies would be eliminated instead.

It is not only inequality restrictions that can be used to generate dominance relations: equality restrictions can be used as well. For example, if the costs of building trust after acquisition are the same in each internal market, $q_i = q$ ($i = 1, 2, 3$), then:

$$c_{1.4} > c_{1.2} > c_{1.3}$$

This means that it is inefficient to acquire production when distribution is wholly owned; it is better to use greenfield production and acquire distribution instead.

If in addition the costs of building trust within IJVs are also the same in all markets, $j_i = j (i = 1, 2, 3)$ then:

$$c_8 > c_{1.3}$$

It is better to combine greenfield production with the acquisition of a distribution facility than to undertake an IJV in production, and franchise distribution to the partner firm.

Finally, consider two further restrictions. The first asserts that the cost of learning about a foreign market through a greenfield distribution facility exceeds the transaction cost of an external intermediate product market, $m > t_3$. It follows that:

$$c_{1.1} > c_{2.1},$$

so that it is cheaper to combine greenfield production with greenfield distribution rather than with an independent distribution facility.

The second restriction asserts that the transaction cost of the external intermediate product market exceeds the cost of building trust in that market following an acquisition; $t_3 > rq_3$. It follows that (given that $q_1 = q_2$ from an earlier restriction):

$$c_{2.2} > c_{1.3}$$

so that it is cheaper to combine greenfield production with acquired distribution than to acquire production and franchise distribution instead.

## Properties of the Solution

By carrying the process of elimination so far, only three of the original strategies are left in contention:

1.3. greenfield production combined with acquired distribution;

2.1. greenfield production combined with franchised distribution; and

6. licensing.

The choice between these strategies is governed by six of the original variables: $a$, $q$, $r$, $s$, $t_2, t_3$.

The solution is to choose:

$$\begin{aligned} &1.3. \quad \text{if } q \leq (t_3+s)/2r, (t_2/r)+a \\ &2.1. \quad \text{if } t_3+s \leq 2qr, t_2+ra \\ &6. \quad \text{if } t_2+ra \leq 2qr, t_3+s \end{aligned}$$

It can be seen that strategy 1.3 is preferred wherever the cost of acquisition $q$ is low. This is reasonable because 1.3 is the only one of the three strategies that involves acquisition. Strategy 2.1 is preferred when the transaction costs of the external market in intermediate out-put, $t_3$, are low, and when the loss of monopoly profits from competitive distribution, $s$, is small. This is reasonable because strategy 2.1 is the only one to involve an arm's length sale of intermediate output, and the only one to leave the local rival in a position to compete. Strategy 6 is preferred when the transactions costs of licensing a technology, $t_2$, and adapting local production facilities, $a$, are low. This is reasonable because the licensing strategy is the only one of the three to utilize existing production facilities; the other two use only existing distribution facilities instead.

## Deriving the Propensity to Adopt a Given Strategy

The logical structure of the model means that a change in any variable that increases the cost of certain strategies tends to inhibit the adoption of these strategies, and to encourage the adoption of alternative strategies instead. These alternative strategies are the ones whose costs are independent of the variable concerned. Indeed, apart from the rate of interest, $r$, and the cost of competition, $s$, every variable that enters into several cost functions enters into each of them in the same way. It is therefore impossible for a change in any variable of this kind to induce any switch between the strategies whose costs depend upon it.

In the case of $r$, however, the impact varies according to the particular set up costs involved, and so the impact of $r$ upon the choice of any strategy cannot be determined unless the relative size of different set-up costs is known. An increase in $r$ reduces the propensity to adopt any strategy that involves a set-up cost compared to any strategy that does not. If a strategy with a positive set up cost has a lower set-up cost than the best alternative strategy; then an increase in $r$ will increase the propensity to adopt this strategy. Because its set-up cost is smaller than that of the best alternative, the strategy is more likely to be chosen when $r$ is high.

In the case of $s$, the impact of an increase favours distribution joint ventures at the expense of wholly owned greenfield distribution facilities, but favours distribution acquisitions and licensing at the expense of both. The net effect on joint venture distribution strategies therefore depends upon whether the best alternative to joint ventures is greenfield distribution, or either acquisitions or licensing instead.

The implications of these general principles for the strategies of acquisition, franchising and licensing discussed above are summarized in Table 4.3. The table indicates whether an increase in a given variable is likely to increase or decrease the propensity to adopt that strategy in preference to the other two. A question mark indicates that the direction of the effect

*Table* 4.3 Comparative static analysis of the effects of changes in the values of the explanatory variables on the choice between the three dominant strategies

| | | $a$ | $q$ | $s$ | $t_2$ | $t_3$ | $r$ |
|---|---|---|---|---|---|---|---|
| 1.3 | Acquisition | + | – | + | + | + | ? |
| 2.1 | Franchising | + | + | – | + | – | + |

*Notes*:
$a$ Adaptation cost of production plant.
$q$ Cost of building trust to access marketing expertise through a newly-acquired distribution facility.
$s$ Value of profit-sharing collusion.
$t_2$ Additional transaction cost incurred by licensing technology.
$t_3$ Additional transaction cost incurred in using an external market for the wholesale product.
$r$ Rate of interest.

cannot be known unless relative set-up costs are specified – in this context, the relative cost of building trust after an acquisition, $q$, and the relative cost of adapting a licensee's production plant, $a$. If $2q>a$, then an increase in $r$ will favour acquisition and discourage licensing, so that $r$ will have a negative effect on licensing. The effect on acquisition will remain indeterminate, however, because although it becomes more favoured relative to licensing, it becomes less favoured relative to franchising. The direction of the effect therefore depends upon whether licensing or franchising is the best alternative to acquisition. If $2q>a$, then an increase in $r$ will favour licensing and discourage acquisition, so that an increase in $r$ will have a negative effect on acquisition. The effect on licensing will remain indeterminate, however, because although it becomes more favoured relative to acquisition, it becomes less favoured relative to franchising.

The wider implications of these principles are summarized in Table 4.4. The results reported in the table apply to the market entry problem in its most general form. The additional assumptions used to derive the dominance relations

*Table* 4.4 Comparative static analysis of the effects of changes in the values of the explanatory variables on the propensity to adopt each possible entry mode

| | $a$ | $j_1$ | $j_2$ | $j_3$ | $m$ | $q_1$ | $q_2$ | $q_3$ | $r$ | $s$ | $t_1$ | $t_2$ | $t_3$ | $z$ |
|---|---|---|---|---|---|---|---|---|---|---|---|---|---|---|
| 1.1 | + | + | + | + | – | + | + | + | + | – | + | + | + | + |
| 1.2 | – | + | + | + | + | – | – | + | ? | + | + | + | + | + |
| 1.3 | + | + | + | + | + | + | – | – | ? | + | + | + | + | + |
| 1.4 | – | + | + | + | – | – | + | – | ? | + | + | + | + | + |
| 2.1 | + | + | + | + | + | + | + | + | + | – | + | + | – | + |
| 2.2 | – | + | + | + | + | – | + | + | ? | + | + | + | – | + |
| 3.1 | – | + | + | + | – | + | + | + | ? | – | – | + | – | + |
| 3.2 | – | + | + | + | + | + | – | + | ? | + | – | + | – | + |
| 4.1 | + | + | + | + | – | + | + | + | + | | [illegible] | + | + | – |
| 4.2 | + | + | + | + | + | + | – | – | ? | + | + | + | + | – |
| 5 | + | + | + | + | + | + | + | [illegible] | [illegible] | – | + | + | – | – |
| 6 | – | + | + | + | + | + | + | + | ? | + | + | – | + | + |
| 7 | – | – | – | + | + | + | + | + | ? | + | + | + | + | + |
| 8 | – | – | + | – | + | + | + | + | ? | + | + | + | + | + |
| 9 | – | + | – | – | + | + | + | + | ? | + | – | + | + | + |
| 10 | + | + | – | – | + | + | + | + | ? | ? | + | + | + | – |
| 11.1 | + | + | – | – | + | + | + | + | ? | ? | + | + | + | + |
| 11.2 | – | + | – | – | + | – | + | + | ? | + | + | + | + | + |

*Notes*:

$a$ Adaptation cost of production plant.
$j_1$ Cost of building trust to support technology transfer in a production joint venture.
$j_2$ Cost of building trust to access marketing expertise through a distribution joint venture.
$j_3$ Cost of building trust to support a flow of the wholesale product to, or from, a joint venture.
$m$ Cost of acquiring knowledge of the market through wholly owned distribution.
$q_1$ Cost of building trust to transfer technology to a newly-acquired production facility.
$q_2$ Cost of building trust to transfer marketing expertise to a newly-acquired distribution facility.
$q_3$ Cost of building trust to support a flow of wholesale product to, or from, a newly-acquired facility.
$r$ Rate of interest.
$s$ Value of profit-sharing collusion.
$t_1$ Additional transaction cost incurred by subcontracting production.
$t_2$ Additional transaction cost incurred by licensing technology.
$t_3$ Additional transaction cost incurred in using an external market for the wholesale product.
$z$ Net additional cost of serving the foreign market by export rather than production in the host market.

above are now set to one side. A wide range of hypotheses are generated by this table. A comprehensive discussion of all of them is beyond the scope of a single paper. Some of the results are fairly obvious, and appear in an intuitive form in the extant literature. Other results are more surprising. In some cases, the element of surprise is a consequence of the specific assumptions that have been made in order to simplify the model. In other cases, the element of surprise indicates a hypothesis which is plausible when considered in depth, but not immediately obvious to the intuition.

## DISCUSSION OF RESULTS

Some of the more obvious results are as follows:

1. An increase in $z$, caused by higher tariffs, transport costs, or a loss of economies of scale in domestic production, encourages production abroad. It encourages both licensing and wholly owned production. This underlines the importance of keeping the distinction between *location* effects and *internalization* effects very clear in any discussion of foreign market entry strategy.
2. An increase in $a$, reflecting a highly specific type of entrant's technology, discourages acquisition and licensing, and favours greenfield production.
3. An increase in the cost of building trust, $q$, discourages acquisition and favours either greenfield investment or arm's length contractual arrangements.
4. A high cost of learning about the foreign market through experience, $m$, encourages acquisition, licensing and franchising, and discourages subcontracting or greenfield investment in distribution.
5. A high transaction cost for intermediate output $t_3$, encourages the vertical integration of production and distribution. This can be achieved either by the foreign entrant investing in both production and distribution, by the entrant exporting to a wholly owned distribution facility, or the entrant licensing the technology to a vertically integrated domestic firm. It can also be achieved by forming a vertically integrated IJV.

6. A high transaction cost for arm's length technology transfer, $t_1$, favours FDI over arm's length arrangements, like subcontracting.
7. In general, subcontracting is not a very attractive mode of foreign market entry. This is because it does not give access to the domestic rival's marketing expertise. It also leaves the domestic rival in a strong competitive position, since the contractual commitment to the entrant is of a short-term nature, and the rival's distribution facility is not committed at all. The reason why subcontracting is so often used is because of another motive for entering a foreign country, and that is for access to local resources – notably cheap labour for off-shore processing. This motive, though important, is excluded from the present paper. This shows how important it is to distinguish different strategic motivations when discussing institutional arrangements in international business.

Three interesting and less obvious results are as follows:

1. The existence of large monopoly rents, associated with a high cost of competition, $s$, favours strategies which give the entrant long-term control over either the domestic rival's production facilities, or the domestic rival's production facilities, or the domestic rival's distribution facilities. It favors acquisition over greenfield investment in either production or distribution. It also favours long-term arrangements, like licensing, over short-term arrangements, like subcontracting and franchising.
2. Joint ventures in distribution are a useful mode of market entry when high costs of learning by experience, $m$, discourage greenfield distribution, high costs of building trust, $q_1$, discourage the acquisition of distribution facilities, high costs in the arm's length intermediate output market, $t_3$, discourage franchising, and high costs of arm's length technology transfer, $t_2$, discourage licensing. However, joint ventures in production do not make much sense as a means of market entry, unless the production joint venture is part of an integrated joint venture that handles distribution as well.
3. In general, the analysis confirms that market structure is a crucial factor in the choice between greenfield investment

and acquisition. Entry through greenfield investment increases local capacity and intensifies competition, whereas entry through acquisition does not. This explains why governments so often compete to attract inward greenfield investment, whilst taking a restrictive attitude to acquisitions at the same time.

## IMPLICATIONS FOR FUTURE RESEARCH

The model is very flexible, in the sense that it is easy to modify the assumptions to address other issues. It can be extended to include two host country rivals, or two entrants vying with each other to enter the same market. This requires extending the analysis from duopoly to three-firm oligopoly. Introducing a third player not only increases the scope for competition, but also introduces new opportunities for cooperation too. The model can be rendered more dynamic by allowing entrants to determine the timing of entry – a particularly important consideration where growing markets, such as China or Eastern Europe, are concerned.

The host government plays a very passive role in the present model. Strategic interactions between the host government and the entrant can be introduced. The host government may offer tax incentives in return for commitments on local value added, or 'job creation', which affect the choice of entry mode. Bargaining may take place over subsidies. Political risk may discourage FDI and encourage the use of arm's length contracts instead. The possibilities for the firm to minimize global tax liabilities through transfer pricing can also be taken into account.

The model can be extended to take account of foreign investment in services, as well as manufacturing. It already takes an important step in the direction of analyzing service industries by introducing marketing and distribution activities in addition to production. By modifying the assumptions about the physical relationship between production and distribution in various ways, the model can be applied to a wide range of service industries.

There are many smaller ways in which the model can be modified as well. The analysis of duopolistic rivalry can be refined using models of Bertrand and Cournot competition

(Gorg, 1998). The formation of IJVs through greenfield investment can be introduced to supplement the 'buy in' strategy assumed above. Finally, the role of host-country production expertise can be modelled in greater detail by making more explicit the function of adapting foreign technology to local production conditions.

## References

Agarwal, Sanjeev and Srindhar N. Ramaswani (1992) 'Choice of foreign market entry mode: Impact of ownership, location and internalization factors', *Journal of International Business Studies*, 23, 1–27.

Anderson, Erin M. and A. T. Coughlan (1987) 'International market entry and expansion via independent or integrated channels of distribution', *Journal of Marketing*, 51, 71–82.

——and Hubert Gatignon (1986) 'Modes of foreign entry: A transaction costs analysis and propositions', *Journal of International Business Studies*, 17, 1–26.

Bakema, Harry G., John H. J. Bell and Johannes M. Pennings (1996) 'Foreign entry, cultural barriers and learning', *Strategic Management Journal*, 17, 151–66.

Beamish, Paul W. (1985) 'The characteristics of joint-ventures in developing and developed countries', *Columbia Journal of World Business*, 20, 13–20.

——(1987) 'Joint ventures in less developed countries: Partner selection and performance', *Management International Review*, 27, 1, 23–37.

——and John C. Banks (1987) 'Equity joint ventures and the theory of the multinational enterprise', *Journal of International Business Studies*, 18, 1–15.

——and J. Peter Killing (eds) (1987) *Cooperative Strategies*, 3 volumes, *North American Perspectives, European Perspectives, Asian Pacific Perspectives*, San Francisco, CA: New Lexington Press.

Benito, Gabriel R. G. and Geir Gripsrud (1992) 'The expansion of foreign direct investments: Discrete rational locational choices or a cultural learning process?', *Journal of International Business Studies*, 23, 461–76.

Blodgett, L. L. (1992) 'Factors in the instability of international joint ventures: An event history analysis', *Strategic Management Journal*, 13, 475–81.

Buckley, P. J. (1983) 'New theories of international business: Some unresolved issues', in Mark Casson (ed.), *The growth of international business*. London: Allen & Unwin, 34–50.

——and Mark Casson (1976) *The future of the multinational enterprise*. London: Macmillan.

——(1981) 'The optimal timing of a foreign direct investment', *Economic Journal*, 92, 361, 75–87.

——(1988) 'A theory of cooperation in international business', in Farok J Contractor and Peter Lorange (eds), *Cooperative strategies in international business*. Lexington, MA: Lexington Books.

——(1996) 'An economic model of international joint ventures', *Journal of International Business Studies*, 27, 5, 849–76.

——and Pervez N. Ghauri (1993) *The internationalization of the firm*. London: Dryden Press.

——and Robert D. Pearce (1979) 'Overseas production and exporting by the world's leading enterprises', *Journal of International Business Studies*, 10, 1, 9–20.

Casson, Mark (1985) 'Multinational monopolies and international cartels', in P. J. Buckley and Mark Casson, *The economic theory of the multinational enterprise*. London: Macmillan.

——(1991) 'Internalization theory and beyond', in Peter J. Buckley (ed.), *New horizons in international business: Research priorities for the 1990s*. Aldershot: Edward Elgar, 4–27.

——(1994) 'Internationalization as a learning process: A model of corporate growth and geographical diversification', in V. N. Balasubramanyam and David Sapsford (eds), *The economics of international investment*. Aldershot: Edward Elgar.

Caves, Richard E. (1971) 'International corporations: The industrial economics of foreign direct investment', *Economica*, 38, 1–27.

Contractor, Farok J. (1984) 'Choosing between direct investment and licensing: Theoretical considerations and empirical tests', *Journal of International Business Studies*, 15, 3, 167–88.

——(1990) 'Ownership patterns of US joint-ventures and liberalisation of foreign government regulation in the 1980s: Evidence from the Benchmark Surveys', *Journal of International Business Studies*, 21, 55–73.

——and Peter Lorange (eds) (1988) *Cooperative strategies in international business*. Lexington, MA: Lexington Books.

Davidson, William H. (1980) 'The location of foreign direct investment activity: Country characteristics and experience effects', *Journal of International Business Studies*, 11, 2, 9–22.

Davidson, W. H. and D. G. McFetridge (1985) 'Key characteristics in the choice of international technology transfer mode', *Journal of International Business Studies*, 16, 2, 5–21.

Dubin, Michael (1975) 'Foreign acquisitions and the spread of the multinational firm', DBA Thesis: Graduate School of Business Administration, Harvard University.

Dunning, John H. (1980) 'The location of foreign direct investment activity, country characteristics and experience effects', *Journal of International Business Studies*, 11, 9–22.

Flowers, E. B. (1976) 'Oligopolistic reaction in European and Canadian direct investment in the United States', *Journal of International Business Studies*, 7, 43–55.

Franko, Lawrence G. (1971) *Joint venture survival in multinational corporations*. New York: Praeger.

Geringer, J. M. (1991) 'Strategic determinants of partner selection criteria in international joint ventures', *Journal of International Business Studies*, 22, 1, 41–62.

——and L. Hebert (1991) 'Measuring performance of international joint ventures', *Journal of International Business Studies*, 22, 2, 249–63.

Gomes-Casseres, Benjamin (1987) 'Joint venture instability: Is it a problem?', *Columbia Journal of World Business*, 22, 2, 97–107.

——(1991) 'Firm ownership preferences and host government restrictions', *Journal of International Business Studies*, 21, 1–22.

Gorg, Holger (1998) 'Analysing foreign market entry: The choice between greenfield investments and acquisitions', Trinity College, Dublin, Technical Paper 98/1.

Graham, Edward M. (1978) 'Transatlantic investment by multinational firms: A rivalristic phenomenon', *Journal of Post-Keynesian Economics*, 1, 82–99.

——(1992) 'The theory of the firm', in P. J. Buckley (ed.), *New directions in international business*. Cheltenham: Edward Elgar.

Gulati, R. (1995) 'Does familiarity breed trust? The implications of repeated ties for contractual choices in alliances', *Academy of Management Journal*, 28, 1, 85–112.

Hallen, Lars and Wiedersheim-Paul, Finn (1979) 'Psychic distance and buyer-seller interaction', *Organisasjon, Marknad och Samhalle*, 16, 5, 308–24. Reprinted in Buckley and Ghauri, 1993, op. cit.

Harrigan, K. R. (1988a) 'Joint ventures and competitive strategy', *Strategic Management Journal*, 9, 141–58.

——(1988b) 'Strategic alliances and partner asymmetries', in F. J. Contractor & Peter Lorange (eds), *Cooperative strategies in international business*. Lexington, MA: Lexington Books.

Hennart, Jean-François (1982) *A theory of multinational enterprise*. Ann Arbor, MI: University of Michigan Press.

——(1988) 'A transaction costs theory of equity joint ventures', *Strategic Management Journal*, 9, 361–74.

——and Young-Ryeoul Park (1993) 'Greenfield vs acquisition: The strategy of Japanese investors in the United States', *Management Science*, 39, 1054–70.

——(1994) 'Location, governance and strategic determinants of Japanese manufacturing investment in the United States', *Strategic Management Journal*, 15, 6, 419–36.

Hill, C. W. L., P. Hwang and C. W. Kim (1990) 'An eclectic theory of the choice of international entry mode', *Strategic Management Journal*, 11, 117–28.

Hirsh, Seev (1976) 'An international trade and investment theory of the firm', *Oxford Economic Papers*, 28, 258–70.

Hofstede, Geert (1980) 'Culture's consequences: International differences in work-related values', Beverly Hills, CA: Sage.

Horst, T. D. (1972) 'Firm and industry determinants of the decision to investment abroad: An empirical study', *Review of Economics and Statistics*, 54, 258–66.

Hymer, Stephen H. (1976) 'The international operations of national firms: A study of direct foreign investment', Unpublished 1960 PhD Thesis, Cambridge Mass: MIT Press.

Inkpen, A. C. and J. Birkinshaw (1994) 'International joint ventures and performance: An interorganizational perspective', *International Business Review*, 3, 3, 201–17.

Johanson, Jan and Jan-Eric Vahlne (1977) 'The internationalization process of the firm – a model of knowledge development and increasing foreign market commitments', *Journal of International Business Studies*, 8, 1, 23–32.

Johanson, Jan and Finn Wiedersheim-Paul (1975) 'The internationalization of the firm – four Swedish cases', *Journal of Management Studies*, 12, 305–22.
Killing, J. Peter (1983) *Strategies for joint ventures*. New York, NY: Praeger.
Kim, W. Chan and Peter Hwang (1992) 'Global strategy and multinational's entry mode choice', *Journal of International Business Studies*, 23, 29–53.
Kindleberger, C. P. (1969) *American business abroad*. New Haven, CT: Yale University Press.
Knickerbocker, Fredrick T. (1973) *Oligopolistic reaction and multinational enterprise*. Boston, MA: Harvard University Press.
Kogut, Bruce (1988) 'Joint ventures: theoretical and empirical perspectives', *Strategic Management Journal*, 9, 319–32.
——(1989) 'The stability of joint ventures: Reciprocity and competitive rivalry', *Journal of Industrial Economics*, 38, 2, 183–98.
——and Harbir Singh (1987) 'Entering the United States by joint venture: Industry structure and competitive rivalry', in F. J. Contractor and Peter Lorange *op cit*.
——and Harbir Singh (1988) 'The effect of national culture on the choice of entry mode', Journal of *International Business Studies*, 19, 3, 411–32.
——and Udo Zander (1992) 'Knowledge of the firm, combinative capabilities and the replication of technology', *Organization Science*, 3, 383–97.
——and Udo Zander (1993) 'Knowledge of the firm and the evolutionary theory of the multinational corporation', *Journal of International Business*, 24, 625–45.
Meyer, K. E. E. (1997) 'Determinants of direct foreign investment in transition economies in Central and Eastern Europe', PhD Thesis: University of London.
Nitsch, Deklev, Paul Beamish and Shige Makino (1996) 'Entry mode and performance of Japanese FDI in Western Europe', *Management International Review*, 36, 27–43.
Penrose, Edith (1959) *The theory of the growth of the firm*. London: Basil Blackwell.
Prahalad, C. K. and Gary Hamel (1990) 'The core competence and the corporation', *Harvard Business Review*, May, 71–91.
Root, Franklin R. (1987) *Entry strategies for international markets*. Lexington, MA: Lexington Books.
Rugman, Alan M. (1981) *Inside the multinationals: The economics of internal markets*. London: Groom Helm.
Shane, Scott (1994) 'The effect of national culture on the choice between licensing and direct investment', *Strategic Management Journal*, 15, 627–42.
Stopford, John M. and Louis T. Wells, Jr. (1972) *Managing the multinational enterprise: Organization of the firm and ownership of subsidiaries*. London: Longman.
Svensson, Roger (1996) *Foreign activities of Swedish multinational corporations*. Uppsala: Department of Economics, Uppsala University, Economic Studies 25.
Tirole, Jean (1988) *The theory of industrial organization*. Cambridge, MA: MIT Press.
Vernon, Raymond (1966) 'International investment and international trade in the product cycle', *Quarterly Journal of Economics*, 80, 190–207. Reprinted in Buckley and Ghauri, 1993, op. cit.

Wilson, Brent (1980) 'The propensity of multinational companies to expand through acquisitions', *Journal of International Business Studies*, 12, 2, 59–65.

Woodcock, Charles P., Paul Beamish and Shige Makino (1994) 'Ownership-based entry mode strategies and international performance', *Journal of International Business Studies*, 25, 253–73.

Yip, George (1982) 'Diversification entry: Internal development versus acquisition', *Strategic Management Journal*, 3, 331–45.

Young, Stephen, James Hamill, Colin Wheeler and J. Richard Davies (1989) *International market entry and development*. Hemel, Hempstead: Harvester Wheatsheaf.

Yu, Chow-Ming and Kiyotaki Ito (1988) 'Oligopolistic reaction and foreign direct investment: The case of the US tyre and textiles industries', *Journal of International Business Studies*, 19, 449–60.

Zejan, Mario C. (1990) 'New ventures or acquisitions: The choice of Swedish multinational enterprises', *Journal of Industrial Economics*, 38, 349–55.

# 5 Atlantic Foreign Direct Investment Flows*

Peter J. Buckley and Jeremy Clegg

**This chapter examines the empirical evidence on Atlantic Foreign Direct Investment (AFDI) flows against the background of the theory of foreign direct investment (FDI). It also examines the function of international alliances and joint ventures in AFDI. We first examine the theory of FDI and then pick out special issues relating to Atlantic FDI. (We confine ourselves to the North Atlantic, taking essentially flows between the European Union (EU) and the members of the North America Free Trade Area (NAFTA)). We then examine the empirical evidence and provide an extensive discussion which relates the evidence to the theoretical perspectives.**

## THE THEORY OF FOREIGN DIRECT INVESTMENT

Foreign direct investment is defined as the acquisition or creation of income-generating assets in a foreign country which entails the control of the organization or operation in which these assets are embodied (see Buckley, 1990a, for a collection of key works). The key issue of FDI is that of control, indeed, control is the defining characteristic which separates FDI from foreign portfolio investment, where ownership of part of the assets is transferred abroad (through a transfer of equity shares, for example) but without this conferring control. Control is not always easy to define. If a foreign company owns 51 per cent of the voting shares, then most would agree that it has control. However, if it owns 25 per cent or 10 per cent, with the rest of the share ownership widely dispersed, then it may

* First published as Chapter 8 in Gavin Boyd (ed.), *The Struggle for World Markets* (Edward Elgar, 1998).

retain control (Buckley and Roberts, 1982). Similarly control may be exercised by control of technology, or of management, as by the supply of crucial inputs. Arbitrary definitions are used in order to avoid marginal cases.

The connection between FDI and foreign joint ventures is evident. Foreign firms may take a majority stake or a minority stake with a local firm and if this stake is substantial, they will be defined as foreign direct investments.

The connection with international strategic alliances is not so clear-cut. Alliances may be defined as 'inter-firm collaboration over a given economic space and time for the attainment of corporate goals' (following Buckley, 1992). Such a definition specifies that alliances must be inter-firm but there is no implication that the input of resources to the alliance from the partners need be in any way equal, nor that the alliance partners share the same goals. The definition of the alliance over space can mean local, national, regional or global cooperation. Its time span will rarely be indefinite but could be in terms of a fixed period of time (e.g. five years) or until certain goals are reached (e.g. the development of a new product, manufacture of a certain amount of output, achievement of a given market share). Alliances are thus essentially temporary (or at least not indefinite) and their very flexibility is a major source of strength. It is clear from this description that we can regard alliances as the general case of collaboration between firms and joint ventures as a special case which exists when the alliance is cemented by an exchange of equity. Joint ventures are thus equity-based alliances. We thus arrive at a key, if self-evident, issue – FDI is carried out almost entirely by multinational firms[1] and it is to the multinational firm that we must turn for the key to explaining the theory of FDI.

The multinational enterprise is generally explained as a special case of the theory of the firm although it is rather better to see it as the general case and the purely national firm as a special sub-set. It is best explained by the theory of internalization (or transactions costs) which states that firms grow until the cost of organizing the marginal transaction within the firm is greater than that of using the market. Thus, firms exist because they are superior means of organizing a core set of transactions and markets bound this range (Buckley and Casson, 1976; Buckley, 1990b, 1988). To this we need to add a theory of location which is simply that firms attempt to minimize the cost of their production by seeking to locate activities so that overall costs are minimized. Consequently, the multinational firm may be viewed as an internally coordinated network where activities are located so as to reduce overall costs, linked by internalized flows of information and physical production (see Casson, 1990). The incentive to internalize (and therefore to internationalize) depends on the interplay of industry-specific, firm-specific, region-specific and nation-specific factors (Buckley and Casson, 1976).

Within this framework, three key motives can be identified for FDI. The first is market-oriented FDI, where firms choose to invest in a market rather than use alternative forms of foreign market servicing such as export or licensing. The second is input-oriented FDI, where investment abroad is chosen as the best means of gaining access to key inputs (raw materials, management skills, R&D facilities and workers for example). The third is cost-oriented FDI where an investment abroad is chosen to reduce the overall cost of production. This will often be targeted on cheaper labour, but tax reduction could also be a reason. Glaister and Buckley (1996) found these key motives directly replicated in UK international strategic alliances.

In addition to the motives for FDI, its form is also important. Two key issues over the form of FDI are the ownership strategy and the choice between takeovers and greenfield entry. The ownership strategy (joint ventures or wholly owned subsidiaries) may boil down to the ability of the firm to secure all the necessary resources on its own versus the ability to recruit them only in partnership with others. The choice between greenfield entry or takeover may rest on the importance of packaged assets. Assets such as brand names, distribution networks, management teams and research facilities can often only be secured by takeover because these assets are embodied in firms and can only be accessed by purchasing the whole firm (although in certain cases they can also be accessed via alliances).

When we examine empirical data on FDI, it is important to look at the role which acquisition plays and also the role of reinvestment. In advanced host countries in particular these elements of total FDI are major components of the total.

## SPECIAL ISSUES OF THEORY RELATING TO ATLANTIC FDI

Several key features of Atlantic FDI impinge on the application of theory to its empirics. First the cultural similarity (of sections) of the flows are striking. These similarities in terms of language, colonial inheritance and culture reduce the transaction costs and make FDI easier because the investor faces lower costs of 'psychic distance' (Hallen and Wiedersheim-Paul, 1979; Buckley and Ghauri, 1993). This is true between the UK and Canada and the US, France and Quebec and Spain and Mexico. Two-way flows between these regions can be expected to be higher than in the presence of cultural barriers.

Second, AFDI flows take place between countries at similar, and high, levels of economic development. This has several potential consequences. First, we would expect there to be a high proportion of intra-industry FDI rather than inter-industry FDI. Second, it is likely that alliances will be an important mode of conducting international business. Glaister and Buckley (1994, 1996) have found that the motives for alliances are very similar to those of FDI. Third, the market size defined at national and regional (EU and NAFTA) level is large and this will encourage marketing seeking FDI in both directions. We should not, however, forget the differences between the two sides of the Atlantic and, in particular, difference in resource endowments, with Canada and the USA in particular being particularly resource-rich.

Third, AFDI takes place in an environment of increasing integration on both sides of the pond (Buckley, Pass and Prescott, 1994, 1995a, 1995b, 1996; Rugman, 1994). The EU has taken enormous steps in creating the Single European Market (SEM) amongst other integrationist actions and moves are well under way to accelerate the economic integration of the NAFTA members. This bi-focal integration has profound consequences for the economic structures of the two areas and will impact further on AFDI. For an analysis of the impact of the development of the European internal market on the incidence of joint ventures see Kay, Ramsay and Hennart (1996). This paper also suggests a growing preference for majority acquisition in the EU.

The long tradition of examining AFDI (from Dunning (1958) onwards) has frequently pointed to the importance of market structure relationships (following Hymer, 1976). In particular it has been suggested that 'exchange of threat' or rivalry across the Atlantic has produced cross-investment to secure world market share (Knickerbocker, 1973; Flowers, 1975; Graham, 1978, 1990). This is now seen more in the context of competitive games where strategic moves are predicated on the strategy of rivals. It may be argued that the closeness of market structures across the Atlantic fosters such strategies.

## EMPIRICAL ANALYSIS

The data employed in this chapter are based on the FDI stock statistics of the USA and Canada. These are among the most accurate in the world. The decision was made early on to use information from the North American side in preference to the European side. The more variable level of accuracy in the different countries of Europe was a factor, as were the problems of consolidation and coherence, which escalate as the number of countries rises. Mexico produces no adequate stock figures, so the discussion of the transatlantic profile of this country is curtailed, and limited to an analysis of the available FDI flow statistics.

### Canadian and US Outward FDI by European Host Country

There are two immediate contrasts between the outward FDI profile of Canada and the USA as presented in Table 5.1. The first concerns the share of Europe in the outward FDI of both countries: this share is considerably lower for Canada (21 per cent in 1995) compared with the USA (51 per cent). This observation can be explained by the pull of the US market on Canadian FDI. The second observation is that Canada has a higher percentage of FDI in the EU(12) relative to the percentage in all of Europe than the USA; however, the USA allocation to the EU(12) has been climbing faster. This acceleration in the attractiveness of the EU market relative to

*Table* 5.1 Outward foreign direct investment stock of Canada and the USA into Europe, percentage distribution, 1985–95

| | *Canada* | | | *USA* | | |
|---|---|---|---|---|---|---|
| | *1985* | *1990* | *1995* | *1985* | *1990* | *1995* |
| **Europe** | **14.43** | **21.70** | **21.42** | **45.68** | **49.88** | **51.08** |
| **EU** | **13.21** | **20.10** | **19.46** | **36.44** | **41.92** | **42.19** |
| Belgium and Luxembourg | 0.24 | 0.61 | 1.72 | 2.49 | 2.59 | 3.58 |
| Denmark | 0.08 | 0.05 | 0.02 | 0.56 | 0.40 | 0.32 |
| France | 0.34 | 1.91 | 1.35 | 3.32 | 4.45 | 4.59 |
| Germany | 1.12 | 0.96 | 1.66 | 7.28 | 6.41 | 6.04 |
| Greece | 0.50 | 0.10 | 0.07 | 0.09 | 0.07 | 0.06 |
| Ireland | 1.47 | 1.09 | 3.11 | 1.60 | 1.37 | 1.54 |
| Italy | 0.34 | 0.42 | 0.59 | 2.57 | 3.27 | 2.35 |
| Netherlands | 0.93 | 1.46 | 1.07 | 3.10 | 4.44 | 5.26 |
| Portugal | 0.01 | 0.13 | 0.05 | 0.10 | 0.21 | 0.24 |
| Spain | 0.49 | 0.59 | 0.13 | 0.99 | 1.83 | 1.36 |
| UK | 7.69 | 12.80 | 9.67 | 14.34 | 16.89 | 16.85 |
| **Other Europe** | **1.22** | **1.61** | **1.96** | **9.24** | **7.96** | **8.90** |
| Austria | 0.05 | 0.01 | 0.13 | 0.21 | 0.26 | 0.29 |
| Norway | 0.10 | 0.06 | 0.02 | 1.40 | 0.98 | 0.69 |
| Sweden | 0.02 | 0.03 | 0.04 | 0.41 | 0.42 | 1.72 |
| Switzerland | 1.02 | 1.38 | 0.97 | 6.85 | 5.83 | 5.11 |
| Other | 0.04 | 0.12 | 0.79 | 0.38 | 0.47 | 1.09 |
| **Rest of world** | **85.57** | **78.30** | **78.58** | **54.32** | **50.12** | **48.92** |
| **Total** | **100.00** | **100.00** | **100.00** | **100.00** | **100.00** | **100.00** |
| **Value in US$ m (current prices)** | **41916** | **78387** | **103706** | **230250** | **430521** | **711621** |

*Source*: Statistics Canada (1996) and United States Department of Commerce (various years).

the rest of Europe is exactly what one would expect to follow from the SEM programme of the EU. The EU(12) share of Canadian FDI has risen since 1985 (roughly when the SEM programme was announced) from 13 per cent to around 20 per cent, while the EU's US share has risen from 36 to 42 per cent. To this extent it does appear that Canada and the USA have increasingly favoured the EU over the rest of Europe, which is consistent with the hypothesis that market integration has behaved as an attractant to FDI.

The observation that the UK is by far the single largest recipient of both Canadian and US FDI throughout 1985–95 is unsurprising. The UK has set out its stall as a primary location for inward FDI into the EU, supported by grants, incentives and lower social overhead costs (the Social Chapter opt-out). It also benefits from the attraction of the English language, and in the case of Canada and the USA, from cultural affinities and similar systems of corporate governance However, while the UK share of US FDI has risen, its share of Canadian FDI has shown no clear trend, first increasing then falling. These developments apart, the primacy of the UK in the outward investment pattern in Europe of both Canada and the USA speaks not simply of political ties between Canada and the UK. It also testifies to cultural and economic links (based on a history of trade), cemented by FDI. Of the other leading European hosts the top 5 are identical between Canada and the USA with the exception of Ireland (number 2 for Canada), and the Netherlands (number 3 for the USA). The leading shared hosts are Germany, France and Belgium-Luxembourg, for which standard explanations of FDI based on market size and growth are tenable. The importance of Ireland for Canada seems likely to be a reflection of cultural affinity – Ireland's share has been disproportionately large over the ten-year period reviewed here. It also reflects Ireland's favourable tax regime as a base for serving EU markets.

The most remarkable thing about the countries of Europe outside the EU(12) is that they collectively add so little in terms of FDI share. The expansion of the EU to fifteen members would therefore not greatly increase the EU's share. Only Switzerland, which remains outside the EU, has a substantial share of US FDI, at just over 5 per cent in 1995.

## Canadian FDI into the UK and EU by Industry

The precise geographical focus of the discussion of FDI patterns in Europe is dictated by the breakdown in the data. In the case of Canada, country by industry data are available only for the EU and the UK within Europe. However, as we know that the EU accounts for the preponderance of Canadian FDI in Europe, this is not too great a handicap. The definition of the EU shifts from EU(12) in 1985 and 1990 to EU(15) in 1995; however, from the data shown in Table 5.1, we know that this will not materially affect the discussion. The industrial analysis must rely on the industry categories given. Generally, these are adequate; however, the category 'Consumer goods and services' clearly mixes manufacturing and services, but probably refers mainly to those goods which are provided jointly with services.

Table 5.2 focuses on the Canadian outward industrial pattern of FDI in the EU, with some data on the World for comparison and to provide a benchmark as to the overall World pattern and trends. The movement away from manufacturing industry and towards services is a clear discernible trend, and this is reflected in the industrial countries of the EU, which have amongst the highest concentrations of manufacturing FDI. The UK in 1985 had a higher concentration of manufacturing FDI than the rest of the EU. However, the UK's percentage of manufacturing FDI fell from 77 per cent in 1985 to reach a low in 1990 (of 44 per cent) rising again to 52 per cent in 1995. In the rest of the EU the trend has been consistently downwards, but the distribution proportion of manufacturing stands at 62 per cent in 1995 (i.e. greater than in the UK).

The shifting pattern from manufacturing to services is encapsulated by the UK, in particular by the impact of the liberalization of service industries. In 1985 Canadian FDI in the UK was dominated by the traditional food, beverages and tobacco sector, largely based on historical links with a tail of less important industries in the shape of metal manufactures (metallic mineral products), finance, and wood and paper. By 1995 communications services had become the leading industry, followed by electrical and electronic products. Both of these sectors are industries in which firm strategy has been a direct response to the liberalization in the UK of the telecommunications market, and of Canadian operators, particularly cable franchise firms (Bell Cable Media, Videotron) and equipment manufacturers (notably Nortel). As we will see again later, the UK has become a highly attractive market to inward FDI because of its leadership in liberalization in telecommunications within Europe.

The figures for the share of telecommunications FDI within the rest of the EU remain stagnant, and will continue to be so until liberalization makes material progress, scheduled for 1998 according to the EU timetable for the telecommunications

*Table* 5.2 Outward foreign direct investment stock of Canada into the UK, other EU, and the world, percentage distribution, 1985–95

| | *UK* | | | *Other EU*[a] | | | *World* | | |
|---|---|---|---|---|---|---|---|---|---|
| | *1985* | *1990* | *1995* | *1985* | *1990* | *1995* | *1985* | *1990* | *1995* |
| *Industry group* | | | | | | | | | |
| **Manufacturing** | **77.24** | **43.62** | **52.19** | **75.52** | **65.21** | **61.46** | **59.03** | **50.84** | **48.99** |
| Food, beverages and tobacco | 28.05 | 9.56 | 9.00 | 12.52 | 23.67 | 16.70 | 9.06 | 8.31 | 6.75 |
| Wood and paper | 13.03 | 5.29 | 2.16 | 5.89 | 8.94 | 7.12 | 3.68 | 3.84 | 3.35 |
| Energy | 8.23 | 7.39 | 11.69 | 12.55 | 3.31 | 1.14 | 14.22 | 7.70 | 8.54 |
| Chemicals, chemical products and textiles | 2.11 | 0.44 | 0.64 | 9.34 | 7.61 | 9.26 | 8.17 | 7.60 | 4.67 |
| Metallic minerals and metal products | 19.16 | 9.48 | 11.52 | 38.77 | 17.49 | 20.18 | 17.89 | 14.38 | 16.22 |
| Machinery and equipment | 2.82 | 2.43 | 1.04 | −5.30 | 1.48 | 1.65 | 0.16 | 1.20 | 0.81 |
| Transportation equipment | 1.09 | 2.92 | 3.11 | −0.10 | 0.16 | 3.66 | 1.13 | 2.32 | 2.72 |
| Electrical and electronic products | 2.75 | 6.11 | 13.02 | 1.85 | 2.55 | 1.76 | 4.71 | 5.48 | 5.93 |

| | | | | | | | | | |
|---|---|---|---|---|---|---|---|---|---|
| **Services** | **22.76** | **56.36** | **47.82** | **19.28** | **32.43** | **34.40** | **40.97** | **49.16** | **51.01** |
| Construction and related activities | 1.25 | 17.50 | 0.91 | .. | .. | .. | 9.94 | 7.48 | 3.28 |
| Transportation services | 1.11 | 1.32 | 0.33 | .. | .. | .. | 3.66 | 4.97 | 3.47 |
| Communications | 3.46 | 6.89 | 29.61 | 3.07 | 3.70 | 1.81 | 5.54 | 8.21 | 10.00 |
| Finance and insurance | 14.34 | 22.24 | 11.85 | 12.13 | 25.65 | 33.45 | 16.61 | 23.80 | 23.67 |
| Accommodation, restaurants, recreation services and food retailing | 0.77 | 3.90 | 0.94 | .. | .. | .. | 0.63 | 2.02 | 6.23 |
| Consumer goods and services | 1.50 | 0.35 | 1.11 | 4.08 | 3.08 | −0.86 | 4.09 | 1.50 | 3.44 |
| Other[b] | 0.32 | 4.15 | 3.07 | .. | .. | .. | 0.51 | 1.18 | 0.92 |
| **Total** | **100.00** | **99.98** | **100.01** | **94.80** | **97.65** | **95.86** | **100.00** | **100.00** | **100.00** |
| **Value in US$ m (current prices)** | **3222** | **10033** | **10025** | **2101** | **5723** | **10307** | **41916** | **78387** | **103706** |

*Notes*:
Figures may not sum precisely to 100 due to rounding and data suppression.
.. denotes data are not available.
[a] Other EU is defined as other EU(12) before 1995 and as other EU(15) in 1995.
[b] Other includes general services to business, government services, education, health and social services, and includes some suppressed data.
*Source*: Statistics Canada (1996).

industry. Within the rest of the EU, the finance and insurance industry is the leading industry for Canadian FDI, with a spectacular rate of growth (from 12 to 33 per cent over the period); but for the growth of telecoms specific to the UK, the trajectory of this industry's share would be the same in the UK. The growth and liberalization of financial markets largely accounts for this acceleration. The share of Canadian FDI in the energy industry in Europe has declined, while shares of food etc. and chemicals have more or less held up, again continuing existing well-established patterns.

## US FDI into the EU and Selected European Countries by Industry

The industrial pattern of US FDI in Europe has a long and distinguished history in catalysing theory and innovative empirical work on international business and the multinational enterprise. Here we can see the vestiges of the historical cross-industry patterns observed in the manufacturing and extractive sectors, and at the same time similar underlying secular shifts to those that have characterized the Canadian FDI position in Europe.

The manufacturing sector was the basis for much of the innovatory work on the multinational enterprise in the last forty years. On the current pattern of US FDI in Europe, the theory of the multinational enterprise would have to be reengineered to give prominence to service industries (Buckley, Pass and Prescott, 1992). This rebalancing of FDI profiles is partly due to the relative decline of extractive industries, here characterized by the petroleum industry, which has declined from over 20 per cent in US FDI in Europe to just 7 per cent (see Table 5.3). These secular trends are not exclusive to US FDI in Europe, but they are more marked within Europe than elsewhere, because of the keenness of competition in the European market.

The single biggest development is the supplanting of the dominance of the manufacturing sector by the services sector. US FDI in Europe has shifted from 35 per cent in services in 1985 to over 50 per cent in 1995. The leading service industry is clearly finance. The other leading industries are wholesale distribution and the familiar manufacturing industries of

*Table* 5.3 Outward foreign direct investment stock of the USA into Europe and the world, percentage distribution, 1985–95

| | *Europe* | | | *World* | | |
|---|---|---|---|---|---|---|
| | *1985* | *1990* | *1995* | *1985* | *1990* | *1995* |
| *Industry group* | | | | | | |
| **Petroleum** | **20.67** | **9.93** | **7.26** | **25.06** | **12.27** | **9.79** |
| **Manufacturing** | **43.14** | **39.60** | **36.06** | **41.13** | **39.53** | **36.20** |
| Food and kindred products | 4.42 | 3.65 | 4.28 | 4.02 | 3.62 | 4.37 |
| Chemicals and allied products | 7.95 | 9.36 | 12.12 | 8.80 | 8.82 | 9.57 |
| Primary and fabricated metals | 1.79 | 2.29 | 1.64 | 2.18 | 2.44 | 1.83 |
| Machinery, except electrical | 11.70 | 9.11 | 5.05 | 8.25 | 7.17 | 4.71 |
| Electric and electronic equipment | 3.54 | 2.72 | 3.16 | 3.70 | 3.61 | 3.59 |
| Transportation equipment | 3.66 | 3.95 | 3.26 | 5.09 | 5.00 | 4.55 |
| Other manufacturing | 10.08 | 8.51 | 6.56 | 9.10 | 8.86 | 7.58 |
| **Services** | **34.59** | **48.56** | **53.42** | **27.98** | **43.54** | **48.02** |
| Wholesale | 11.20 | 12.02 | 10.05 | 9.90 | 10.15 | 10.03 |
| Banking | 5.96 | 4.25 | 3.96 | 6.28 | 4.80 | 4.28 |
| Finance (except banking), insurance and real estate | 15.02 | 28.24 | 34.24 | 9.77 | 25.47 | 29.80 |
| Other services | 2.41 | 4.05 | 5.17 | 2.03 | 3.12 | 3.91 |
| **Other industries** | **1.60** | **1.91** | **3.26** | **5.83** | **4.66** | **6.00** |
| **Total** | **100.00** | **100.00** | **100.00** | **100.00** | **100.00** | **100.00** |
| **Value in US$ m (current prices)** | **105171** | **214739** | **363527** | **230250** | **430521** | **711621** |

*Source*: United States Department of Commerce (various years).

chemicals (which includes pharmaceuticals) and non-electrical machinery.

The calculation of a definitive aggregate FDI position for the EU alone is made difficult by the changing membership of the EU and data suppression. Therefore the discussion will concentrate on the four leading EU hosts which collectively dominate inward US FDI, plus Switzerland – the prime non-EU host within Europe. Table 5.4 traces the industrial patterns in these five countries that account for the lion's share of US FDI in Europe. Within the UK and Switzerland, finance has been the first-ranking industry since 1985, but the share has mushroomed in the UK (from just under 20 per cent to 46 per cent in 1995) and peaked at 53 per cent in Switzerland in 1990. In France, Germany and the Netherlands the share of finance has increased from single-digit levels to 20 per cent, and to almost 50 per cent in the Netherlands. This globalization of US FDI in finance is a worldwide phenomenon, but the growth has spread from the existing financial centres to elsewhere in Europe.

The chemicals industry is a strong attractant to US FDI, particularly in continental Europe (unfortunately, data are suppressed for Switzerland). The distribution of US FDI in this industry which includes the pharmaceutical sector, has risen most in France, and slightly in Germany. The importance of US FDI in the old staple transportation equipment industry has stagnated in the UK (at a low share of around 2–3 per cent) to be supplemented by Japanese and Korean inward FDI, and in Germany (at around 13 per cent), and declined in France to just 3 per cent. The machinery and electrical industries equally have a very low prominence in what would have been their natural domain since the 1950s. Switzerland, which stands outside the EU, has the most static profile of the selected European hosts, with the US inward FDI structure loaded towards the services. Apart from finance, banking and the wholesale trade are the leading industries, and there appears to be little pressure for this pattern to change.

The impact of European market integration is difficult to discern in the industry pattern of US FDI in Europe, probably because US MNEs have taken a pan-European strategic perspective for a considerable time before the advent of the SEM

*Table* 5.4 Outward foreign direct investment stock of the USA into the UK, France, Germany, the Netherlands and Switzerland, percentage distribution, 1985–95

| | *UK* | | | *France* | | | *Germany* | | | *Netherlands* | | | *Switzerland* | | |
|---|---|---|---|---|---|---|---|---|---|---|---|---|---|---|---|
| | *1985* | *1990* | *1995* | *1985* | *1990* | *1995* | *1985* | *1990* | *1995* | *1985* | *1990* | *1995* | *1985* | *1990* | *1995* |
| *Industry group* | | | | | | | | | | | | | | | |
| **Petroleum** | **28.03** | **14.23** | **11.70** | **7.58** | .. | **3.56** | **15.48** | .. | **5.16** | **25.81** | **7.47** | **5.21** | .. | **2.48** | **2.86** |
| **Manufacturing** | **38.64** | **31.91** | **23.23** | **64.74** | **60.31** | **50.71** | **63.93** | **58.46** | **55.05** | **49.03** | **34.24** | **27.93** | **7.15** | **5.34** | **10.57** |
| Food and kindred products | 5.44 | 3.77 | 2.75 | 4.59 | 1.82 | 9.27 | 3.63 | 3.89 | 5.00 | 8.77 | 4.27 | 3.71 | .. | .. | .. |
| Chemicals and allied products | 6.60 | 5.39 | 4.95 | 10.39 | 16.21 | 18.54 | 6.75 | 10.29 | 11.14 | 16.26 | 14.78 | 10.96 | 1.45 | 0.59 | 2.34 |
| Primary and fabricated metals | 1.60 | 2.21 | 1.50 | 1.90 | 2.64 | 1.99 | 3.77 | 4.75 | 3.70 | 3.38 | 2.77 | 1.67 | .. | 0.34 | 0.47 |
| Machinery, except electrical | 8.05 | 6.40 | 4.74 | 25.40 | 19.05 | 7.13 | 19.61 | 13.20 | 10.43 | 8.89 | 5.76 | 3.28 | 0.49 | 0.83 | 1.09 |
| Electric and electronic equipment | 2.53 | 2.41 | 2.70 | 3.96 | 2.26 | 1.87 | 5.39 | 3.46 | 3.83 | 1.80 | 3.31 | 2.32 | 0.70 | 0.65 | 1.19 |
| Transportation equipment | 1.94 | 3.16 | 1.38 | 6.25 | 3.20 | 2.72 | .. | 13.11 | 13.22 | 0.50 | 0.32 | 0.32 | 0.00 | 0.02 | .. |
| Other manufacturing | 12.47 | 8.57 | 5.20 | 12.27 | 15.12 | 9.19 | .. | 9.75 | 7.72 | 9.43 | 3.04 | 5.66 | 3.75 | .. | 2.35 |

*Table* 5.4 (*contd.*)

| | *UK* | | | *France* | | | *Germany* | | | *Netherlands* | | | *Switzerland* | | |
|---|---|---|---|---|---|---|---|---|---|---|---|---|---|---|---|
| | *1985* | *1990* | *1995* | *1985* | *1990* | *1995* | *1985* | *1990* | *1995* | *1985* | *1990* | *1995* | *1985* | *1990* | *1995* |
| **Services** | **31.98** | **51.79** | **60.69** | **25.70** | **32.02** | **42.64** | **18.07** | **30.79** | **34.76** | **21.59** | **56.92** | **63.09** | **77.17** | **91.90** | **86.14** |
| Wholesale | 4.37 | 5.36 | 5.53 | 15.71 | 17.22 | 13.50 | 3.78 | 8.09 | 7.73 | 9.31 | 8.40 | 11.90 | 29.12 | 30.78 | 25.61 |
| Banking | 5.68 | 3.89 | 4.33 | 4.79 | 1.54 | 1.11 | 7.95 | 5.72 | 5.41 | 1.78 | 0.73 | 0.37 | 8.16 | 5.62 | 6.20 |
| Finance (except banking), insurance and real estate | 19.75 | 38.47 | 46.03 | 2.97 | 9.34 | 20.85 | 6.08 | 13.73 | 19.40 | 2.47 | 39.01 | 48.04 | 36.41 | 52.68 | 50.36 |
| Other services | 2.18 | 4.06 | 4.81 | 2.22 | 3.92 | 7.12 | 0.27 | 3.25 | 2.22 | 8.02 | 8.78 | 2.78 | 3.48 | 2.83 | 3.96 |
| Other industries | 1.36 | 2.08 | 4.37 | 2.00 | .. | 3.09 | 2.52 | .. | 5.03 | 3.56 | 1.37 | 3.77 | .. | 0.27 | 0.42 |
| **Total** | **100.00** | **100.00** | **100.00** | **100.01** | **100.00** | **100.00** | **100.00** | **100.00** | **100.00** | **99.99** | **100.01** | **100.00** | **100.00** | **100.00** | **100.00** |
| **Value in US$ m (current prices)** | **33024** | **72707** | **119938** | **7643** | **19164** | **32645** | **16764** | **27609** | **43001** | **7129** | **19120** | **37421** | **15766** | **25099** | **36342** |

*Notes*:
Figures may not sum precisely to 100 due to rounding.
.. denotes data are not available.
*Source*: United States Department of Commerce (various years).

(Clegg, 1996). Unlike other countries investing in Europe, US MNEs had already adjusted to serving the European market on a regional basis.

## European Foreign Direct Investment into North America

The countries of Europe play a proportionately greater role in the inward FDI of the USA than they do in Canada. This is again quite simply because of the importance of intra-North American FDI, into Canada from the USA. By 1995, 24 per cent of Canadian FDI was of European origin while for the USA the figure was 64 per cent (Table 5.5). Over the period 1985 to 1995 there was no clear trend in these shares, although they temporarily dipped in 1990 in the USA and peaked in Canada. This result may have been brought about by the impact of European integration and North American economic integration, and a preference for European investors to locate in the USA compared with Canada.

To a large extent the inward profiles mirror the outward pattern of North American FDI to Europe. The leading foreign investing nations in both Canada and the USA are the usual group of European countries: the UK, which is in both cases in premier position throughout, followed by France, Germany, the Netherlands and Switzerland, in a variety of rankings. The UK accounts for almost a quarter of US total inward FDI, and just under 10 per cent in Canada. France has risen from fourth place in Canada to second, but remained at fourth in the USA, which may reflect increased FDI bolstered on cultural and linguisticties in Canada. Switzerland remains throughout the fifth most important investor in North America, and the only leading investor of non-EU origin from Europe. The questions that these aggregate positions raise can only satisfactorily be addressed at by inspecting the industrial profile for strengths and weaknesses (see Tables 5.6, 5.7 and 5.8).

The conclusions on the geographical pattern of aggregate FDI into North America are that the leading inward investing nations are also the leading hosts to North American FDI. To this extent the intensity of cross-FDI is greatest for an established group of countries, the UK, France, Germany, the Netherlands and Switzerland. This suggests the importance

*Table* 5.5 Inward foreign direct investment stock of Canada and the USA from Europe, percentage distribution, 1985–95

| | *Canada* | | | *USA* | | |
|---|---|---|---|---|---|---|
| | *1985* | *1990* | *1995* | *1985* | *1990* | *1995* |
| **Europe** | **19.55** | **27.65** | **24.02** | **65.77** | **62.63** | **64.41** |
| **EU** | **17.08** | **23.91** | **20.53** | **57.86** | **55.93** | **55.23** |
| Belgium and Luxembourg | 0.41 | 0.51 | 1.64 | 1.43 | 1.54 | 1.48 |
| Denmark | 0.04 | 0.01 | 0.11 | 0.31 | 0.21 | 0.54 |
| France | 1.68 | 2.92 | 3.15 | 3.61 | 4.72 | 6.83 |
| Germany | 2.89 | 3.87 | 2.96 | 8.03 | 7.15 | 8.55 |
| Greece | 0.01 | 0.01 | 0.02 | .. | .. | .. |
| Ireland | 0.21 | 0.06 | 0.12 | .. | 0.34 | 1.28 |
| Italy | 0.04 | 0.24 | 0.15 | 0.67 | 0.39 | 0.40 |
| Netherlands | 2.21 | 2.41 | 2.56 | 20.07 | 16.38 | 12.08 |
| Portugal | .. | .. | .. | .. | 0.00 | .. |
| Spain | 0.02 | 0.03 | 0.02 | 0.15 | 0.20 | 0.46 |
| United Kingdom | 9.57 | 13.85 | 9.80 | 23.59 | 24.99 | 23.62 |
| **Other Europe** | **2.48** | **3.74** | **3.49** | **7.90** | **6.70** | **9.18** |
| Austria | 0.06 | 0.19 | 0.05 | 0.07 | 0.16 | 0.29 |
| Norway | 0.05 | 0.46 | 0.32 | 0.21 | 0.20 | 0.34 |
| Sweden | 0.42 | 0.48 | 0.65 | 1.28 | 1.39 | 2.10 |
| Switzerland | 1.71 | 2.20 | 2.03 | 5.72 | 4.48 | 5.90 |
| **Rest of world** | **80.45** | **72.35** | **75.98** | **34.23** | **37.37** | **35.59** |
| **Total** | **100.00** | **100.00** | **100.00** | **100.00** | **100.00** | **100.00** |
| **Value in US$ m (current prices)** | **66187** | **112385** | **122452** | **184615** | **394911** | **560088** |

*Notes*:
Figures may not sum precisely to 100 due to rounding.
.. denotes data are not available.
*Source*: Statistics Canada (1996) and United States Department of Commerce (various years).

of long-lived and stable economic, cultural and even political ties.

The examination of transatlantic FDI would not be complete without the inclusion of the third North American OECD country, Mexico. Unfortunately, data on Mexican FDI abroad are not available in a form adequate to conduct a country, let alone a country by industry, analysis. The quality of Mexican inward FDI information is still fairly rudimentary, and relies on the reporting of foreign direct investment projects. The

*Table 5.6* Inward foreign direct investment stock of Canada from the UK, other EU, and the world, percentage distribution, 1985–95

| | *UK* | | | *Other EU*[a] | | | *World* | | |
|---|---|---|---|---|---|---|---|---|---|
| | *1985* | *1990* | *1995* | *1985* | *1990* | *1995* | *1985* | *1990* | *1995* |
| *Industry group* | | | | | | | | | |
| **Manufacturing** | **47.77** | **56.53** | **50.94** | **57.28** | **55.99** | **61.04** | **69.54** | **66.62** | **64.86** |
| Food, beverages and tobacco | 14.07 | 17.16 | 20.70 | 0.77 | 0.58 | 12.43 | 6.63 | 7.03 | 9.49 |
| Wood and paper | 4.15 | 1.26 | 1.51 | 3.56 | 0.67 | 1.20 | 3.94 | 5.81 | 4.70 |
| Energy | 16.56 | 17.18 | 11.37 | 30.12 | 18.32 | 13.09 | 23.67 | 16.42 | 11.68 |
| Chemicals, chemical products and textiles | 5.02 | 9.11 | 8.68 | 4.92 | 16.73 | 15.11 | 8.97 | 10.36 | 10.90 |
| Metallic minerals and metal products | 2.34 | 5.58 | 2.80 | 4.40 | 7.34 | 6.33 | 4.80 | 7.44 | 6.07 |
| Machinery and equipment | 1.09 | 1.39 | 2.16 | 2.41 | 2.88 | 2.76 | 4.18 | 3.98 | 4.20 |
| Transportation equipment | 3.00 | 3.10 | 2.03 | 8.31 | 6.00 | 4.68 | 10.93 | 10.02 | 10.72 |
| Electrical and electronic products | 1.55 | 1.74 | 1.69 | 2.30 | 3.47 | 5.44 | 6.42 | 5.56 | 7.10 |
| **Services** | **52.24** | **43.46** | **49.06** | **42.74** | **44.03** | **38.96** | **30.46** | **33.38** | **35.14** |
| Construction and related activities | 8.09 | 5.79 | 6.80 | 18.57 | 10.95 | 6.72 | 5.53 | 5.36 | 6.49 |
| Transportation services and communications | 0.65 | 1.73 | 1.27 | 0.44 | 0.95 | 0.57 | 1.30 | 2.47 | 3.02 |
| Finance and insurance | 34.91 | 29.96 | 33.79 | 20.17 | 28.48 | 24.25 | 15.46 | 18.87 | 18.04 |
| Consumer goods and services | 7.36 | 2.91 | 4.36 | 2.01 | 2.30 | 2.92 | 5.18 | 3.86 | 4.64 |
| Other[b] | 1.24 | 3.06 | 2.84 | 1.55 | 1.36 | 4.50 | 2.99 | 2.83 | 2.95 |
| **Total** | **100.01** | **99.99** | **100.00** | **100.01** | **100.02** | **100.01** | **100.00** | **100.00** | **100.00** |
| **Value in US$ m (current prices)** | **6331** | **15562** | **12004** | **4962** | **11314** | **14343** | **66187** | **112385** | **122452** |

*Notes*:
Figures may not sum precisely to 100 due to rounding.
[a] Other EU is defined as other EU(12) before 1995 and as other EU(15) in 1995.
[b] Other includes general services to business, government services, education, health and social services, accommodation, restaurants and recreation services, and food retailing.
*Source*: Statistics Canada (1996).

*Table* 5.7 Inward foreign direct investment stock in the USA by Europe and the world, percentage distribution, 1985–95

| | *Europe* | | | *World* | | |
|---|---|---|---|---|---|---|
| | *1985* | *1990* | *1995* | *1985* | *1990* | *1995* |
| *Industry group* | | | | | | |
| **Mining** | **1.01** | .. | .. | **2.19** | .. | .. |
| **Petroleum** | **21.11** | **13.86** | **7.44** | **15.31** | **10.86** | **6.36** |
| **Manufacturing** | **37.76** | **46.83** | **43.70** | **32.27** | **38.69** | **37.55** |
| Food and kindred products | 8.36 | 8.05 | 4.86 | 5.80 | 5.71 | 4.65 |
| Chemicals and allied products | 13.67 | 15.97 | 19.01 | 10.20 | 11.58 | 13.66 |
| Primary and fabricated metals | 2.17 | 3.41 | 2.57 | 3.77 | 3.47 | 2.72 |
| Machinery | 5.20 | 7.85 | 7.01 | 5.00 | 7.00 | 6.54 |
| Other manufacturing | 8.35 | 11.55 | 10.26 | 7.50 | 10.93 | 9.97 |
| **Services** | **36.96** | **34.10** | **42.96** | **44.80** | **45.48** | **51.17** |
| Wholesale trade | 11.35 | 8.49 | 7.91 | 15.74 | 12.89 | 12.79 |
| Retail trade | 4.25 | 2.69 | 2.00 | 3.70 | 2.34 | 2.40 |
| Banking | 4.73 | 3.16 | 5.84 | 6.16 | 4.67 | 7.47 |
| Finance, except banking | 2.06 | 0.24 | 8.22 | 2.30 | 2.12 | 8.56 |
| Insurance | 7.23 | 8.38 | 10.19 | 6.39 | 6.87 | 8.44 |
| Real estate | 7.35 | 4.38 | 3.20 | 10.51 | 8.85 | 4.73 |
| Other services | .. | 6.76 | 5.60 | .. | 7.75 | 6.77 |
| **Other industries** | **3.16** | **5.21** | **5.90** | **5.43** | **4.97** | **4.92** |
| **Total** | **100.00** | **100.00** | **100.00** | **100.00** | **100.00** | **100.00** |
| **Value in US$ m (current prices)** | **121413** | **247320** | **360762** | **184615** | **394911** | **560088** |

*Notes*:
Figures may not sum precisely to 100 due to rounding.
.. denotes data are not available or not separately available
*Source*: United States Department of Commerce (various years).

best stock estimate that is available is the culmination of reported FDI project inflows since 1971. These are the data routinely used and published by the Dirección General de Inversion Extranjera of the Secretaria de Comercio y Fomento Industrial (SECOFI) in order to assess inward investment.

Foreign direct investment into Mexico is naturally dominated by the USA (with a cumulated share of around 60 per cent), with Canada accounting for around 2.5 per cent.

*Table* 5.8 Inward foreign direct investment stock in the USA by the UK, France, Germany, the Netherlands and Switzerland, percentage distribution, 1985–95

| | *UK* | | | *France* | | | *Germany* | | | *Netherlands* | | | *Switzerland* | | |
|---|---|---|---|---|---|---|---|---|---|---|---|---|---|---|---|
| | *1985* | *1990* | *1995* | *1985* | *1990* | *1995* | *1985* | *1990* | *1995* | *1985* | *1990* | *1995* | *1985* | *1990* | *1995* |
| *Industry group* | | | | | | | | | | | | | | | |
| **Mining** | **0.55** | .. | .. | .. | .. | .. | **1.65** | .. | .. | **0.60** | .. | .. | .. | .. | .. |
| **Petroleum** | **27.91** | **16.11** | **8.31** | .. | .. | .. | .. | **0.51** | **-0.14** | **30.98** | **20.51** | **19.16** | .. | **0.78** | **1.46** |
| **Manufacturing** | **26.83** | **42.93** | **43.01** | **85.71** | **69.91** | **55.23** | **40.60** | **55.67** | **51.09** | **36.03** | **38.25** | **31.75** | **65.11** | **60.26** | **43.50** |
| Food and kindred products | 6.32 | 8.86 | 7.59 | 5.22 | 5.72 | 5.48 | 0.21 | 0.45 | -0.15 | .. | 11.40 | 4.49 | .. | .. | .. |
| Chemicals and allied products | 8.35 | 13.35 | 16.90 | 44.90 | 21.87 | 24.69 | 25.15 | 29.65 | 28.10 | 9.61 | 12.59 | 12.86 | 20.36 | 18.54 | 24.46 |
| Primary and fabricated metals | 1.76 | 1.70 | 2.53 | 9.43 | .. | 2.91 | 1.42 | 4.21 | 3.16 | .. | 2.24 | 0.81 | .. | .. | 2.27 |
| Machinery | 4.54 | 4.80 | 3.55 | 3.21 | .. | 12.10 | 6.97 | 11.55 | 10.07 | 4.85 | 6.08 | 6.26 | 6.64 | 16.53 | 5.10 |
| Other manufacturing | 5.88 | 14.22 | 12.45 | 22.95 | 19.84 | 10.06 | 6.85 | 9.80 | 9.91 | 8.84 | 5.93 | 7.34 | 11.73 | 9.30 | .. |
| **Services** | **41.55** | **32.23** | **36.66** | **5.50** | **10.11** | **41.25** | **55.55** | **41.75** | **38.25** | **29.51** | **37.87** | **46.24** | **30.97** | **37.89** | **54.45** |
| Wholesale trade | 9.23 | 5.25 | 4.16 | 6.61 | 6.57 | 3.23 | 29.83 | 22.60 | 15.65 | 5.82 | 7.23 | 8.38 | 6.57 | 4.63 | 3.75 |
| Retail trade | 6.45 | 2.46 | 1.75 | 2.08 | 1.07 | 0.92 | 5.44 | 4.68 | 3.00 | 3.08 | 2.69 | 1.32 | 0.72 | 1.24 | 0.60 |
| Banking | 5.73 | 1.53 | 4.51 | 7.02 | 6.56 | 6.53 | 1.48 | 2.75 | 4.66 | 4.22 | 3.69 | 6.61 | 0.87 | 0.34 | 2.92 |
| Finance, except banking | 0.82 | 2.69 | 7.01 | -12.25 | -16.92 | 10.05 | .. | -4.42 | .. | 5.31 | 1.60 | 3.55 | 6.48 | 6.85 | 25.03 |
| Insurance | 8.23 | 9.07 | 9.95 | 1.42 | 1.31 | 7.79 | 11.38 | 10.27 | 11.52 | 5.11 | 6.18 | 11.93 | 12.10 | 20.50 | 15.98 |
| Real estate | 10.94 | 3.64 | 3.21 | 0.61 | 0.96 | 0.18 | 7.42 | 4.64 | 2.64 | 5.97 | 7.62 | 7.31 | 4.23 | 1.14 | 0.25 |
| Other services | .. | 7.58 | 6.06 | .. | 10.56 | 12.55 | .. | 1.23 | 0.78 | .. | 8.85 | 7.13 | .. | 3.19 | 5.91 |
| **Other industries** | **3.15** | **8.72** | **12.01** | **5.95** | .. | .. | **3.11** | **2.07** | .. | **2.88** | **3.36** | **2.85** | **3.25** | **1.06** | **0.60** |
| **Total** | **100.00** | **100.00** | **100.00** | **97.17** | **80.02** | **96.48** | **100.91** | **100.00** | **89.20** | **100.00** | **100.00** | **100.00** | **99.33** | **100.00** | **100.00** |
| **Value in US$ m (current prices)** | **43555** | **98676** | **132273** | **6670** | **18650** | **38240** | **14816** | **28232** | **47907** | **37056** | **64671** | **67654** | **10568** | **17674** | **33070** |

*Notes*:
Figures may not sum precisely to 100 due to rounding.
.. denotes data are not available or not separately available.
*Source*: United States Department of Commerce (various years).

*Table* 5.9 Inward foreign direct investment stock of Mexico for available European countries, * value and percentage distribution, 1995

| | *Value in US$ m (current prices)* | *Percentage* |
|---|---|---|
| **Europe** | **13005** | **24.89** |
| **EU** | **10741** | **20.55** |
| France | 1662 | 3.18 |
| Germany | 2687 | 5.14 |
| Italy | 81 | 0.16 |
| Netherlands | 1597 | 3.06 |
| Spain | 994 | 1.90 |
| United Kingdom | 3720 | 7.12 |
| **Other Europe** | **2264** | **4.33** |
| Sweden | 385 | 0.74 |
| Switzerland | 1879 | 3.60 |
| **Rest of world** | **36989** | **70.78** |
| **Total** | **52257** | **100.00** |

*Notes*:
* The stock estimate of FDI is the culmination of annual inflows since 1971.
Figures may not sum precisely to 100 due to rounding.
*Source*: SECOFI (1996).

Table 5.9 shows that the leading countries of Europe contribute over 20 per cent of Mexico's inward FDI. The leading share is that of the UK (7 per cent), but close behind are Germany (5 per cent), Switzerland (4 per cent), and France (3 per cent). The source country detail provided is not exhaustive of the countries of the EU or Europe. The shares of other source countries are extremely small. Some data on annual flows by source country (not reported here) show that the omitted countries often have near zero flows to Mexico. The importance of cultural and linguistic ties between Mexico and Spain is supported by the share of Spanish FDI into Mexico, which approached 2 per cent in 1995. This can be compared with the Spanish share of FDI into Mexico's North American neighbours, standing at less than 0.5 per cent in the USA and just 0.02 per cent in Canada in 1995.

**European Foreign Direct Investment into Canada by Industry**

From an overview of the FDI shares in Canada by industry, there is some evidence that European investors capitalize on their marketing and organizational, and perhaps financial, advantages, to compete in Canada. The share of other EU FDI into Canada in the food, beverage and tobacco industry has been expanding rapidly between 1985 and 1995 (from 0.77 per cent to 12 per cent), and the UK's share in this traditional industry has also increased, from some 14 to 21 per cent. This growth stands out in comparison to the more sedate increase in inward FDI in the industry from the world as a whole. The leading share position of European inward investment in finance and insurance into Canada confirms the global importance of this industry, reflected in the intensity of transatlantic cross-FDI.

The UK's FDI is heavily weighted towards finance and insurance, but other important industries are very much in common with other countries of the EU: chemicals, construction, and energy (though in relative decline in terms of share).

**European Foreign Direct Investment into the USA by Industry**

Since 1985 the importance of the petroleum industry's share in European FDI into the USA in 1985 has plummeted from 21 per cent to 7 per cent, very much in line with trends observed before (Table 5.7). The other extractive industry for which there are some data, mining, is deleted as a separate item by 1990, from which it can be inferred that this industry becomes so minor as to cease warranting its own category. The counterpart of these changes is again the growth of the service sector. In the case of US inward FDI, finance and insurance are separately identified, totalling an 18 per cent share. Otherwise the leading industries remain in the manufacturing sector. The chemicals industry in particular accounts for high shares, suggesting European industrial competitive strength and the attractiveness of the US market in these industries.

The importance of market-seeking strategies in the US market are evident also in the industry structure of European countries' FDI (see Table 5.8). The importance of European FDI in the wholesale trade is a case in point. It is a prominent industry for each of the selected European source countries. All the selected European hosts show a high share of their FDI in the USA as being in the chemicals industry, which includes pharmaceuticals. Prominent here is Switzerland, with its domestic industrial strength in this industry, and France. France had a 45 per cent share of its activity in this industry in 1985, slipping to 25 per cent by 1995, but still ranking in first place. The general nature of this distribution suggests that the US, or North American market, is increasingly attractive as a production base.

Apart from the general secular trends, European FDI in the USA does exhibit some source-country-specific patterns. UK foreign investment in real estate, which peaked in the mid-1980s at the time of the low exchange value of the dollar to sterling, has subsequently fallen. The two European countries with the strongest bases in finance, the UK and Switzerland, have made the greatest inroads into the USA. The UK's share rose from less than 1 per cent in 1985 to 7 per cent in 1995, and the Swiss share from 6 per cent to 25 per cent. The negative FDI position of France in this industry in 1985 and 1990 clearly is a reflection of French affiliates in the finance industry expanding their lending to their parent firms in France. Although counterintuitive as an indicator of foreign activity, negative FDI positions actually signify the use of highly integrated financial practices.

## CONCLUSIONS ON THE REVIEW OF THE DATA

The geographical pattern of Canadian and US FDI into Europe is dominated by the EU, and in particular by the UK. The increase in the EU's share of North American FDI is consistent with the hypothesized impact of the SEM on North American firms' business strategies to build up their investment in the EU. Cultural affinities seem to dominate over political affinities in explaining the especially high US FDI in the UK and the significant Canadian FDI in Ireland.

The Canadian industrial pattern in the UK and the rest of the EU centres around the replacement (or overlaying in the case of Europe) of the traditional industrial profiles based on low-technology manufacturing industry. In the EU this has been dominated by finance and insurance, and in the UK by telecommunications FDI and by high-technology supplier activities in the form of electrical and electronic industries. The leading cause of these changes has been the liberalization of the telecommunications market in the UK, and the liberalization of financial markets within the EU. These policy initiatives have largely changed the complexion of Canadian FDI, and have brought forth a dynamism in Canadian FDI that was lacking in the old pattern.

From an overview of the industry pattern of North American FDI in Europe it appears that liberalization in finance, and the globalization of markets, has driven the upsurge in US FDI in Europe in this industry. The traditional manufacturing industries, such as automobiles, machinery and electrical are now very minor elements in US FDI in the EU, and have been supplanted principally by the service sector, especially finance and by the prominence of the chemicals industry group. Most of the adjustments in industrial structure in US FDI in Europe have been the outcome of secular trends rather than the impact of market integration *per se*, as US MNEs have adjusted to a pan-European strategy over a long period.

European FDI into North America is characterized by growth, particularly as a result of market liberalization in finance and telecommunications (especially in the UK). This has altered the industry balance, but preserved the overall identity of the established partner countries – the UK, France, Germany, the Netherlands and Switzerland – reflecting national industrial specialization. The growth of services in general has reinforced the tendency for established cross-investors to invest most heavily in markets abroad most similar in terms of economic structure to their own, i.e., to bolster the cross-intensity of transatlantic FDI. The cultural affinity thesis with Canada appears to be borne out best in European strengths in the traditional sectors in North America, for example, in the food, drink and tobacco industry group.

While the growth of the service sector has accompanied and has been part of the intensification of transatlantic FDI, nevertheless, US inward FDI from Europe in key manufacturing industries remains relatively strong. Market-seeking FDI characterizes all European involvement in the USA. i.e., production for the US or North American market. North American integration appears to have reinforced these tendencies, for example, in the chemicals group. The strong and growing attractiveness of the US market for FDI in this group certainly signifies market-seeking FDI, probably allied to the need to locate pharmaceuticals production in North America. It is likely that North American market size and integration have combined to shift market servicing strategies increasingly towards direct local production. (See also the analysis by Dunning (1993) examining the period 1950 to 1990).

## CONCLUSION

It is frequently said that there is nothing so practical as a good theory. In this case theory tells us where to look for the salient features of transatlantic FDI and does not fail in highlighting the key regularities.

First, there is a clear influence from cultural similarities. Even within the integrating units (EU and NAFTA), the UK (and Ireland) are picked out by Canadian and US investors and Spanish FDI goes disproportionately to Mexico. Language is a good proxy for cultural affinity but does not tell the whole story.

Second, the impact of integration is felt on the direction of AFDI flows. The preference of European AFDI for the US over Canada and that for the UK over the rest of the EU for US and Canadian AFDI is increased by integration. Multinationals no longer need manufacturing outputs in markets fragmented by tariffs. They can centralize their market-wide activities to gain economies of scale and supplement these units by warehousing and distribution investments throughout the unifying market.

Third, cross-investment by country and industry is intense as we would expect between countries of similar income levels. This reflects both 'exchange of threat' strategies and also the underlying determinants of FDI (notably its use, as the key strategic weapon of market access, of its relationship to advertising and R&D-intensive activity (Buckley and Casson 1976, Buckley and Dunning 1976), and therefore to differentiated product industries).

Fourth, in terms of industry breakdown, AFDI in both directions has shown a marked shift from manufacturing to services and a decline in the proportion of extractive industries in the total. The key story concerns the rise of financial services in AFDI, but there is also a strong upward trend in wholesale activity, which marks a shift to centralized production plus satellite distribution in markets becoming larger as integration proceeds.

Extensions of this research could take the form of an analysis of the breakdown of AFDI by merger and acquisition (M&A) versus greenfield investments. At present, the classification of the data does not allow a country by industry analysis of M&A activity.

## APPENDIX

### Definition of Foreign Direct Investment

A foreign direct investment (FDI) exists when a business enterprise (or a natural person) has a lasting interest in and a degree of influence over the management of a business enterprise in another country. The normal criterion for a foreign investment to be deemed a foreign direct investment is the ownership or control of 10 per cent or more of an enterprise's voting securities. If this condition is met, the enterprise can be designated as a foreign affiliate. Any foreign investment not meeting this condition is considered to be a portfolio foreign investment. The USA adopted this definition of FDI in the International Investment and Trade in Services Act. The Canadian definition of FDI also sets ownership at 10 per cent of equity. The OECD also considers the Mexican definition of FDI to comply with the definition of FDI set out in the Fifth Edition of the IMF *Balance of Payments Manual* and the OECD *Detailed Benchmark Definition*. The value of FDI in the foreign affiliate attributed to the parent enterprise is then arrived at through the normal process of the consolidation of accounts. For an account of the pitfalls in using FDI data (in the UK case) see Buckley and Pearce 1991.

## Statistical Sources

*Canada*

Statistics Canada, Balance of Payments Division (1996), *Canada's International Investment Position, 1995*. Ottawa: Minister of Industry Canada.

*Mexico*

Secretaria de Comercio y Fomento Industrial (SECOFI) (1996), *Evolucion de la Inversion Extranjera en Mexico. Enero de 1995*. SECOFI.

*USA*

United States Department of Commerce, Bureau of Economic Analysis, International Investment Division, data provided in electronic form for various years.

## Notes

The authors are grateful for comments from John Dunning, Gavin Boyd, Alan Rugman and the HEC Montreal Conference participants.

1. FDI by 'natural persons' is a very minor item in statistical terms.

## References

Buckley, Peter J. (1988) 'The limits of explanation: testing the internalisation theory of the multinational enterprise', *Journal of International Business Studies*, xix, 2, Summer, 181–93.

——(ed.) (1990a) *International Investment*. Cheltenham: Edward Elgar.

——(1990b) 'Problems and developments in the core theory of international business', *Journal of International Business Studies*, 21, 4, 155–71.

——(1992) 'Alliances, technology and markets: a cautionary tale' in Peter J. Buckley, *Studies in International Business*. London: Macmillan.

——and Mark Casson (1976) *The Future of the Multinational Enterprise*. London: Macmillan.

——and John H. Dunning (1976) 'The industrial structure of US investment in the UK', *Journal of International Business Studies*, 7, 2, Fall, 5–13.

——and Pervez N. Ghauri (eds) (1993) *The Internationalisation of the Firm*. London: Dryden Press.

——and Robert D. Pearce (1991) *The International Aspects of UK Economic Statistics*. London: Chapman and Hall.

——and Brian R. Roberts (1982) *European Direct Investment in the USA before World War I*. London: Macmillan.

——, C. L. Pass and Kate Prescott (1992) 'The internationalisation of service firms: a comparison with the manufacturing sector', *International Business Review*, 1, 1, 39–56.

——, C. L. Pass and Kate Prescott (1994) 'Economic integration: the Single European Market and the NAFTA and their Implications for Canada-UK Bilateral Trade and Investment', *British Journal of Canadian Studies*, 9, 2, 375–400.

——, C. L. Pass and Kate Prescott (1995a) 'The Single European Market initiative – a perspective from Canadian companies', *British Journal of Canadian Studies*, 10, 1, 77–86.

——, C. L. Pass and Kate Prescott (1995b) *Canada–UK Bilateral Trade and Investment Relations*. London: Macmillan.

——, C. L. Pass and Kate Prescott (1996) *Canadian–European Union Strategic Alliances*. Report for Canadian High Commission in London.

Casson, Mark (ed.) (1990) *Multinational Enterprises*. Cheltenham: Edward Elgar.

Clegg, J. (1996) 'United States foreign direct investment in the European Community: the effects of market integration in perspective', in F. N. Burton, M. Yamin and S. Young (eds), *International Business and Europe in Transition*. London: Macmillan, 189–206.

Dunning, John H. (1958) *American Investment in British Manufacturing Industry*. London: George Allen and Unwin.

——(1993) 'Transatlantic foreign direct investment and the European Economic Community', in *The Globalization of Business*. London: Routledge, 166–89.

Flowers, E. B. (1975) 'Oligopolistic reactions in European and Canadian direct investments in the United States', *Journal of International Business Studies*, 7, 43–55.

Glaister, Keith and Peter J. Buckley (1994) 'UK international joint ventures: an analysis of patterns of activity and distribution', *British Journal of Management*, 5, 1, 33–51.

——and Peter J. Buckley (1996) 'Strategic motives for UK international alliance formation', *Journal of Management Studies*, 33, 3, 233–45.

Graham, E. M. (1978) 'Transatlantic investment by multinational firms: a rivalistic phenomenon?', *Journal of Post Keynesian Economics*, 1, 82–99.

——(1990) 'Exchange of threat between multinational firms as an infinitely repeated non-cooperative game', *The International Trade Journal*, 4, 259–77.

Hallen, L. and F. Wiedersheim-Paul (1979) 'Psychic distance and buyer-seller interaction', *Organisasjon, Marknod och Samhalle*, 16, 5, 308–24. Reprinted in Buckley and Ghauri (1993).

Hymer, Stephen H. (1976) *The International Operations of National Firms*. Cambridge, MA: MIT Press.

Kay, Neil M., Harvie Ramsay and Jean-François Hennart (1996) 'Industrial collaboration in the European internal market', *Journal of Common Market Studies*, 34, September, 465–75.

Knickerbocker, Frederick T. (1973) *Oligopolistic Reaction and Multinational Enterprise*. Cambridge, MA: Harvard University Press.

OECD (1995) *International Direct Investment Statistics Yearbook*. Paris: OECD.
Rugman, Alan M. (ed.) (1994) *Foreign Investment and NAFTA*. University of South Carolina Press.

# 6 Transfer Pricing and Economic Functions Analysis: The Japanese Paradigm*

Peter J. Buckley and
Jane Frecknall-Hughes

**This chapter examines the difficulties facing tax authorities in valuing cross-border flows from a transactions based analysis, in conditions where intangibles and services are important and where the multinational firm concerned is operating a system in which group-wide economic functions dominate decision making. Its key contention is that the economic functions of any entity should be examined in order to determine whether transactions analysis can be used to produce an acceptable value. This is done in the particular context of Japanese multinational enterprises and uses two hypothetical situations to demonstrate the inadequacy of transactions based analysis as a panacea for transfer pricing problems, especially for transfers of value involving intangibles and services, which it redefines into two categories, perceptible and imperceptible.**

## INTRODUCTION

In recent months transfer pricing issues have been given extensive coverage in financial, professional and academic articles. The underlying tone of many articles has often been condemnatory, especially in financial press reports about Japanese multinationals, taking the line that such enterprises

* First published in *Applied Economics*, 30, 5 (1998).

deliberately manipulate transfer pricing mechanisms to obtain various tax advantages. The reasons for this increased level of interest in the affairs of multinational enterprises, particularly Japanese based groups, is detailed by Pentelow (1996):

(i) The globalization of economic activity will result in more companies becoming part of multinational enterprises than has traditionally been the case, as a result of regional and global competition and the reduction of exchange controls and other barriers to the movement of goods and services across the world. A multinational enterprise will therefore produce in whichever country provides the most effective, efficient and beneficial facilities [The idea of what constitutes 'beneficial' will be explored later];
(ii) Many of the newer growing business [such as the software industry] acquire or create international affiliates at a much earlier stage of their development than do the more traditional industries;
(iii) As part of global competition, economies compete to provide attractive locations for inward investment and so the trend is for tax rates to be reduced progressively [This is apparent for the UK – see Higson and Elliott, 1994];
(iv) There is a consequent erosion of the tax base at a time when, in the developed economies, there are growing demands on the state because of demographic and other changes. Jurisdictions will therefore seek to protect their tax base against any perceived exporting of profits through transfer pricing or other means; and
(v) The supranational mechanisms for regulating the competition between taxing jurisdictions [such as the OECD, the EU Arbitration Convention, mutual agreement procedures in tax treaties etc.] are not highly developed.

It could also be added that some of the above pull in opposite directions, which adds to the complexity. The multinational enterprise is therefore developing against a backcloth of ill-defined regulations (as witnessed by attempts to expand the UK's network of international tax treaties – see *Accountancy Age*, 18 April 1996, p. 10).

Pentelow's analysis is done from the viewpoint of the professional tax practitioner, and suggests that, for the same reasons, the existing situation is likely to become even more complex. However, these are not the only reasons for the current scale of the problems and the recent heightened interest. The Inland Revenue has developed an interest also, from a different professional perspective. This seems to be the natural corollary of the establishment of 'Pollard' districts in the early to mid-1980s, to bring together the affairs of groups of companies within one district (previously each company's affairs had been dealt with in the tax district where the company was actually registered) and the subsequent recent establishment of large business offices to look at all tax aspects (including PAYE and NIC) of large businesses, not only groups. The inclusion of all companies in a group under one umbrella obviously provides the Inland Revenue with a better overview of group affairs and will significantly reduce administration costs. However, there is a strong suggestion, though again in the press (see *Accountancy Age*, 31 July 1997, p. 1) that this bringing together has resulted in a deeper level of probing by the Revenue, although this is not made specific to transfer pricing issues. Also evident has been the perceived inadequacy of the existing transfer pricing legislation which is drafted in very general terms.

Added to the professional interest of tax practitioners and the Inland Revenue is the increasing interest of academics in all aspects of Japanese business, especially in defining reasons for its great success (see Cole, 1980; Drucker, 1981; Hayes, 1981; Robinson, 1985; Kharbanda and Stallworthy, 1991 and Kharbanda, 1992) and, in particular, examining the role of management accounting as part of that success (see Monden and Sakurai, 1989; Morgan and Weerakoon, 1989 and McMann and Nanni, 1995).

The allegations of the use of transfer pricing for profit manipulation purposes was examined in our earlier article (see Buckley and Frecknall Hughes, 1997). The chief allegation (which we considered there) seems to have been that companies set out deliberately to engineer a pricing structure which results in a sales/purchase price which is artificially low/high for goods which, typically, are traded across one or more national boundaries. This is in practical terms difficult to prove, and tax authorities normally seek to make adjustments based on attempts to establish a 'fair' or 'arm's length' price for goods for which an independent market seldom exists. Press allegations have assumed that multinationals operate similarly to one another in the area of transfer pricing – to the disadvantage of the host countries in which they operate. Tax avoidance, however, would not be the only rationale for transfer pricing. The desire to realize profits in Japan might also reflect a desire to minimize exposure to exchange rate risk, which cannot be built into a tight costing/pricing schedule. Moreover, if tax avoidance were so great a motivation, then one might actually expect Japanese subsidiaries to declare more profit in the UK, as corporation tax rates in Japan are currently around 50 per cent – higher than the UK rates. (See also Cravens, 1997, on motivations other than taxation.) In our first article we contended that such mechanisms are the fundamental, natural results of operating from a different perspective and culture. The key thrust of this second article is to develop a wider appreciation of the effects of operating from a different business perspective in an area fundamentally related to costing/pricing issues of this kind, namely the use of a transactions based approach to value cross-border activities. We shall attempt to show, by the use of hypothetical examples, how difficult it can be to identify any transaction and its origin, even before the problems of valuation are considered, and how many activities might escape detection completely. Further, we shall demonstrate that there are certain occasions when transfers of value occur, where the fundamental benefit would be overlooked completely if examined from a transactions based perspective (see below, hypothetical example 2). It is our contention that before any transactions based analysis is done, one should look at the economic functions involved to see *whether* this is an appropriate method of valuation. It is our further contention that transactions based analysis frequently will not be appropriate because of basic differences between Japanese and Western methods of doing business, some of which are so fundamental that trying to import a Western-developed method such as transactions based valuation will be, in the words of the old axiom, 'like trying to fit a square peg in a round hole'.

## THE CURRENT CONTEXT

Current thinking, as typified in the latest *OECD Guidelines on Transfer Pricing*, suggests that any adjustments to taxable profits should be calculated on a transactions basis, that is, each individual transaction (or groups of similar transactions) which occurs between entities operating in different tax jurisdictions should be examined and adjustments made if it is not valued in accordance with an 'arm's length' principle. There are several different practical methods permitted to achieve such a result, such as (i) use of a comparable uncontrolled price, (ii) a resale price method, (iii) cost plus method together with (iv) transactional net margin and (v) profit split, if the first three cannot be used. All of these methods are transactions based, though their ways of defining the transaction differ. It is the contention of this article that such analysis is sometimes not possible for the following reasons:

(i) In practical terms, in an international context, there will be insufficient documentation available to the taxing authorities to 'prove' a lack of arm's length price. If one considers a purchase from an associated foreign entity, all the documentation relating to costing and manufacture will be held in the foreign country, and Revenue authorities ideally need access to costings to see whether an import price charged is too high (but see later).

(ii) More importantly, for a typical Japanese group of companies, such analysis simply cannot be done because of their different methods of costing (see Buckley and Frecknall Hughes, 1997) and, in a wider sense, different methods of doing business. A much wider contextual appreciation is required: one needs to look at the actual economic function that is taking place first before homing in on details of individual transactions. Indeed, it may not be possible to identify the transaction that has actually occurred, although an economic result may be evident even it is not easy to quantify.

We would argue that it is the achievement of economic results on a global scale that is the particular objective of any Japanese based group. The Japanese paradigm is adopted here because it is a well-established fact that Japanese entities favour the use of target costing as the best means of putting into operation their business concepts, rather than as a manipulative pricing device. Over 80 per cent of major Japanese companies in assembly-type operations are believed to have adopted target costing (Sakurai, 1989, 1990). However, target costing by its very nature does permit an entity to locate a predetermined amount of profit in a predetermined location because of the way a product is priced onwards into its target market. We have argued in an earlier article that Japanese companies, especially because of their powerful position as large entities, are able to achieve their desired profit level by controlling costs in their suppliers. A recent study of cost control in the UK operation of Nissan reports that members of the Nissan operation became actively involved in helping their suppliers and sub-suppliers reduce the costs of supplied goods where these exceeded Nissan's own target costs, some companies willingly adopting an 'open-book' arrangement to allow Nissan free access to their internal costings (Carr and Ng, 1995). Although some suppliers appeared initially wary of this approach, it seems to have succeeded because Nissan's approach was aimed at reducing the supplier's costs, but *not* eroding their profit margins. This must be much easier to achieve where a supplier is a group company: the difficulty is in costing out any given product to include within those costings/pricings the amount of profit which will be allowed to remain with a subsidiary to cover its operating costs. (We have already suggested that this will not be a significant amount (see Buckley and Frecknall Hughes, 1997) and could thus vary significantly between different locations.) This in itself is not a difficult concept when it is remembered that 'target costing is not a costing system as such; rather it is an activity which is aimed at reducing the life cycle costs of new products, while ensuring quality, reliability and other customer requirements, by examining all ideas for cost reduction at the product planning, research and development process' (Kato, 1993, p. 1). Numerous other researchers examining Japanese cost systems have taken a similar line, from management accounting and from international business perspectives (see Monden and Hamada, 1991; Yoshikawa *et al.*, 1993, pp. 33–55; and Cravens, 1997). The Japanese multinational enterprise operates as one entity, we would argue, aiming to generate a central profit in its home base: this is the concept which drives its pricing structure in relation to foreign entities, especially its own subsidiaries (see Buckley and Frecknall Hughes, 1996). The subsidiaries do not exist to make a profit for themselves, which would be dysfunctional, but for the parent company, thus transcending any notion of individual company and national boundaries. Whatever legal form they take, the foreign subsidaries are regarded as operational agents. A useful analogy to demonstrate the difference from traditional Western/European thinking is to consider them as arms or legs of a body, helping that body to function properly as one whole, rather than as a mother company with distinct 'offspring' with separate, identifiable lives of their own. If this underlying concept determines pricing, as we argued in our earlier article, it is similarly likely to underlie all other aspects of Japanese business, which should surely be examined from this perspective.

However, the 1995 *OECD Guidelines*, with their emphasis on a transactions based method of valuing transfers, are based on Western/European thinking. For example, they emphasize the need for documentation to be maintained to include such items as the details of the group, the parties to the transactions, the transactions themselves, the methods used to determine the transfer prices, proof that the transfer prices are at arm's length and evidence of a search for comparable transactions and companies. This approach would require a great deal of documentation to be maintained, although, again, it is difficult to see how some of the necessary evidence could be obtained from foreign countries. The *Guidelines* inherently acknowledge that this approach is not wide enough, as witnesses the inclusion of the phrase 'functional analysis', although its meaning remains unclear. The practical and theoretical difficulties of such an approach may best be demonstrated by the use of some hypothetical examples.

## Hypothetical Situation (1)

Figure 6.1 shows part of a hypothetical multinational group of companies, based on Japan. For the purposes of this example, Figure 6.1 is deemed to show a subgroup operating in Europe

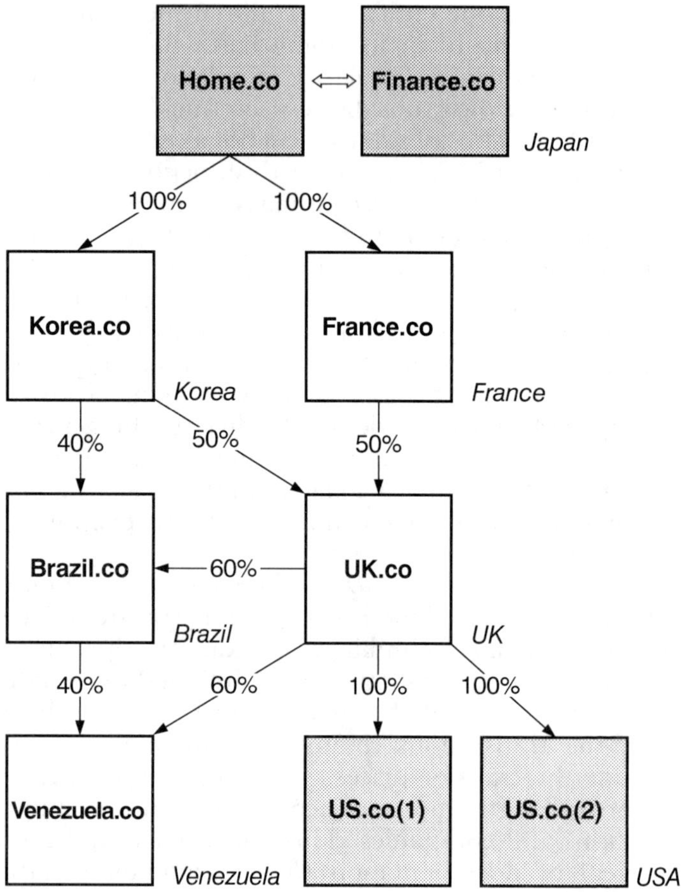


→ Direction of and percentage of share ownership

□ National boundary of individual company (identical shading indicates companies within the same national boundary, hence, **US.co(1)** and **US.co(2)** are both in the USA, and so on).

⇔ Indicates linked Japanese companies (Home.co and Finance.co) in the same group in the home country. Because holding companies are forbidden in Japan (see *Economist*, 17 February 1996, p. 74, 'The Ties that Bind'), a quasi-group structure would be achieved by a complicated series of cross-holdings of shares in several different companies. Such cross holdings also tend to feature in the shareholding structures outside Japan, although the above is such simplified.

*Figure* 6.1 Hypothetical group of Japanese based companies

and the Americas. It is emphasized that this subgroup structure is purely conjectural and is not to be identified with any existing group of companies, even if there appear to be similarities: any such similarities are coincidental. The subgroup structure and operation are simplified here: a Japanese multinational might typically comprise numerous similar subgroups operating worldwide with a greater complexity and volume of intragroup trade.

For this first scenario, the following business operations are assumed:

(i) Company **UK.co** in this group is a UK based company owned 50:50 by **Korea.co** and **France.co** which are manufacturing companies (making electronic components) based in Korea and France respectively, the majority of their raw materials being imported from **Home.co** in Japan, with a small proportion from a nominally independent supplier in Korea (which company is effectively controlled by the group as it has no other customers, although it is not technically owned outright). **Korea.co** and **France.co** export goods directly to the South American based subsidiaries **Brazil.co** and **Venezuela.co**, but these goods are invoiced via **UK.co**, which is a distribution and assembly company, and through which orders for **Korea.co**'s and **France.co**'s goods are routed by the two South American companies. These particular goods never enter the UK at all. **UK.co** is remunerated by the South American companies, receiving 1.5 per cent of the ultimate sales value of the goods in the market in which they are eventually sold.

(ii) **UK.co** also imports goods from **Korea.co** and **France.co** for direct onward sale to its own 100 per cent owned US based subsidiaries. These goods do enter the UK, and are repackaged here in a form suitable for their ultimate US market.

(iii) **UK.co** also imports goods from **Korea.co** and **France.co** which is assembles with other components imported directly from **Home.co** in Japan, forming a differentiated product, which it also sells to **US.co(1)** and **US.co(2)** in the US and to **Brazil.co** and **Venezuela.co** in South America.

(iv) **UK.co** also acts as a coordinator for all **Korea.co**'s and **France.co**'s sales within the rest of Europe (although no goods physically enter the UK) and processes all the paperwork for orders from customers. It is not responsible for collection of debts for those companies, and is not remunerated in any way for doing this.

The UK tax authorities will be concerned solely with the activities of **UK.co** from a transfer pricing perspective as it is the only company located within its jurisdiction. (There may be controlled foreign company implications in respect of the US subsidiaries, but these do not concern us here.)

Although this is a relatively simple set-up as far as international business activities are concerned, untangling the cross-border transfers which give rise to transfer pricing implications is far from easy, especially in the light of any transactions based analysis. For the goods exported directly to South America by **Korea.co** and **France.co**, **UK.co** provides an invoicing service only, as no goods enter the UK. It is likely that the remuneration of 1.5 per cent of the ultimate sales value which it receives for this service would have been determined centrally, as part of the target costing for this product, and would be part of the administrative expenses associated with selling the product on a world scale (see Sparkes *et al.*, 1987). Determining the origin of the activity is difficult: it is not merely a question of revenue coming to **UK.co** on the basis of its own activities, as **Korea.co**, **France.co**, **Brazil.co** and **Venezuela.co** are all involved. On the strength of the central determination referred to above, the origin of the activity may be felt to be ultimately in Japan. Trying to determine an 'arm's length' price for tax purposes becomes infeasible as the UK company's operation is not independent, but part of a chain inseparable into its individual links. The group has set up this function purely for its own purposes: it may be unique and not susceptible of analysis on a transactions based concept. From the Japanese point of view, the revenue coming into **UK.co** is not a stand-alone transaction: it is more like, say, an internal movement within a warehouse with a nominal charge to cover the cost of the paperwork. The transaction would occur when the goods were finally sold outside the group, namely by the Brazilian or Venezuelan company to the outside market: that would be the profit-generating point. The series of internal processes or transactions through which goods have passed within the group are not relevant, but it is these which Western tax authorities seek to identify. Under the existing remuneration system, the South American companies are paying for the benefit both they and **Korea.co** and **France.co** receive. On a transactions based approach the benefit to the latter two companies (for which they pay nothing) would also have to be taken into account. In many ways it is like trying to value work-in-progress: everyone understands that there may be several stages of manufacture or processing to go through before completion. From a Japanese point of view, a transaction may be stretched over space and time, but it is planned and executed as one operation. The Western/European concept aims to break it down into subcomponents, and these are not always clearly definable because they were not planned as separable stages.

Such an operational set-up does beg the question as to why any entity would choose to do business in this way. There could be a variety of reasons. It may be that the Japanese company took over existing operations in various countries which already operated in this way and kept what it found. A historical set-up is very often the reason for an apparently illogical way of operating. However, bearing in mind that the Japanese selling operation will have been based on an appreciation of its target market, using one company to collate all details of orders for particular products is a useful and easy way of collecting together the product sales orders from a variety of countries in an immediately available form, such that any adverse trends can be readily detected and any appropriate corrective action taken, e.g., additional advertising or price discounts which would be determined when the data were fed back to the home base. Possibly the UK would be selected as a base because English is a first language for the UK and USA, and a second one for most other countries, particularly in Europe. (The cross-share holdings could be either a historical feature or a reflection of normal share-owning practices in Japan.) As a control mechanism, this collation is effective and its overall benefit to the group would not be measurable. Here there is an obvious instance of an economic effect or function, but the actual transactions which produce it cannot easily be separately distinguished or quantified. Such activity cannot be dealt with effectively using the *OECD Guidelines* as they stand. The way the transaction is planned and executed from start to finish is designed to benefit the group as a whole as much as possible, hence the use of an invoicing route which may seem unnecessary or illogical if looked at from a different perspective. In many ways this is very similar to, say, a UK based company taking advantage of economies of scale. In some respects, when a multinational does so, it seems to act against the spirit of the tax legislation prevailing in countries of operation.

In addition **UK.co** imports goods from Korea and France which it repackages and sells on to the US subsidiaries. It also carries out an assembly operation on some goods by combining them with other components from Japan which it sells on to the US as well as to South America. As the goods physically enter the UK, the problem of their import price arises. It would be expected, under target costing, that there would be no significant profit margin either on the import to the UK for the Korean or French companies, or to **UK.co** on the subsequent export after repackaging or assembly. The price to the buying companies would take into account the additional work (= added value) of the processes undergone in the respective countries, but this in turn is accounted for in the target price for the target market. Export will be at import price plus added value for processes incurred, plus a margin for administrative costs (depending on what market prices will permit), the pricing structure being set up so that the majority of the profit ends up in the home base. In the case of goods bought by **UK.co** here, if a transactions based concept is followed, the trial goes back to the Japanese company **Home.co** as this is the origin of the raw materials. The Korean company which also is a supplier cannot provide a truly independent comparative price as it is effectively under group control (see Sparkes *et al.*, 1987). It would be difficult for any tax authority to get back to such records without the willing cooperation of the companies involved.

This also raises the question of allocation of overheads. For example, does **Home.co** include in its price to Korea and France a proportion of its own indirect overheads, as would be a usual expectation, or does it not need to because it can recover these from selling the same products in a home market which is protected from foreign competition? As regards the development costs of the original products, are these recovered from a home market in the same way or is some proportion recovered in a charge to the companies in Korea and France, because they are benefiting from the home company developing originally the product which they now manufacture commercially? It is arguable that this idea of a local entity benefiting is a very Western/European one and does not sit happily with the interpretation of the Japanese concept of doing business which is fundamental to our arguments here. It is more likely to be the case that such costs are either regarded as an integral part of Japanese production costs (raising the inevitable question of how they are allocated so as to prevent over-recovery) or are recovered via a home market.

The idea of research and development is also a two-way concept. Although one company may develop a product, which a second company manufactures, and a third company in reality sells and distributes, that third company is in an excellent position to feed back to its home base information about consumer reaction to the product – what customers like, what they do not like, and what, based on their selling experience, would make the product sell even better. Feedback of information of this kind from a well-placed distribution company, such as **UK.co** in our example, could be instrumental in its effect on group sales of products worldwide. This is valuable group service, carried out in the UK, but for which the UK company would not be in any way remunerated. It would be impossible to value this on a transactions basis, yet the function could be essential to group profitability as a whole. Ensuring that the UK company acts as a coordinator of all European sales for **Korea.co**'s and **France.co**'s sales would enable this function to be performed the more effectively. In our example, this latter function is not remunerated in **UK.co**. The function may involve keeping detailed customer files, negotiating particular customer contracts, providing product support, authorizing price rebates if goods sold to the outside world could not be sold on to a final consumer, arranging advertising rebates if a customer significantly displayed the product's brand name and so on. The value in monetary terms, using the company's own criteria, may be hard to evaluate, let alone trying to calculate it on an arm's length basis. The entire function might be performed by one or two personnel, who might be Japanese nationals working in the UK, putting to work their original training acquired at home. Their mere presence and training would ensure that such activities would be carried out in a manner concordant with group policy, which by their involvement would be exported to the UK. These are services which, in our opinion, are impossible to value objectively because they are so fundamental to the way in which business is done.

The second part of the *OECD Guidelines*, published in March 1996, tackles the issue of intangibles, such as research and development and services. However, our analysis above develops the idea of intangibles further than the *Guidelines* in their present form. It is thus arguable that there are two types of intangibles and services, namely those which can be perceived, such as research and development (perceptibles) and those which cannot, such as the value of having a Japanese national working for **UK.co** (imperceptibles). This latter point is clarified below.

## Hypothetical Situation (2)

Referring to Figure 6.1 again, there remains one company hitherto unmentioned, namely **Finance.co.** In this second scenario, it is envisaged that **Finance.co** is a company dealing exclusively with finance. It is further envisaged that the UK company operation is to be expanded and a new warehousing facility is required which will cost several million pounds sterling to develop. **Finance.co**, as the Group's finance company, is responsible for raising the loan required for this expansion. First of all, as **Finance.co** has the backing of an international group, the loan need not be raised within the UK at all: in practice it may be raised entirely from a Japanese bank. There are, however, several methods by which finance could in theory be raised. The following are necessarily simplistic to demonstrate to cross-border problems for the UK company. (There may well be considerable tax problems associated with the type of loan involved in its own right, but this is beyond our consideration at this point.)

If the loan is raised in the UK (using the expert negotiation of **Finance.co**) cross guarantees may be accepted from other group companies, so there is a benefit to the UK company from this. Further, the loan may have been granted to the UK company simply because it was recognized as part of an international group; hence the lender perceived less risk. A loan may not have been granted to a non-group, non-internationally backed UK company in the same situation. There may be nothing unusual about the actual terms of the loan itself: it might be on the same terms as any other loans made by that particular lender, but it is the group backing which ensured that it was given in the first place. How indeed can this be valued on an arm's length principle? The loan terms are certainly at arm's length, but the acquisition has not been. While the fundamental issue of the loan being granted in the first place would concern Revenue authorities (and is in our opinion *the* fundamental transfer pricing issue) yet it is likely that Revenue authorities could only in such circumstances address the issue of whether payment of interest was on commercial terms. It would be difficult, if not impossible, to value the act of granting the loan. Such a transaction would be even more difficult to deal with if the loan were from a source outside the UK.

**Finance.co** may have elected to raise finance elsewhere in the world, and ferry the loan across to the UK by means of a back-to-back loan, either directly from itself, or it might have involved yet another group company in the chain, all three being located in different tax jurisdictions and all using different currencies (Figure 6.2). (Although this is a feasible means of finance, it is more usually found in European than in Japanese groups. However, it may be attractive to a European subgroup of a Japanese entity, such as we have envisaged here.)

**Finance.co** is well placed to manipulate currency exchange differences to the benefit of the group, and the play-off between one currency and another may have been deliberately undertaken for no other reason. However, the arrangement might have been put in place to take account of the different companies' cash flows. The middle company in the chain might be able to raise cash for interest payments as required by the original loan terms, pass this on to **Finance.co**,

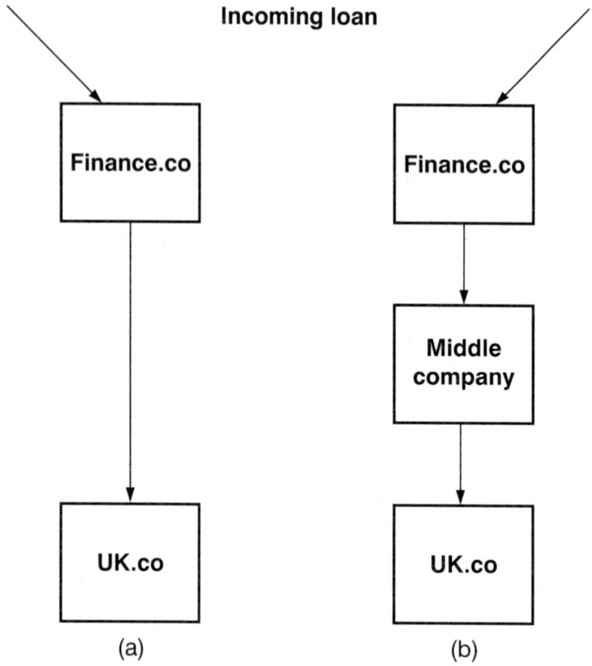


↓ Direction of loan into and out of **Finance.co**
(a) **Finance.co** loans directly to **UK.co**
(b) **Finance.co** loans to a middle company, the normal currency of which is different from both **Finance.co** and **UK.co**: this middle company then passes on the loan to **UK.co**

*Figure* 6.2 Hypothetical loan scenario

and this latter company then pay the lender. The UK company may only be capable of paying interest at one point in its financial year as a result of the way its cash flow arises, especially if sales are seasonal, and may thus be empowered to pay the relevant interest on to the middle company annually instead of quarterly. Filtering the loan through group companies therefore provides a service to the UK company, although it need not be violating the arm's length principle.

If **Finance.co** raised finance *en bloc* for several different companies from a variety of world banks, and allocated a proportion of funds raised to the UK company, either directly or via the mechanism outlined, as it may very well do, the situation would be more complex, and all any Revenue authority could do would be to determine whether interest was being paid at a commercial rate. It would not be able to trace the direct source of the funds. Even **Finance.co** might not know!

It almost goes without saying that **Finance.co** in this scenario is also well placed to deal with the implications of world trade using different currencies. These would arise in the first example above as a matter of course. There would be a benefit to all group companies, not only to **UK.co**, of having an overseer in this area – again an unquantifiable benefit.

## CONCLUSION

Throughout this chapter we have suggested that the economic functions of any company need to be identified before taxation can be applied relevantly. The term *economic functions analysis* is to be differentiated from the term *functional cost analysis* (FCA) which has been used by Yoshikawa *et al.* (1989) and Tanaka *et al.* (1994).

> FCA is a technique employed by many Japanese firms as a means of achieving the target costs which they have established...[It] is an adaptation of value analysis and value engineering techniques which were developed in the West over 30 years ago. The Society of Japanese Value Engineering (1992, p. 1) defines value engineering as 'a systematic approach to studying the functions of products or services in order to achieve their necessary functions with minimum costs'... It involves expressing each function as a verb and a noun, so, for example, the primary function of a staple remover might be 'separate paper' or the primary function of a pen might be 'make mark', with, in the latter instance, secondary functions such as 'flow ink', 'store ink', 'prevent stains' and 'hold pen'. (Yoshikawa *et al.*, 1995, pp. 415–16, following upon an already extensive body of work on Japanese costing – see also Yoshikawa *et al.*, 1993a and 1993b).

Extensive cost databases, known as cost tables, have been developed to support FCA by permitting the quick costing of design changes and new products right at the beginning of the design process. Cost tables include information internal and external to the organization, and can incorporate the use of alternative materials, capital equipment, means of assembly and are the result of years of experience. A survey by Yoshikawa *et al.* (1990, p. 68) of Japanese companies using cost tables found that 71 per cent based their cost tables on the parts of products and 29 per cent on the functions of products. The whole process, including FCA and the use of tables to implement, monitor and control the process is now commonly referred to as target cost management.

This information, readily available to Japanese companies, if relayed to Revenue authorities, would be of some help in establishing appropriate costs and prices, and would go far in eliminating uncertainty about product costs, including overheads, and thus make transfer pricing problems easier to resolve. Indeed, the current *OECD Guidelines*, with the use of the wording 'functional analysis' (see earlier) suggests some thinking in this direction. However, this would depend on the Japanese companies making such data freely available to the Revenue authorities, often of an overseas jurisdiction. It is conceivable that they would object to doing so, but, in a way, their position is similar to that of their own suppliers: here they are the suppliers of tax revenue to a higher, more powerful authority. They have been able to persuade suppliers to be 'open-book', by revealing their internal costings, so perhaps they need to be persuaded of the validity of doing so before tax authorities.

It is conceivable that there would still be some problems associated chiefly with, for example, the specific location of profits, which Revenue authorities would wish to see justified, but the underlying costing and pricing problems could be more easily resolved. There is, of course, the distinct possibility that functions perceived as having a value by a Revenue authority would not be so perceived by a Japanese company. A typical example of this might be the employment of a Japanese national in an overseas country. The cost would most obviously be his/her wage or salary, but a Revenue authority might contend that the mere presence of an individual trained in the methods of a parent company, and disseminating expertise learned there, would be a function carrying value. Thus, while some problems might be resolved, the focus of the debate could change.

It would seem (on the basis of the hypothetical examples above) that a transactions basis for valuing cross-border transfers starts too far down the chain of events: one needs to go much further back into the operational process to find out what exactly is going on, that is, to determine the economic function that is taking place. To try to value cross-border transfers using a transactions basis may be a laudable aim, but it is not always clear whence stems any transaction (which is often a chain of multi-linked integral activity designed to benefit a group using that particular group's structure to the best effect) or what it actually comprises. (Even defining the nature of a function can be problematic, as we have seen, though perhaps less so in overall terms.) In other cases, looking at intragroup activity from this perspective actually misses the substance of a cross-border transfer, as it does not look deeply enough. Similarly, apparently unproblematic arm's length activity may be exactly the opposite! It is our contention that, in a Japanese context, chosen because it is so different from traditional Western business circumstances, an economic functions analysis would go far in addressing these particular problems. Once the problems have been so addressed, then it will be time to think in a more focused way about valuation methods. We do not offer this analysis as an instant solution to the valuation problems inherent in cross-border transfers: if anything they make it harder. However, we have tried to delve to the root of the problem, and not until or unless the problem is understood at this level will any solution proposed get to grips with it, and transactions based valuation principles will continue to fall short of so doing.

## References

*Accountancy Age*, 18 April 1996, 10.

——'Costs fear over tax raids', 31 July 1997, 1.

Buckley, P. J. and Frecknall Hughes, J. (1997) 'Japanese transfer pricing; a note', *Applied Economics Letters* 4, 13–17.

Carr, C. and Ng, J. (1985) 'Total cost control. Nissan and its UK supplier partnerships', *Management Accounting Research*, 6, 347–65.

Cole, R. E. (1980) 'Learning from the Japanese: prospects and pitfalls', *Management Review*, September, 22–4.

Cravens, K. S. (1997) 'Examining the role of transfer pricing as a strategy for multinational firms', *International Business Review*, 6, 2, 127–45.

Drucker, P. F. (1981) 'Behind Japan's success', *Harvard Business Review*, March–April, 110–22.

*Economist*, 'The Ties that Bind', 17 February 1996, 74.

*Financial Times*, 23 November 1995, 11.

Hayes, R. H. (1981) 'Why Japanese factories work', *Harvard Business Review*, July–August, 55–66.

Higson, C. and J. Elliott (1994) 'The incentive to locate a multinational firm: the effect of tax reforms in the United Kingdom', *International Tax and Public Finance*, 1, 1, 81–97.

Kato, M. (1993) 'Target costing support systems: lessons from leading Japanese companies', *Management Accounting Research*, 4, 1, 33–47.

Kharbanda, O. P. (1992) 'Japan's lessons for the West', *CMA Magazine*, February, 26–9.

—— and E. A. Stallworthy (1991) 'Let's learn from Japan', *Management Accounting*, March, 26–33.

McMann, P. J. and A. J. Nanni Jr (1995) 'Means versus ends: a review of the literature on Japanese management accounting', *Management Accounting Research*, 6, 313–46.

Monden, Y. and K. Hamada (1991) 'Target costing and kaizen costing in Japanese automobile companies', *Journal of Management Accounting Research*, Fall, 3, 16–34.

—— and M. Sakurai (eds) *Japanese Management Accounting: A World Class Approach to Profit Management*. Productivity Press, Cambridge, MA, 413–23.

Morgan, M. J. and P. S. H. Weerakoon (1989) 'Japanese management accounting: its contribution to the Japanese miracle', *Management Accounting*, July/August, 42–3.

*OECD Guidelines on Transfer Pricing*, November 1995 and March 1996.

Pentelow, L. (1996) 'Transfer pricing: the issue for the 90's', *Taxation Practitioner*, April, 13–14.

Robinson, R. D. (1985) *The Japanese Syndrome: Is there One?* Georgia State University Press, Atlanta, GA.

Sakurai, A. (1989) 'Target costing and how to use it', *Journal of Cost Management*, Summer, 39–50.

—— (1990) 'The influence of factory automation on management accounting practices: a study of Japanese companies', in R. Kaplan (ed.), *Measures for Manufacturing Excellence*. Harvard Business School Press, Cambridge, MA.

Society of Japanese Value Engineering (1992) *A Guide Book of Value Engineering Terms*, (in Japanese). Society of Japanese Value Engineering, Tokyo.

Sparkes, J. R., P. J. Buckley and H. Mirza (1987) 'A note on Japanese pricing policy', *Applied Economics*, 19, 6, June, 729–32.

*Sunday Times*, 'Insight', 22 March 1992, 1 and 16.

Tanaka, M., T. Yoshikawa, J. Innes and F. Mitchell (1994) *Contemporary Cost Measurement*. Chapman & Hall, London.

Yoshikawa, T., J. Innes and F. Mitchell (1989) 'Cost management through functional analysis', *Journal of Cost Management*, Spring, 14–19.

——, J. Innes and F. Mitchell (1990) 'Cost tables: a foundation of Japanese cost management', *Journal of Cost Management*, Fall, 30–6.

——, J. Innes and F. Mitchell (1993a) 'Japanese management accounting: a comparative survey', *Management Accounting*, November, 20–3.

——, J. Innes and F. Mitchell (1993b) *Contemporary Cost Management*. Chapman & Hall, London.

——, J. Innes and F. Mitchell (1995) 'A Japanese case study of functional cost analysis', *Management Accounting Research*, 6, 415–32.

# 7 Foreign Direct Investment in Japan: Theoretical Explanation and Evidence from European Direct Investors*

Peter J. Buckley

**The low level of foreign direct investment (FDI) has been said to be a theoretical puzzle and is also adduced to be a source of economic conflict between Japan and its major trading and investing partners. This chapter attempts to evaluate inward FDI into Japan from an orthodox position (relying on the stream of theory generated by Buckley and Casson's (1976) internalization approach). It also draws on empirical work developed by Buckley, Mirza and Sparkes (1985) and Mirza, Buckley, and Sparkes (1989) in examining European direct investors in Japan.**

## THEORETICAL BACKGROUND

### Internalization

The internalization approach to FDI (Buckley and Casson, 1976, 1985; Buckley, 1989, 1992, 1995), posits that multinational firms exist because they internalize imperfect markets across national boundaries. They do this in order to create

* First published in Noritake Kobayashi (ed.), *Management: A Global Perspective* (Japan Times Ltd, Tokyo, 1997).

internal futures markets by bringing previously interdependent activities under common control, to utilize discriminatory pricing over intermediate products, to avoid the bilateral concentration of market power and 'buyer uncertainty' in the transfer of information and knowledge and to utilize international transfer pricing to minimize the global tax bill. Within this general framework, the theory suggests that certain market types are more likely to be internalized than are others. Notably, markets in knowledge-intensive products, primary products requiring monitoring of product quality, raw materials whose deposits are geographically concentrated, capital-intensive industries requiring the services of sophisticated plant and machinery, skill, knowledge and communication-intensive services, and location-dependent services are most likely to be internalized (Buckley 1988).

We must, however, not ignore the costs of internalization. These are higher resource costs of adjusting scales of activity to incorporate internal markets, communications costs, the administrative costs of running an internal market, and the specifically international cost of bearing discrimination against a foreign-owned firm. These costs must be set against the benefits of internalization in every case, and the balance between the costs and benefits of internalization determines the optimal scope of the firm (after Coase, 1937).

On this reading, the extent of internalization depends on:

1. industry-specific factors – the nature of the product, the structure of the external market, and the relation between the optimal scales of the activities linked by the market;
2. region-specific factors – the geographical and 'psychic' distance (Hallen and Weidersheim-Paul (1975) between the regions involved);
3. nation-specific factors – the political and fiscal relations between the nations involved; and
4. firm-specific factors, such as the degree of professionalization of management.

**Location**

To this theory of internalization, we need to add a theory of location to 'fix' the firm's optimal scope in real economic space. This is perhaps best done by examining the key motives which firms have in seeking direct investments in foreign markets. Essentially, there are three key motives: (1) Market seeking FDI, (2) Resource seeking FDI, (3) Cost-reduction or efficiency seeking FDI.

Market seeking FDI occurs because investment is a better means of achieving market access than either exporting or technology transfer mechanisms, such as licensing. Resource seeking FDI classically refers to the acquisition of raw materials, but this should be widened to include intermediate products, key assets which are locationally bound and fixed sources of external economies. Cost reducing FDI again has traditionally been confined to cheap labour seeking investment but can also refer to other sources of cost reduction, such as cheap capital and low taxation rates.

The issue of location is best developed by examining the internationalization strategies of companies. This issue has been developed by a number of authors (see Buckley and Ghauri, 1993) and suggests a pattern which runs from exporting, through intermediate forms, such as foreign agencies, sales subsidiaries, and licensing arrangements, to foreign direct investment. The mechanics of the debate do not concern us here, but what is crucial is the process of growing commitment and gradual building of confidence which precedes FDI. If various stages of this sequence are blocked (e.g., by export inhibitions) then firms may not move on to deeper stages of involvement because of their perceptions of risk and lack of commitment. Further, we should not forget that in the internationalization process, there are choices, so that development in one direction (e.g., toward Europe) may, in a situation of capital rationing, take precedence over another (investment in Japan).

The details of this process, too, are crucial. Foreign market entry strategy involves choices. Two of the crucial choices are between takeovers and 'greenfield ventures' (building up from scratch on a greenfield site) and between wholly owned operations and joint ventures with local firms. Firms may have distinct preferences as to the choices, and should these choices be blocked, they may decide to abort the FDI entry.

**Strategy**

Some readers will be surprised by the apparent lack of attention to the strategy of multinational firms in the preceding discussion. In particular, the lack of attention that has been paid to competition. In fact, both internalization and location have strategic aspects. Internalization can be used in order to tie-in key resources (inputs, skilled labour, managers) and prevent access to these elements by rivals. Entry, too, can have a strategic motive as Knickerbocker's (1973) work illustrated. As the theory emphasizes long-run issues, it is less concerned with tactical issues than much of the writing on strategic management. Foreign direct investment (usually) involves a large commitment of resources, notably capital and management time. Consequently, the actions of rivals can be factored in to a long-run view of the basic issues – what market share of what market size will be gained by the investment and what are the long-run implications for costs in the market and global costs? These issues are more likely to be driven by fundamentals rather than the action of rivals. Although, to quote Keynes, 'in the long run we are all dead' and so intermediate effects can be influential in some cases. Most particularly, in this start-up period immediately after entry, strategic actions (e.g., a price war) by (local) competitors can considerably increase costs, and the threat of such action may deter entry.

## RELEVANCE TO FDI IN JAPAN

The above overbrief theoretical background needs to be applied to Japan. This requires an appraisal of the internalization paradigm and particular attention to the locational characteristics of Japan as a host to inward FDI. Although it is the 'peculiar' locational factors of Japan that have attracted most attention (Yoshitomi and Graham, 1996), it is to internalization factors that we first turn.

**Internalization factors**

We begin by examining the set of factors listed above which determine the exact scope and direction of internalization elements: industry-, region-, nation-, and firm-specific factors.

Entry into Japan must be predicated on achieving one of the main goals set for FDI – market, resource acquisition, or cost reduction. Given the high cost structure of Japan, it is unlikely that the last motive will loom large in the planning of non-Japanese multinationals. This can be confirmed by the exodus of Japanese-based multinationals seeking cost-reducing investments elsewhere, most notably in Pacific Asia. Resource acquisition may, in certain industries, be a potential motive – not in raw materials but perhaps in access to key components or classes of labour (scientific, managerial), but again there are severe barriers in terms of the keiretsu structures, loyalty to Japanese companies by key workers and severe cultural and business practice barriers to the acquisition of companies (which is the most important way of acquiring key packaged assets such as brands, distribution networks, managerial and scientific teams). In short, the key motive for FDI in Japan is market access.

Two key areas where market access is sought are industrial products and consumer goods. In examining the market for industrial components and supplies in Japan, the logic of internalization works against inward foreign investors – many of the intermediate markets are already internalized within conglomerate groups or are quasi-internalized by long-run supply contracts of a strong, binding and long-term nature. Breaking in to this supply network, except where product uniqueness is involved, is a difficult, expensive and long-run problem.

In consumer goods, again the distribution issue is crucial. Access to the key distribution channels, retailers and the support services (advertising agencies, service suppliers) presents a problem for the foreign entrant. A great deal of up-front capital is required. This is a similar story in the provision of services where severe cultural barriers are also present.

Turning to region-specific factors, it is undeniable, on any indicator, that the 'psychic distance' between Japan and the major potential investors (European, US) is greater than between these countries, each other, and other potential markets (such as Africa, South America, and Australasia). These cultural and psychic barriers, including language, put up the costs of doing business in Japan versus other potential markets.

Although nation-specific barriers, such as prohibition of foreign investment, tariff barriers and so on, have come down in Japan, they have done so in an ordered fashion. As Japanese industry gathers competitive strength so the barriers come down. As one European executive said to the author regarding FDI in Japan, 'It is like being invited to the cinema when all the seats have been taken!'

Finally, firm-specific factors, too, have served to raise barriers to international internalization and FDI in Japan. These include the lack of a long-term commitment to Japan by foreign investors (which is excusable if relative rates of return are considered) and the lack of professional vision in non-Japanese multinationals of the importance of securing a foothold in the Japanese market. The strength of Japanese competition and the speed of reaction of domestic companies to a competitive threat have also surprised the unwary, inward investor, convinced of its technical superiority.

These factors, classified above as industry-, region-, nation-, and firm-specific inhibitors to inward FDI can be examined also as peculiarities of the particular location – Japan – under consideration.

## JAPAN AS A HOST COUNTRY FOR FDI

FDI in Japan must be evaluated against two alternatives: FDI in another location and using another method of foreign market servicing (exporting, licensing). Because there are disincentives to FDI, many firms choose one or both of the alternatives.

Often the first choice of European and US foreign investors will be to enter a market via a takeover of an existing facility rather than by greenfield entry. In the overwhelming majority of cases, this will not be possible in Japan where companies (or divisions of companies) can rarely be bought. Similarly, entry via wholly owned (as at least majority owned) subsidiaries is preferred, other things being equal, to joint ventures. For reasons to do with cultural barriers (and the need to learn) and with the tightly-knit industrial structure in Japan, joint ventures (particularly the elsewhere unpopular 50:50 joint ownership pattern) are almost universally chosen as the first entry mode for FDI in Japan.

The joint venture in Japan is also frequently different from the typical firm. It is often housed in the Japanese partner's premises, uses personnel seconded from the Japanese partner company (whose loyalty remains to that partner and whose promotion prospects depend on return to the Japanese company's hierarchy), and conducts its business in exactly the same way as the Japanese partner. Control (the distinguishing feature of FDI) is therefore difficult to exercise by the foreign partner. Such ventures can work, but frequently a foreign investor who takes Japan seriously has to effect a 'second entry', using a wholly owned subsidiary and effectively bypassing the original joint venture.

The internalized and quasi-internalized vertical purchasing structure in Japan, both inside and outside keiretsu structures, also poses problems. A frequently used entry strategy by foreign investors is to find a 'niche' in the vertical structure and then expand backward and forward from this bridgehead (often by acquisition). Such moves are blocked in Japan by pre-existing supply relationships, often cemented by ownership links, which prevent such a strategy. Again foreign investors (e.g., ICI) have had to effect a parallel 'second entry' into Japan, using a complete vertical chain from R&D to manufacture and distribution in order to have the room to manoeuvre and expand along the supply chain.

The intensity of competition in Japan cannot be overestimated. The highly competitive domestic market is a real barrier to entry for foreign firms. There is price competition, but also quality and service competition, which foreign investors find difficult to meet. Japanese consumers demand high standards of products service and aftercare. It is essential for a foreign firm to at least match these standards. Pressure for high quality and high service content are transmitted down the supply chain so that 'world-class standards plus' are required for successful operation in Japan.

Meeting these standards requires huge investments, long-run commitment and learning (often painful and costly learning). There are, of course, easier markets in which to operate, but if non-Japanese firms are to compete at the highest level, then they must meet Japanese quality standards in Japan.

Three other factors often adduced to represent barriers to FDI in Japan include: government restrictions, cultural barriers and xenophobia, and longtermism. Each of these does have some explanatory content, though perhaps not so great as some commentators (often looking for single-issue explanation) have attributed to them. Government regulation, on classic 'infant-industry argument' lines, built up sectors before deregulation. It is now difficult to discern (except in small, peculiar areas) any significant deterrent to inward FDI from government interference, although this was not true in the past. Cultural barriers and xenophobia are perhaps more apparent in the labour market than in purchasing behaviour. The Japanese consumer is open to innovation from wherever it comes, but Japanese workers and managers show a marked preference for Japanese firms over all but a tiny few inward investors. Despite the fact that inward investors have successfully tapped the market for female workers, they are still at a disadvantage in recruitment. Finally, the charge of shortermism is difficult to refute in many cases of failure of foreign firms in Japan. There are many stories of Western managers in Japan appealing to head office for the time and resources necessary to do a good job in Japan and being refused. However, we should again note that head offices are charged with global responsibilities and have to examine the resources devoted to Japan versus other locations.

## Process Issues

It is very rare indeed for a firm to undertake foreign direct investment with out some previous involvement with the market. FDI can be considered as the culmination of a process of 'deepening involvement' which is likely to include exporting, licensing, agencies, and other forms of lesser involvement in building a long-run relationship with a market or a foreign location. If this process is inhibited or attenuated by, for instance, barriers to imports or barriers to building relationships, then the potential foreign investor is unlikely to reach the stage of actual investor.

This attenuation has occurred in Japan. Exports to Japan have been inhibited by deliberate government policy in the past, by the demands of the Japanese consumer (e.g., requiring super-fresh products and expensive aftercare) and by cultural barriers. Paradoxically, the answer to these difficulties for the entrant firm is to build a presence in Japan. But that presence requires investment and that investment requires confidence which is absent because of the lack of success.

Thus, successful operation in Japan requires FDI but FDI is inhibited because, without FDI, little success is achieved! Only the biggest, bravest, or luckiest investors (or those with inside help, e.g., joint-venture partners) can make it through the whole process.

## THE LEVEL OF FDI IN JAPAN

The above application of orthodox theory to FDI in Japan suggests that it is not surprising that its level is much lower than in North America or the European Union.

Theory suggests that the main barriers are:

1. difficulties in internalizing intermediate markets in Japan across a wide range of industries and sectors;
2. high costs of entry because of cultural barriers;
3. the high level of intense competition in Japan;
4. lack of profitable opportunities for inward investors, compared to returns elsewhere;
5. 'process issues', difficulties of entering by takeover, difficulties of (initial) entry by wholly owned subsidiary, difficulties of building a pre-FDI position without a presence;
6. global competitive weakness of non-Japanese firms versus Japanese firms in quality and price, service, and aftercare.

These issues are not immutable, nor fixed for all time. There is considerable evidence that, even in areas of traditional Japanese strength, European and North American firms are gaining ground and have the capability of competing in Japan. Further, there is evidence that in certain sectors firms of non-Japanese ownership are increasingly prevalent and profitable in Japan, e.g., pharmaceuticals. The adjustment process is likely to be a long one, but FDI in Japan will rise in parallel to the global competitive strength of non-Japanese firms.

## References


Buckley, Peter J. (1988) 'The limits of explanation: testing the internalization theory of the multinational enterprise', *Journal of International Business Studies* xix, 2, (summer): 181–93.

——(1989) *The Multinational Enterprise: Theory and Applications*. London: Macmillan.

——(1992) *Studies in International Business*. London: Macmillan.

——(1995) *Foreign Direct Investment and Multinational Enterprises*. London: Macmillan.

—and Mark Casson (1976) *The Future of the Multinational Enterprise*. London: Macmillan.

——(1985) *The Economic Theory of the Multinational Enterprise*. London: Macmillan.

——and Pervez N. Ghauri (eds) (1993) *The Internationalization of the Firm*. London: Dryden Press.

——, Hafiz Mirza and John R. Sparkes (1985) 'Direct investments in Japan as a means of market entry: The case of European firms', *Journal of Marketing Management* 2, 3, 241–58. [Reprinted in Buckley and Ghauri, op. cit.]

Coase, Ronald H. (1937) 'The nature of the firm', *Economica* (n.s.) 4, 386–405.

Hallen, Lars, and Finn Wiedersheim-Paul (1979) 'Psychic distance and buyer-seller interaction', *Organisasjon, Marknad och Samhalle* 16, 5, 308–24. [Reprinted in Buckley and Ghauri, op.cit.]

Knickerbocker, Frederick T. (1973) *Oligopolistic Reaction and Multinational Enterprise*. Cambridge, Mass: Harvard University Press.

Mirza, Hafiz, Peter J. Buckley and John R. Sparkes (1989) 'Swimming against the tide? The strategy of European manufacturing investors in Japan', in *Japanese and European Management: Their International Adaptability*, eds. Kazuo Shibagaki, Malcolm Trevor, and Tetsuo Abo. Tokyo: University of Tokyo Press. [Reprinted in Buckley 1992. op. cit.]

Yoshitomi, Masoru and Edward M. Graham (eds) (1996) *Foreign Direct Investment in Japan*. Cheltenham: Edward Elgar.

# Part III

# International Cooperation: Joint Ventures and Alliances

# 8 Measures of Performance in UK International Alliances*

Peter J. Buckley and Keith W. Glaister

**This study examines measures of performance for a sample of UK international alliances. The chapter builds on previous studies in comparing objective and subjective measures of performance and examining the influence of national culture on performance evaluation, but it goes beyond them by examining in detail the ways in which measures of performance are affected by differences in perception arising from the parent companies. Corporate culture is also included with national culture as a key determinant in the evaluation of performance. The chapter also reports on new work on the differences in subjective performance evaluation between organizational modes of alliances and develops this in the context of alliance termination, and perceptions of differences in national culture and corporate culture.**

## INTRODUCTION

The alliance is a relatively old organizational form traditionally used by multinational companies as a mode of entry to the markets of developing countries. More recently, alliances have increasingly been established between firms from advanced market economies (Hergert and Morris, 1988; Glaister and Buckley, 1994). Anderson (1990) maintains that more alliances and cooperative arrangements have been announced since 1981 than in all previous years. The current wave of alliance activity between firms from advanced market

* First published in *Organization Studies*, 19, 1 (1998).

economies is expected to persist (Gomes-Casseres, 1996) and alliances are increasingly being recognized as a significant organizational form. Teece (1992, p. 24) notes that 'In retrospect, the emergence and proliferation of alliances, dating from about 1970, may turn out to be as significant an organisational innovation as the moving assembly line and the multidivisional structure.'

Alliances have the potential to be used as a flexible form of organization. This flexibility means that firms using alliances have the freedom to respond to changing external circumstances and alterations in internal strategic intent by manipulating the ambiguous and ill-defined nature of some of the parameters of the venture. Buckley and Casson (1996) show that international alliances occupy a 'middle range' between full ownership and (internalization or merger) and an arm's length licensing arrangement. The area where alliances are optimal depends on the firm being situated in an area of intermediate market size and moderate volatility of technology. This intermediate strategic area makes international alliances difficult to model (because extreme values of particular factors do not explain international alliances) and difficult to evaluate in performance terms – particularly as changes in key explanatory variables may make alliances non-optimal, dictating a switch of strategy, say to full merger of the partner companies. This is an alternative way of viewing the problem that the cessation of an alliance does not necessarily indicate failure.

The issue of technological volatility and alliance types has been considered by a number of authors. In reviewing the literature, Osborn and Baughn (1990) suggest that technological stability of individual sectors is crucial in explaining different patterns of equity and non-equity ownership, with joint ventures dominating in sectors with low degrees of R&D intensity, while contractual agreements predominate in R&D intensive sectors. Hagedoorn and Narula (1996) demonstrate that high-tech sectors have a high share of contractual agreements, whereas joint ventures predominate in medium and low-tech industries.

Two basic organizational modes of alliance may be identified: equity joint ventures (EJVs) and non-equity alliances (NEAs) (Contractor and Lorange, 1988). EJVs are created when two or more partners join forces to create a newly incorporated company in which each has an equity share and each thereby may expect an appropriate allocation of dividend as compensation, representation on the EJV's board of directors, and active participation in the decision-making activities of the venture (Harrigan, 1985; Geringer, 1991). The outcome may depend on the strategic purpose of the EJV: for example, many EJVs are established as cost centres with the benefits accruing in activities of the partners. Similarly, EJVs may be established more for promoting the development of technology or facilitating learning in other areas, such as marketing, rather than with a specific immediate financial or dividend goal. NEAs in contrast, are agreements between partners to cooperate in some way, but they do not involve the creation of new firms. In NEAs, sharing or exchange of equity may occur between partners (although this was not a feature of the NEAs reported in this study). In NEAs, the compensation to each firm may be less dependent on the level of profits earned than in EJVs. For instance, it may be based on the percentage of output consumed, but there is at least a moderate degree of inter-organizational dependence (Contractor and Lorange, 1988). In practice, both NEAs and EJVs tend to be governed by agreements and contracts which can readily specify the basis by which compensation is shared or allocated to the partners. EJVs may be established merely, for example, as clearing mechanisms for transactions involving partner firms (e.g. a downstream marketing arm for partners who contribute components or other inputs). Compensation for activities supplied from one partner to another may be based on profits, volume or the relative valuation of inputs involving fees such as management fees or technology fees. Again, this is an example of the use of alliances to attain flexibility. An alliance may be considered to be international if at least one partner has its headquarters outside the venture's country of operation or if the alliance has a significant level of operation in more than one country (Geringer and Hebert, 1989).

The performance of alliance relationships has been an important theme in the literature, although relatively little of the research relating to alliance performance has directly examined ventures between firms from advanced market economies. Given the increased emphasis on alliances as an organizational form in the latter context, this chapter attempts to provide new perspectives on aspects of performance in alliances with partners from developed countries. The main goals of this chapter are as follows: (1) To consider the relationship between objective and subjective measures of alliance performance from a sample of UK international ventures. The aim of this part of the research is partly to replicate the work of Geringer and Hebert (1991) in the context of UK firms' alliances. (2) To extend the work of Geringer and Hebert (1991) by considering the effect of the perception of national cultural differences on the relationship between objective and subjective measures of alliance performance and to develop this work by a consideration of the effect of the perception of corporate cultural differences on this relationship. (3) In the context of the first two goals, to develop new work which examines performance measures by organizational mode of alliance, and, in particular, to consider the performance of NEAs, which has hitherto been neglected in the literature.

This study extends previous empirical work in the area of international alliances because it draws on a unique database of UK companies which have alliances with parents from other advanced economies. It is thus differentiated from previous work, which either utilizes a sample of North American parents (Geringer and Hebert, 1991, in their paper, examined a sample of EJVs involving one or more US parents, and a sample of two- and three-parent EJVs located in Canada) or concentrates on alliances in developing countries (Beamish, 1987). Moreover, since a substantial proportion of the alliance literature has focused on the United States and Japan (e.g. Yoshino and Rangan, 1995), alliance relationships with a different national focus merit attention.

The UK context is highly relevant. Because of the United Kingdom's long-standing international commercial contacts and its membership of the European Union (EU), we can expect international links to be strong, broad and deep. The cultural outlook of UK executives is likely to differ from that of North American executives and the perceptions of UK executives on cultural distance or psychic distance (Hallen and Wiedersheim-Paul, 1979; Hofstede, 1980) are explored below.

The focus on alliances with advanced countries is also significant. In the context of our research, the international strategy of UK firms across the 'Triad' (North America, Europe, Japan) is likely to create a major role for alliances with competitors, suppliers and customers. The nature of the cooperative exchange (Buckley and Casson, 1988) is likely to differ from the case of less developed country partners. Performance issues, too, are likely to be more critical when the context is the dynamic partnership with firms from industrialized nations.

The remainder of the chapter is set out in the following way: issues in the performance of alliances are discussed in the following section, together with the research hypotheses. The research methods are set out in the third section. The fourth section presents the results and a discussion of the findings. Conclusions are in the final section.

## ISSUES IN ALLIANCE PERFORMANCE AND RESEARCH HYPOTHESES

### Conceptual Considerations

The measurement of organizational performance is a controversial area (Goodman and Pennings, 1980; Cameron, 1986; Chakravarthy, 1986; Lewin and Minton, 1986; Venkatraman and Ramanujam, 1986; Jacobson, 1987; Buckley *et al.*, 1988; Varadarajan and Ramanujam, 1990; Eccles, 1991). A major problem is the choice of the appropriate yardstick(s) to be used when assessing organization performance. Essentially, this debate concerns the appropriateness of traditional financial measures (for example ROI, growth) as providing a unique measure of performance, versus the relevance of other indicators (such as maximizing shareholders' wealth; qualitative returns to non-financial stakeholders, such as customer satisfaction). A further issue is the influence of factors outside the firm's control. Performance would be expected to vary with the nature of the organization's environment and its resource capability. An acceptable level of performance for a small firm in a hostile environment might be considered unsatisfactory for a large firm in a benevolent environment (Anderson, 1990). More fundamentally, controversy surrounds the lack of differentiation between indicators of performance and determinants of performance.

The controversy over the measurement of organizational performance appears set to continue, with theoretical issues currently unresolved and the debate hindered by the relative paucity of well-founded empirical studies. In this regard, it is not surprising that the operationalization of alliance performance has proved difficult, with no consensus on the appropriate definition and measure of this concept (Geringer and Hebert, 1989, 1991). The debate over alliance performance measures is clearly a sub-set of wider concerns regarding the assessment of organizational performance in general, of which the evaluation of alliance performance is a particular challenge.

Anderson (1990) has summarized a number of key points concerning the evaluation of alliance performance. One involves the perspective from which the venture should be evaluated. In an EJV, for instance, there are a number of different viewpoints on the venture, including the parent firms and the EJV management (assuming that the venture has a separate workforce, which is not necessarily the case), which means that there might be different views on which aspects of performance to measure and how successful these measures indicate the performance to be. The EJV may be performing well, but at the expense of one parent's interests, for example because the EJV chooses not to source inputs from this parent. From one parent's perspective the EJV is performing poorly, with the venture being rated differently depending on the parent viewpoint adopted. In principle, therefore, performance evaluation should incorporate multiple viewpoints. Schaan (1983) and Beamish and Banks (1987) in empirical work have measured alliance performance by a managerial assessment where only when both partners were satisfied was the venture considered successful. In contrast, Anderson (1990) argues that alliances should be evaluated primarily as stand-alone entities seeking to maximize their own performance, not the parents. This perspective would then free the alliance from parent politics and parochial viewpoints. This may be excessively naive and, in practice, impossible. It is frequently imperative to consider alliances in the context of their fit within the network of the parents' (international) ventures. The linkages which most alliances have with other units of the network may render them inseparable, politically, from the power structure of the network as a whole.

Anderson (1990) notes that alliances (as distinct from other organizational forms) may be more commonly used in highly uncertain settings with a very long-term performance horizon and no current performance baselines for comparison. In high-risk/uncertain settings, short-term financial measures would tend to indicate poor performance, although the venture may be making satisfactory progress towards long-term goals, or achieving current non-financial goals. In this respect, it should be recognized that alliances may not be intended to fulfil standard financial objectives such as profit generation, but, instead, are formed to fulfil a range of motives, for example to enhance parent learning (Kogut, 1988a), or to improve the strategic positioning of the parent firms (Contractor and Lorange, 1988; Glaister and Buckley, 1996), in order, for example, to gain a presence in new markets. It should also be noted that alliances are commonly used for exploiting opportunities with a short-term horizon. NEAs are particularly appropriate in contexts where opportunities are uncertain and the likely return is short term. The failure of financial and objective measures to adequately reflect the extent to which an alliance has achieved its aims is stressed by Geringer and Hebert (1991), who argue that despite poor financial results, liquidation or instability, an alliance may have met or exceeded the parents' objectives and so be considered successful by one or all of the parents. Conversely, an alliance may be viewed as unsuccessful despite good financial results or continued stability. Anderson (1990) takes this point further by arguing that parents should recognize that most alliances should be evaluated more subjectively over a longer time horizon than is typically used. Resort to formal, financial measures of performance are likely to lead to early termination before an alliance has had enough time to realize its potential. In this respect, alliances require a more balanced, often subjective approach, if their promise is to be realized.

## Prior Empirical Research

Many of the prior empirical studies examining alliance performance relate to MNCs from developed countries forming alliances with firms from developing countries. In these studies, a large number of criteria have been used to assess performance (Chowdhury, 1992). In summarizing prior empirical research, Geringer and Hebert (1991) point out that early studies relied on a variety of financial indicators, such as profitability, growth and cost position (e.g. Tomlinson, 1970; Lecraw, 1983). Other studies have used objective measures of performance such as survival of the alliance (Franko, 1971; Stopford and Wells, 1972; Killing, 1983; Geringer, 1990; Geringer and Woodcock, 1995), its duration (Harrigan, 1986; Kogut, 1988b), instability of its ownership (i.e. significant changes in the equity holdings of the parents in EJVs) (Franko, 1971; Gomes-Casseres, 1987; Beamish and Inkpen, 1995), and re-negotiation of the alliance contract (Blodgett, 1992). Performance has also been evaluated using an event-study perspective to examine the stock-market reaction to the announcement of a joint venture (Lummer and McConnell, 1990; Koh and Venkatraman, 1991).

Due to concerns over the ability of financial and objective measures to effectively capture alliance performance, as noted above, several researchers have turned to perceptual measures of a parent's satisfaction with alliance performance (Killing, 1983; Schaan, 1983; Beamish, 1985; Inkpen and Birkinshaw, 1994; Lyles and Baird, 1994; Dussauge and Garrette, 1995). Perceptual measures are able to provide information regarding the extent to which the alliance has achieved its overall objectives. Several authors (Killing, 1983; Schaan, 1983; Beamish, 1985; Janger, 1980) have also made use of subjective performance measures for each of a limited number of individual dimensions of the alliance.

A key contribution of the study by Geringer and Hebert (1991) is the comparison of objective and subjective measures of EJV performance. Noting that the most frequently used objective measures of performance in the alliance literature are survival, stability and duration, Geringer and Hebert (1991) hypothesized a significant and positive correlation between these objective and subjective measures of EJV performance, and discovered this to be the case for their sample of US EJVs. The objective measures were found to be positively correlated, although not perfectly, with parent firms' reported satisfaction with EJV performance, and with perceptions of the extent to which an EJV performed relative to its initial objectives. In an attempt to replicate these findings for UK parents of EJVs and to extend the analysis to UK parents of NEAs, this study's first hypothesis is:

*H1: There will be a significant and positive correlation between objective and subjective measures of alliance performance.*

Geringer and Hebert examined only EJVs, which are a mode of alliance frequently discussed in the management literature. Factors affecting the choice of mode of alliance is a relatively under-researched area (but one that is attracting increased attention, e.g. Gulati, 1995), as is the appropriate measure of performance and whether this differs between alliance mode. In principle, where contingent factors determine the choice of alliance mode, it may be expected that specific performance outcomes would be expected by alliance partners, for example, technology development or quality control. In general, however, there appears to be no reason why overall measures of satisfaction should not be equally applicable to both EJVs and NEAs. In this sense, Hypothesis 1 applies to alliances, irrespective of organizational form. Furthermore, it would be expected that the same measures of subjective performance would be equally effective in capturing the level of satisfaction perceived by the parties to the venture and that, providing, initially, the optimal mode had been chosen, the performance outcomes would not vary between alliance form. This is expressed in the second hypothesis:

*H2: The mean measure of subjective performance will not vary between organizational mode of alliance.*

A somewhat contentious issue in the alliance performance literature is the extent to which termination signifies a failure on the part of the venture. As has been indicated above, several authors (e.g. Geringer and Hebert, 1991; Anderson, 1990) have argued that termination does not necessarily mean that the venture has failed. Indeed the alliance may be terminated because it has successfully achieved its objectives. Nevertheless, some alliances will be terminated because of poor performance and this is likely to be reflected in subjective measures of performance. If more alliances are terminated because they fail rather than because they succeed in attaining their objectives, and to the extent that continuing ventures are perceived as being more successful than terminated ventures, mean subjective performance measures of overall satisfaction should differ between those alliances which have terminated and those which have not. Moreover, this difference should be equally applicable to both organizational modes of alliance. This argument is the basis of the third hypothesis:

*H3: The mean measure of overall satisfaction obtained from subjective measures of performance will be lower in those alliances which have been terminated, compared to those alliances which are continuing.*

Geringer and Hebert (1991) also considered the influence of national culture on performance evaluation. They note that agreement on a EJV's performance between its parents may be influenced by the national cultural similarity among them. Where there are national cultural dissimilarities, this may lead to differences in the partners' perceptions of each other and the EJV and result in a lower degree of agreement regarding EJV performance. In contrast, similarities in national culture will tend to produce a greater agreement among the parents regarding the venture's performance. Geringer and Hebert's statistical analysis of their Canadian sample supported these arguments: correlations between partners' assessments of specific aspects of EJV performance were significantly positive as well as being stronger for partners where there was a cultural similarity.

By extension, their line of argument may be broadened to encompass corporate cultural similarities or differences between alliance parents. To the extent that corporate culture differs between parent firms this may lead to differences in the partners' perception of each other and the alliance, and result in a lower degree of agreement regarding performance. Conversely, where organizational culture is similar, it may be expected that there will be a greater agreement among the parents regarding the alliance's performance.

The degree of cultural similarity was crudely proxied in Geringer and Hebert's (1991) study by the location of the partners. Cultural similarity was assumed to exist only if all of the venture's parent firms were headquartered in North

America. In contrast, if at least one parent was located outside North America, then cultural similarity was assumed not to exist. When dealing with perceptions of performance, however, we contend that it is the perceptions of the respondents with regard to the cultural similarity of the foreign partner which is of importance. Furthermore, even if the respondent does perceive cultural dissimilarity, the further perception of the respondent may be that this dissimilarity does not effect the performance of the alliance. In order to avoid crude characterizations of cultural similarity and to deal consistently with subjective perception of performance, we argue that it is necessary to take into account both the respondent's perception of cultural similarity and the extent to which this is perceived to affect the performance of the alliance. This line of argument we also apply to the perception of corporate culture.

This leads to the study's fourth and fifth hypotheses, as follows:

*H4: Correlations between objective and subjective measures of alliance performance will be stronger in alliances where the perception and effect of national cultural differences are not apparent to the reporting parents, compared to those for whom such differences are apparent.*

*H5: Correlations between objective and subjective measures of alliance performance will be stronger in alliances where the perception and effect of corporate cultural differences are not apparent to the reporting parents, compared to those for whom such differences are apparent.*

The logic of the argument leading to Hypotheses 4 and 5, also implies that where one partner perceives no dissimilarity in the national (or corporate) culture of the other partner, or where there is a perceived dissimilarity, but one that makes no difference to the performance of the alliance, then there is more likely to be a higher level of satisfaction observed in subjective performance measures. This leads to the final two hypotheses:

*H6: The mean measure of overall satisfaction obtained from subjective measures of performance will be higher in those alliances where the perception and effect of national cultural differences are not apparent to the reporting parents, compared to those for whom such differences are apparent.*

*H7: The mean measure of overall satisfaction obtained from subjective measures of performance will be higher in those alliances where the perception and effect of corporate culture differences are not apparent to the reporting parents, compared to those for whom such differences are apparent.*

## RESEARCH METHODS

### Data Collection Method

The research hypotheses developed in the preceding section were tested using a sample of UK parents of international alliances with partner firms from Western Europe, the United States and Japan, formed since 1980. A list of qualifying alliances was obtained from announcements in the *Financial Times* between 1980 and 1989. It was assumed that this source represented a good approximation to the population of qualifying alliances and that any selection biases would be minimal. It should be noted, however, that the qualifying alliances do not include those organized through national or international government agencies, particularly European Community programmes such as ESPRIT. These ventures were excluded in order to ensure that the sample was derived from alliances created from the free association of firms and not those encouraged by incentives provided by external agents. As an environmental factor, the run up to the creation of the Single European Market at the end of 1992 may have had an influence on the strategy of some firms, when deciding to form an alliance. This still involves the 'free association' of the firms. We are making a distinction between these types of alliances and those which were induced under governmental programmes in a deliberate effort to boost international competitiveness.

To work within time and cost constraints, a postal questionnaire was used to gather the data. A set of semi-structured interviews with a senior manager from each of eight UK partners confirmed understanding of the nature of the research topic and helped to shape the form of the final questionnaire. Results from a pre-test questionnaire confirmed the appropriateness of the data-collection instrument. Telephone contact was made with each UK partner to ascertain the name and position of the most appropriate senior manager and the questionnaire was personally addressed to this person. The questionnaire cited the alliance referred to in the *Financial Times* of which the UK firm was a partner, but invited the respondent to complete the questionnaire with respect to another alliance with which they were more familiar, providing the foreign partner(s) was from either Western Europe, the United States or Japan, and that this alliance had been formed since 1980. The request for information on the alliance with which the respondent had the most detailed knowledge was designed to improve the quality of the data. In total, 9 respondents chose to do this (7 of the EJVs and 2 of the NEAs in the sample), providing data on alliances formed in the 1990–91 period. The sample, therefore, contains data on alliances not in the original sample frame. The benefit of this is that respondents provided data on more recent alliances, hence obviating the danger of memory decay. Moreover, the respondents have self-selected to report on the alliance that they know most about. To provide motivation and accurate responses, respondents were guaranteed anonymity and were promised a summary of the research findings.

The qualifying alliances recorded in the *Financial Times* involved 277 separate UK firms. Of these, several firms proved impossible to contact either because they had been taken over and restructured or had gone out of business altogether. Other firms had moved location and could not be traced. In some cases, although the firm could be contacted, there was no longer anyone in employment with sufficient knowledge to provide the depth of answers the study required. This left a total of 203 UK partners to whom the questionnaire was administered in the autumn of 1992. After one reminder, 94 questionnaires were returned, a response rate of 46.3 per cent. No respondent provided responses to more than one alliance.

It is apparent that this study relies on data collected from one parent. The extent to which data collected from one element of the alliance – one parent or the alliance general manager – represents a reliable measure of alliance performance and a reliable estimate of the other elements' perception of this performance was a topic of concern in the study by Geringer and Hebert (1991). Noting that EJVs are organizations in which ownership and decision making are shared, Geringer and Hebert assume that one parent will be aware of the other parent's or EJV general manager's satisfaction and assessment of EJV performance. They therefore hypothesize that one parent's evaluation of the other partner's or EJV general manager's satisfaction regarding EJV performance will be positively correlated. Data from Geringer and Hebert's Canadian sample of EJVs provided support for this hypothesis. Geringer and Hebert conclude that where it is only possible to obtain responses from one of the partners, 'use of a single respondent per IJV [international joint venture] appears to allow researchers to obtain fairly reliable and efficient data for overall IJV performance' (Geringer and Hebert, 1991: 261). The findings of Geringer and Hebert provide some justification for the research method adopted here and confidence in the performance data so obtained.

About 18 per cent of the alliances had more than one foreign partner. As Geringer (1991) has pointed out, there may be difficulties associated with analyzing multiple partner alliances in that two-partner ventures may demonstrate significant differences from ventures with three or more partners. Such difficulties are likely to be exacerbated when studying one parent's perception of another parent's view of performance. Hence this study only concerns the single foreign-partner alliances. Also, in recognizing that performance data for very new alliances might not be meaningful, it was decided to analyze only those alliances that had been in existence for at least one year at the time the data was collected. The time span of the study is therefore 1980 to 1991.

The sample consists of 75 alliances (51 EJVs and 24 NEAs). The majority of these were formed with partners from Western Europe (26 EJVs and 8 NEAs) followed by the United States (14 EJVs and 11 NEAs) and Japan (11 EJVs and 5 NEAs). A total of 48 alliances are in the manufacturing sector (33 EJVs and 15 NEAs) and 27 in the tertiary sector (18 EJVs and 9 NEAs).

### Measures of Performance

The subjective and objective performance measures were broadly derived in the manner followed by Geringer and

Hebert (1991). The UK parent's *subjective level of satisfaction* with the alliance's overall performance was assessed using a five-point Likert-type scale (from 1='Very Dissatisfied' to 5='Very Satisfied'). On the same scale, the UK respondents were also asked to provide a measure of satisfaction that they believed applied to their foreign partner and the managers of the alliance. Hence the following three subjective measures of alliance performance were obtained:

SATUKP: Subjective measure of satisfaction of alliance performance made by the UK partner.

SATFP: Assessment by the UK parent of the foreign partner's measure of satisfaction of alliance performance.

SATALLM: Assessment by the UK parent of the alliance management's measure of satisfaction of alliance performance.

As a check on the UK parent's own satisfaction rating for alliance performance, an alternative measure of subjective performance was derived at a non-sequential point in the questionnaire. The respondent was asked whether the benefits to the UK parent's overall strategy from having the alliance, outweighed the costs of the alliance. Responses were measured on a three-point Likert-type scale (with 1='Benefits exceed costs'; 2='Benefits equal costs'; 3='Benefits are less than costs'). This alternative attempt to measure overall alliance performance (the variable CBALL) was not used by Geringer and Hebert. It should be noted that a negative sign is expected on correlations between CBALL and the other satisfaction measures, given the way each of these variables has been measured.

As well as providing subjective measures of overall alliance performance, respondents were asked to rate the alliance's actual performance versus initial projections at the time the venture was formed (if such an initial projection had been made) for 15 individual venture dimensions. The 15 items were ones previously used by Geringer and Hebert (1991). While the latter assessed the individual performance dimensions using a five-point Likert-type scale, this study utilized a three point scale (1='Worse than expected'; 2='Same as expected'; 3='Better than expected'). A three-point scale was adopted in this study, because it was felt that more numerous response categories would exceed the respondents' ability to discriminate, with the likelihood that 'noise' rather than more precise data would result. It was also considered likely that a trichotomous measure would tend to facilitate greater cooperation and return rates (Jacoby and Matell, 1971).

*Objective performance measures* of survival, stability (for EJVs) and duration were each derived in the manner adopted by Geringer and Hebert (1991). Alliance *survival* was measured using a dichotomous variable based on the survival or non-survival (i.e. termination) of the alliance from the time of its formation until the data collection point in 1992. For EJVs, venture *stability* was measured with a dichotomous variable based on whether changes in the division of the venture's equity (excluding termination) had occurred since the venture's formation. Alliance *duration* was measured by the number of years between the alliance's formation and either its termination or the collection of performance data, whichever came first.

As Geringer and Hebert (1991) note, these three objective measures of performance are the ones most frequently used in the alliance literature. For the sample of alliances as a whole, 48 ventures were still in existence (33 EJVs and 15 NEAs), while 27 alliances had been terminated (18 EJVs and 9 NEAs). The average duration of all alliances was 4.7 years (4.8 years for EJVs and 4.6 years for NEAs). The average duration of surviving (non-terminated) alliances was 5.1 years, while the average duration of terminated alliances was 4.1 years. The number of EJVs subject to instability in their ownership structure (excluding terminated EJVs) was 6 (the equity share increasing for 3 UK partners and decreasing for 3) with 27 EJVs experiencing no change in equity shareholding.

## Cultural Difference

Cultural difference relating to national culture was measured dichotomously and derived in the following manner. Perception and effect of national cultural difference was deemed to be 'not apparent' if the respondent either answered 'No' to the question 'Do you believe that the *national* culture of the foreign partner is different to Britain's?', or after responding 'Yes' to this question, answered 'of no importance' to the question 'How important have differences in national culture been on the overall performance of the alliance'. In contrast, the perception and effect of national cultural differences was deemed to be 'apparent' where the respondent answered 'Yes' to the first question and either 'of some importance' or 'of major importance' to the second question. This construct of national cultural difference is not one that is typically employed (Geringer and Hebert, 1991; Anderson and Weitz, 1989), but, as argued above, when dealing with subjective performance measures, this approach appears warranted. Even if, in reality, national cultural differences do occur between the partners, this is largely irrelevant for subjective performance measures if the perception of the respondent is such that national culture is either no different or is believed not to have an effect on performance, even if national culture is considered to be different.

Cultural difference relating to corporate culture was measured dichotomously and derived following the same procedure for national culture, this time substituting the word 'corporate' for 'national' in the relevant questions. This study therefore uses two concepts of culture, one relating to the national culture of the respective partners to the alliance and one to the corporate culture of the partners themselves.

**Data Analysis**

Spearman rank-order correlation coefficients were computed using SPSS in order to test the hypotheses H1, H4 and H5. As Geringer and Hebert (1991) argue, this non-parametric statistic appears the most appropriate given the measures used and the sizes of the samples and sub-samples. To assess reliability of results, Kendall tau-B and Pearson correlation coefficients were computed, and results consistent with the Spearman-based analysis were obtained on each test.

To test for differences in means associated with hypotheses H2, H3, H6 and H7 (and in order to set out the findings meaningfully), each of the hypotheses was tested by conducting parametric two sample T-Tests. The nature of the data made it judicious, however, to 'shadow' this parametric test by an equivalent non-parametric one (Mann–Whitney U) as a check on interpretation. In each case, the non-parametric test (not reported here) confirms the findings of the parametric test reported below.

## RESULTS AND DISCUSSION

Before considering the extent to which the data supports the hypotheses, it is first useful to examine the UK parents' subjective measures of alliance performance. Recalling Geringer and Hebert's (1991) assumption that one parent will be aware of the other parent's or alliance general manager's satisfaction and assessment of performance, Table 8.1 sets out the correlations between the respondents' own assessment of performance (SATUKP) and the respondents' assessment of the measure of satisfaction of the partners (SATFP) and the alliance management (SATALLM). There are positive and strong correlations (all significant at 0.001 or less) between the three elements of the alliance for both EJVs and NEAs. For EJVs (but not NEAs) the relationship appears marginally stronger between the UK parent and the alliance management than it is between the UK parent and the foreign partner. In addition, for both EJVs and NEAs, the relationship is marginally stronger between the UK parent and the alliance management, than it is between the foreign partner and the alliance management. As all of the correlations are less than 1.0, it is clear that the UK respondents recognize a difference between their level of satisfaction of alliance performance and that of their partners and alliance managers.

Also shown in Table 8.1 is the alternative subjective measure of the respondents' assessment of overall performance expressed in cost/benefit terms (CBALL). The anticipated negative correlations associated with CBALL are confirmed in Table 8.1. While moderate to high significant correlations (at better than 0.05) are obtained between the respondents' own assessment of performance (SATUKP) and CBALL for both EJVs and NEAs, given that the correlations are less than 1.0, it is clear that these two subjective measures of overall performance are capturing different aspects of perceived performance. Also, the most direct measure of satisfaction (SATUKP) achieves a stronger set of correlations between the foreign partners' and alliance managements' perceived satisfaction level than does the more indirect measure of overall performance (CBALL), with the weakest set of correlations associated with NEAs.

*Table* 8.1 Spearman rank-order correlations between UK parents' subjective measures of alliance performance

| | *EJVs* *(n = 51)* | | | *NEAs* *(n = 24)* | | |
|---|---|---|---|---|---|---|
| | CBALL | SATUKP | SATFP | CBALL | SATUKP | SATFP |
| SATUKP | $-.64^{***}$ | | | $-.44^{**}$ | | |
| SATFP | $-.45^{***}$ | $.79^{***}$ | | $-.33$ | $.89^{***}$ | |
| SATALLM | $-.56^{***}$ | $.91^{***}$ | $.84^{***}$ | $-.51^{**}$ | $.89^{***}$ | $.81^{***}$ |

*Notes*: SATUKP: Subjective measure of satisfaction of alliance performance made by UK partner.
SATFP: Assessment by UK parent of foreign partner's measure of satisfaction of alliance performance.
SATALLM: Assessment by UK parent of alliance management's measure of satisfaction of alliance performance.
CBALL: UK parent's subjective measure of the extent to which the costs of the alliance outweigh the benefits of the alliance.
$^{***}$ $p \leq 0.001$; $^{**}$ $p \leq 0.05$.

**Hypothesis 1**

Results relating to H1 are set out in Table 8.2. Data for EJVs show that of the objective measures, survival dominates duration and stability in terms of strength of correlation with subjective measures. Survival evidences significant correlations (at 0.01 or less) with all four of the overall satisfaction measures and (at 0.05 or less) with five of the fifteen individual dimensions of performance. Correlations between survival and the subjective measures of overall satisfaction and the individual dimensions relating to general performance – e.g. market share, profitability and overall EJV performance – were clearly stronger and significant compared to correlations between more specific individual dimensions of performance, such as customer service. Some ten correlations between individual dimensions of performance and survival did not show significance at the 0.05 level, however, and, contrary to expectations, the dimensions, technology development and labour productivity showed non-significant negative relationships.

The correlations between the objective measure of duration and the subjective performance measures are very weak, with 11 of the 19 correlations displaying non-significant relationships in a direction contrary to that proposed in H1, including the overall satisfaction measure of the UK partner (SATUKP). Perversely, the non-significant sign of the correlation on the subjective cost/benefit measure (CBALL) is also contrary to the direction hypothesized.

The correlations between the objective measure of stability and the subjective performance measures for EJVs are all weak and non-significant (at the 0.05 level). Although non-significant, in total, four of the signs in this set of correlations are the reverse of that anticipated.

For NEAs the correlations between the objective measure of survival and the subjective measures of overall satisfaction are weak and non-significant (at the 0.05 level). However, four of the correlations between survival and the individual dimensions of performance are moderately strong and significant at the 0.05 level or less. Unlike the findings for EJVs, these correlations are less clearly associated with the general performance level of the alliance, in particular the individual dimensions of marketing and customer service which evidence moderately strong significant correlations. Two of the non-significant correlations have the reverse sign from that expected, those on technology development and product design.

For NEAs although there are several correlations which display moderate levels of strength, all the correlations between duration and the subjective measures of performance are non-significant. Two of the correlations have a sign the reverse of that anticipated.

With respect to H1, the results reported in Table 8.2 (and summarized in Table 8.9) are at best mixed. Most support for the hypothesis comes from the set of correlations between the objective measure of survival and the subjective performance measures, particularly those relating to overall satisfaction and general levels of satisfaction for the individual dimension of performance, and especially for EJVs. In this respect, these findings support those of Geringer and Hebert (1991) (whose US sample most closely matches that of EJVs in this study), although they found marginally stronger correlations from the ones reported here. No real support for Hypothesis 1 comes from the correlations based on the objective measures of duration or (for EJVs) stability. This contradicts the findings of Geringer and Hebert (1991) whose results evidenced several moderately strong and significant correlations between these objective measures of performance and subjective performance measures.

The findings of this study relating to H1 identify a number of issues. First, it is clear from Table 8.2 that not all alliance parents make initial projections of performance, particularly with respect to specific performance dimensions. The individual projections that are made probably reflect the relative importance of this particular aspect of the alliance operations. In this respect, a better understanding of the relationship between subjective and objective performance measures is likely to come in the context of an examination of the underlying motives for the formation of the alliance. Second, the contrast between EJVs and NEAs in terms of correlations between survival and the subjective measures of overall performance indicate that survival may be a less important objective measure of performance for NEAs than for EJVs. This is perhaps not surprising given the anticipated greater

*Table* 8.2 Spearman rank-order correlations between objective and subjective measures of alliance performance: EJVs and NEAs

| | Objective performance measures | | | | | | | |
|---|---|---|---|---|---|---|---|---|
| | Equity joint ventures | | | | | Non-equity alliances | | |
| *Subjective performance measures* | *(n)* | *Survival* | *Duration* | *(n)* | *Stability* | *(n)* | *Survival* | *Duration* |
| *Overall Satisfaction* | (51) | | | (33) | | (24) | | |
| SATUKP | | .45*** | –.02 | | .19 | | .17 | .08 |
| SATFP | | .40*** | .01 | | .18 | | .13 | .15 |
| SATALLM | | .37*** | .12 | | .21 | | .37* | .18 |
| CBALL | | –.44*** | .02 | | –.24 | | –.18 | –.09 |
| *Individual Dimensions* | | | | | | | | |
| Sales level | (50) | .14 | .13 | (33) | .20 | (14) | .58** | .33 |
| Market share | (50) | .33** | .03 | (33) | .24 | (13) | .47 | .12 |
| Profitability | (51) | .32** | .13 | (33) | .26 | (15) | .63** | .15 |
| Cost control | (48) | .31** | –.04 | (32) | –.01 | (17) | .00 | .05 |
| Management of alliance | (48) | .37** | .05 | (31) | .12 | (18) | .26 | .17 |
| Technology development | (33) | –.03 | –.07 | (21) | .22 | (11) | –.09 | .29 |
| Product design | (30) | .00 | –.19 | (20) | .25 | (11) | –.07 | –.12 |

| | | | | | | | | |
|---|---|---|---|---|---|---|---|---|
| Quality control | (37) | .09 | −.12 | (26) | −.05 | (13) | .37 | .43 |
| Labour productivity | (39) | −.07 | −.25 | (26) | −.33* | (10) | .11 | .42 |
| Marketing | (46) | .11 | −.10 | (31) | .18 | (14) | .63** | .08 |
| Distribution | (41) | .29* | .14 | (27) | .29 | (12) | .33 | .11 |
| Reputation | (44) | .22 | −.07 | (30) | .14 | (16) | .48* | .23 |
| Customer service | (45) | .16 | −.14 | (31) | .22 | (14) | .56** | .17 |
| Need for involvement | (43) | .20 | −.12 | (28) | −.09 | (15) | .43 | .23 |
| Overall performance | (50) | .36** | .06 | (33) | .22 | (21) | .26 | −.01 |

*Notes*: SATUKP, SATFP, SATALLM, CBALL: see notes to Table 8.1.
*** $p \leq 0.01$; ** $p \leq 0.05$; * $p \leq 0.10$

commitment to EJVs in terms of resources. There is often a presumption that EJVs, which formally embody the creation of a new firm, represent a longer-term commitment by the parent organizations than do NEAs, which are often viewed as more temporary organizational modes. It may also be the case that the amount of investment required in the establishment of an EJV is, on average, greater than that for the establishment of a NEA and that the former absorbs more managerial time and effort than the latter. Given these potential differences, it may be supposed that the survival of the alliance has a higher priority for EJVs than for NEAs and that the success of the EJV is seen in terms of its survival and evolution to a wider domain of activity. In contrast, the NEA may be created with fewer resources for a specific purpose, and once this purpose is achieved it may be terminated. Finally, and most importantly, the contrasting results (for EJVs) between this study and that of Geringer and Hebert (1991), and, in particular, the way this study would support survival over duration and stability when examining relationships between objective and subjective performance measures, clearly flags up the need to replicate studies in different contexts. As part of the rationale for the first published study in this area Geringer and Hebert (1991, p. 251) noted that 'the consistency between subjective and objective measures of IJV [international joint venture] performance is unknown and, while often assumed, has not been formally tested'. The role of replication in furthering understanding and developing a consensus view on empirical relationships deserves to be emphasized and encouraged. This paper serves to make a contribution in that respect.

**Hypothesis 2**

The findings relating to H2 are shown in Table 8.3. This study finds support for H2 in that there is no significant difference between the mean measures of subjective performance between EJVs and NEAs. Although the differences are not significant, Table 2 shows that, for the direct measure of performance (SATUKP), the mean level of satisfaction is higher for NEAs than for EJVs. In line with H2, it may be concluded that the overall measures of subjective performance are equally applicable to EJVs and NEAs and that, for this sample,

*Table* 8.3 Subjective performance means: *t*-tests by organizational mode

| | *Group* | *n* | *Mean* | *SD* | *t-value* |
|---|---|---|---|---|---|
| SATUKP | EJVs | 51 | 3.47 | 1.39 | |
| | NEAs | 24 | 3.75 | 1.15 | −0.92 |
| SATFP | EJVs | 50 | 3.70 | 1.27 | |
| | NEAs | 24 | 3.87 | 1.08 | −0.62 |
| SATALLM | EJVs | 49 | 3.61 | 1.32 | |
| | NEAs | 22 | 3.55 | 1.26 | 0.20 |
| CBALL | EJVs | 51 | 1.58 | 0.85 | |
| | NEAs | 24 | 1.58 | 0.88 | 0.02 |

*Notes*: SATUKP, SATFP, SATALLM, CBALL: see notes to Table 8.1.
SATUKP, SATFP and SATALLM are each measured on a five-point scale from 1 = 'Very Dissatisfied' to 5 = 'Very Satisfied'.
CBALL is measured on a three-point scale from 1 = 'Benefits exceed Costs' to 3 = 'Benefits less than Costs'.

subjective performance outcomes do not vary between organizational mode of alliance.

## Hypothesis 3

Evidence relating to H3, which argues that mean values of subjective performance measures will show less satisfaction in terminated alliances compared to those which have not been terminated is shown in Table 8.4. For EJVs, the findings clearly support H3. The mean values for the surviving EJVs show higher means of satisfaction than for the terminated EJVs and the difference in means are significant (at 0.05 or better). For NEAs, although the mean measures of subjective performance show higher levels of satisfaction in the surviving alliances than in those that have been terminated, the differences are not statistically significant. These findings add further support to the argument advanced above in connection with H2, i.e. the conjecture that the survival of the alliance has a higher priority for EJVs than for NEAs, and that

*Table* 8.4 Subjective performance measures: *t*-tests by survival

| | | *Equity joint ventures* | | | | *Non-equity alliances* | | | |
|---|---|---|---|---|---|---|---|---|---|
| | *Group* | *n* | *Mean* | *SD* | *t-value* | *n* | *Mean* | *SD* | *t-value* |
| SATUKP | Terminated | 18 | 2.61 | 1.38 | | 9 | 3.44 | 1.42 | |
| | Not terminated | 33 | 3.93 | 1.17 | $-3.46^{***}$ | 15 | 3.93 | 0.96 | −0.91 |
| SATFP | Terminated | 17 | 3.00 | 1.28 | | 9 | 3.67 | 1.22 | |
| | Not terminated | 33 | 4.06 | 1.12 | $-2.90^{***}$ | 15 | 4.00 | 1.00 | −0.69 |
| SATALLM | Terminated | 17 | 2.94 | 1.35 | | 8 | 3.00 | 1.20 | |
| | Not terminated | 32 | 3.97 | 1.18 | $-2.66^{**}$ | 14 | 3.85 | 1.23 | −1.60 |
| CBALL | Terminated | 18 | 2.11 | 0.96 | | 9 | 1.78 | 0.97 | |
| | Not terminated | 33 | 1.30 | 0.64 | $3.20^{***}$ | 15 | 1.45 | 0.83 | 0.80 |

*Notes*: SATUKP, SATFP, SATALLM, CBALL: see notes to Table 8.1.
SATUKP, SATFP and SATALLM are each measured on a five-point scale from 1 = 'Very Dissatisfied' to 5 = 'Very Satisfied'.
CBALL is measured on a three-point scale from 1 = 'Benefits exceed Costs' to 3 = 'Benefits less than Costs'.
$^{***}$ $p \leq 0.01$; $^{**}$ $p \leq 0.05$

the success of the alliance in terms of its survival is a more significant measure of performance for EJVs than for NEAs. In this respect, it may be noted that for the direct and indirect measures of subjective performance, the mean values show greater levels of satisfaction for the terminated NEAs than they do for the terminated EJVs.

**Hypothesis 4**

Evidence relating to H4, which is based on the argument that the underlying perceptions of respondents must be taken into account when considering the effect of national cultural differences on subjective measures of alliance performance, is presented in Table 8.5 for EJVs, and Table 8.6 for NEAs. Table 8.5 shows correlations between the objective measure of survival (chosen because of the better results evidenced in Table 8.2) and subjective performance measures for EJVs stratified according to whether the perception and effects of national cultural differences are 'apparent' or not. As hypothesized, the strength of correlation is greater where the perception and effects of national cultural differences are 'not apparent'. In three of the four overall satisfaction measures, the correlations for the 'not apparent' group show greater strength (and all are significant at 0.05 or less). In 13 of the 15 individual dimensions of performance, the correlations show greater strength. While many of the latter correlations are non-significant, the two correlations from the 'not apparent' group which are significant (at 0.05 or better) display greater strength than the corresponding correlation from the 'apparent' group.

Somewhat contrary findings are evidenced for NEAs, shown in Table 8.6. Only the correlations relating to the overall satisfaction measures are shown in Table 8.6 because the relatively small number of observations for sub-groups which anticipated performance for the individual dimensions makes these correlations unreliable, hence they are not reported. Table 8.6 shows that for national cultural differences, while not significant (at the 0.05 level) greater strength is evidenced in those correlations where the differences in national culture are 'apparent', and all of the coefficients for the 'apparent' group have the anticipated sign. None of the 'not apparent' group of coefficients is significant and that

*Table* 8.5 Perceptions and effects of cultural differences and Spearman rank-order correlations between measures of alliance performance: EJVs

| *Subjective performance measures* | | *Objective performance measure – survival* | | | | | | |
|---|---|---|---|---|---|---|---|---|
| | | *Perceptions and effects of:* | | | | | | |
| | | *National cultural differences* | | | | *Corporate cultural differences* | | |
| *Overall satisfaction* | *(n)* | *Not apparent* | *(n)* | *Apparent* | *(n)* | *Not apparent* | *(n)* | *Apparent* |
| SATUKP | (16) | .59** | (35) | .37** | (16) | .40 | (35) | .48*** |
| SATFP | (15) | .59** | (35) | .30* | (15) | .41 | (35) | .43*** |
| SATALLM | (16) | .56** | (33) | .25 | (15) | .42 | (34) | .35** |
| CBALL | (16) | –.33 | (35) | –.49*** | (16) | –.29 | (35) | –.51*** |
| *Individual dimensions* | | | | | | | | |
| Sales level | (16) | .48* | (34) | –.05 | (16) | .19 | (34) | .10 |
| Market share | (16) | .34 | (34) | .27 | (16) | .40 | (34) | .29* |
| Profitability | (16) | .42* | (35) | .24 | (16) | .37 | (35) | .30* |
| Cost control | (13) | .31 | (35) | .29* | (13) | .24 | (35) | .34** |
| Management of alliance | (14) | .75*** | (34) | .18 | (14) | .34 | (34) | .38** |
| Technology development | (11) | –.15 | (22) | .19 | (9) | –.06 | (24) | .00 |
| Product design | (8) | .37 | (22) | –.16 | (7) | – | (23) | –.02 |
| Quality control | (10) | .61* | (27) | –.14 | (10) | .32 | (27) | .03 |

| | | | | | | | | |
|---|---|---|---|---|---|---|---|---|
| Labour productivity | (11) | .00 | (28) | −.07 | (11) | −.13 | (28) | −.04 |
| Marketing | (14) | .29 | (32) | .06 | (14) | .13 | (32) | .07 |
| Distribution | (9) | .47 | (32) | .23 | (9) | .25 | (32) | .30* |
| Reputation | (13) | .26 | (31) | .19 | (13) | .07 | (31) | .28 |
| Customer service | (14) | .23 | (31) | .13 | (14) | .27 | (31) | .11 |
| Need for involvement | (13) | .31 | (30) | .18 | (12) | .52* | (31) | .14 |
| Overall performance | (16) | .54** | (34) | .23 | (16) | .42 | (34) | .32* |

*Notes*: SATUKP, SATFP, SATALLM, CBALL: see notes to Table 8.1.
– coefficient cannot be calculated
*** $p \leq 0.01$; ** $p \leq 0.05$; * $p \leq 0.1$.

*Table* 8.6 Perceptions and effects of cultural differences and Spearman rank-order correlations between measures of alliance performance: NEAs

| *Subjective performance measures* | *Objective performance measure – survival* | | | | | | | |
|---|---|---|---|---|---|---|---|---|
| | *Perceptions and effects of:* | | | | | | | |
| | *National cultural differences* | | | | *Corporate cultural differences* | | | |
| *Overall satisfaction* | *(n)* | *Not apparent* | *(n)* | *Apparent* | *(n)* | *Not apparent* | *(n)* | *Apparent* |
| SATUKP | (7) | .15 | (17) | .28 | (8) | .12 | (16) | .27 |
| SATFP | (7) | .15 | (17) | .15 | (8) | .12 | (16) | .15 |
| SATALLM | (7) | .22 | (15) | .50* | (8) | .23 | (14) | .48* |
| CBALL | (7) | .32 | (17) | −.39 | (8) | .18 | (16) | −.37 |

*Notes*: SATUKP, SATFP, SATALLM, CBALL; see notes to Table 8.1.
* $p \leq 0.1$.

between survival and the indirect cost/benefit measure of satisfaction (CBALL) does not have the anticipated sign.

## Hypothesis 5

Evidence relating to H5, which concerns the perception and effects of corporate culture is also shown in Table 8.5 for EJVs and Table 8.6 for NEAs. For EJVs, the overall satisfaction measures provide no support for H5. Table 8.5 shows that in three out of the four correlations greater strength is evidenced in the 'apparent' group and these are the only correlations which are significant (at 0.05 or less). For the individual dimensions of performance, although ten of the fifteen correlations show greater strength in the 'not apparent' group none of these correlations is significant (at the 0.05 level), while two of the correlations in the 'apparent' group are significant (at the 0.05 level).

For NEAs, Table 8.6 broadly shows the same findings for corporate cultural differences as for national cultural differences: although not significant (at the 0.05 level), greater strength is evidenced in those correlations where the differences in corporate culture are 'apparent', and all the coefficients for the 'apparent' group have the anticipated sign. None of the 'not apparent' group of coefficients is significant and that between survival and the indirect cost/benefit measure of satisfaction (CBALL) does not have the anticipated sign.

At this point, it is worth reviewing the findings relating to H4 and H5. For EJVs, in broad terms, it may be argued that there is some support for Hypothesis 4, which relates to national culture. From the evidence presented in this study, it may be argued that researchers should avoid broad categorizations of national cultural similarity or difference and attempt instead more subtle measures based on the perceptions of respondents, otherwise conclusions drawn from alliance performance analysis may be misleading. This would appear to be particularly important when dealing with respondents' subjective measures of performance. In such instances, respondents' perception of and views concerning the effect of national cultural differences on performance should also be measured. In general, the evidence reported here supports the conclusions on national cultural differences reported by Geringer and Hebert (1991), although the support comes from making the distinction between those respondents for whom national cultural differences are, or are not, 'apparent', rather than from the location of the partner firms. Hence the basis of the findings differs between the two studies. For NEAs, however, there is no support for H4.

For both EJVs and NEAs, there is no real support for H5, which relates to corporate culture. For EJVs, this means that the findings of the study clearly differ between the effect of national and corporate cultural differences on the correlation between objective and subjective measures of alliance performance. The effects of culture differences are further explored in the final two hypotheses which are examined next.

**Hypothesis 6**

The findings relating to H6 are shown in Table 8.7. For EJVs, this study offers no support for H6. Although the differences in means are not statistically significant (at the 0.05 level), the mean values for each of the overall performance measures indicates a higher level of satisfaction, where the perception and effect on performance of national culture differences are 'apparent'. This is counter to the argument of H6. By way of

*Table* 8.7 Subjective performance means: $t$-tests by national cultural differences on performance

| | | Equity joint ventures | | | | Non-equity alliances | | | |
|---|---|---|---|---|---|---|---|---|---|
| | *Group* | *n* | *Mean* | *SD* | *t-value* | *n* | *Mean* | *SD* | *t-value* |
| SATUKP | Not apparent | 16 | 3.25 | 1.53 | | 7 | 4.14 | 0.90 | |
| | Apparent | 35 | 3.57 | 1.34 | −0.72 | 17 | 3.58 | 1.23 | 1.23 |
| SATFP | Not apparent | 15 | 3.60 | 1.50 | | 7 | 4.00 | 1.15 | |
| | Apparent | 35 | 3.74 | 1.17 | −0.33 | 17 | 3.82 | 1.07 | 0.35 |
| SATALLM | Not apparent | 16 | 3.44 | 1.55 | | 7 | 3.71 | 1.13 | |
| | Apparent | 33 | 3.70 | 1.21 | −0.59 | 15 | 3.47 | 1.36 | 0.45 |
| CBALL | Not apparent | 16 | 1.94 | 0.93 | | 7 | 1.71 | 0.95 | |
| | Apparent | 35 | 1.43 | 0.78 | 1.91* | 17 | 1.52 | 0.87 | 0.44 |

*Notes*: SATUKP, SATFP, SATALLM, CBALL: see notes to Table 8.1.
SATUKP, SATFP and SATALLM are each measured on a five-point scale from 1 = 'Very Dissatisfied' to 5 = 'Very Satisfied'.
CBALL is measured on a three-point scale from 1 = 'Benefits exceed Costs' to 3 = 'Benefits less than Costs'.
* $p \leq 0.10$

contrast, in NEAs, for the direct measures of subjective performance, the means are higher where the perceived differences and effect of national culture on performance are 'not apparent', which is in accord with H6. However, the differences in means are not statistically significant.

### Hypothesis 7

Evidence relating to H7 is set out in Table 8.8. For EJVs, there is no support for H7. For each of the measures of performance, the mean values indicate a higher level of satisfaction where the perception and effect on performance of corporate cultural differences are 'apparent', although the difference in means is not statistically significantly. In the case of NEAs, the mean values of the direct measures of satisfaction indicate a higher level of satisfaction for the 'not apparent' group, which conforms to H7, but the differences in means are not significant.

It may be argued that the logic underlying each of H4, H5, H6 and H7 may be faulty. This view comes from recognizing that some cultural differences may be necessary for alliance success. For instance, cultural difference may underlie the strategic motive of the venture to enter new markets where the capabilities of the foreign partner in terms of understanding the foreign culture may be accessed by the UK partner. Culture difference may indeed be the basis for choosing the organizational mode of the venture. So long as partners recognize and appreciate the differences in culture and regard this as an opportunity to learn new things and thus expand the capabilities of the organization, then this may be a source of strength to the alliance. On the basis of this argument, it would be expected that correlations between objective and subjective measures of performance will be stronger in alliances that involve parents with *dissimilar* national (or corporate) cultures The logic of this argument is contrary to that expressed by Geringer and Hebert (1991) and also runs counter to their empirical findings The recognition of cultural differences may reflect a greater willingness to maintain the venture, to persist in attempting to make it work and to overcome any problems that differences in culture may cause. Clearly, this issue warrants further investigation in future

*Table* 8.8 Subjective performance means: *t*-tests by corporate cultural differences on performance

| | | *Equity joint ventures* | | | | *Non-equity alliances* | | | |
|---|---|---|---|---|---|---|---|---|---|
| | *Group* | *n* | *Mean* | *SD* | *t-value* | *n* | *Mean* | *SD* | *t-value* |
| SATUKP | Not apparent | 16 | 3.25 | 1.43 | | 8 | 4.12 | 0.83 | |
| | Apparent | 35 | 3.57 | 1.38 | −0.75 | 16 | 3.56 | 1.26 | 1.30 |
| SATFP | Not apparent | 15 | 3.40 | 1.40 | | 8 | 4.00 | 1.07 | |
| | Apparent | 35 | 3.83 | 1.20 | −1.03 | 16 | 3.81 | 1.11 | 0.40 |
| SATALLM | Not apparent | 15 | 3.27 | 1.49 | | 8 | 3.75 | 1.04 | |
| | Apparent | 34 | 3.77 | 1.23 | −1.14 | 14 | 3.43 | 1.40 | 0.61 |
| CBALL | Not apparent | 16 | 1.62 | 0.89 | | 8 | 1.62 | 0.92 | |
| | Apparent | 35 | 1.57 | 0.85 | 0.20 | 16 | 1.56 | 0.89 | 0.16 |

*Notes*: SATUKP, SATFP, SATALLM, CBALL: see notes to Table 8.1.
SATUKP, SATFP and SATALLM are each measured on a five-point scale from 1 = 'Very Dissatisfied' to 5 = 'Very Satisfied'.
CBALL is measured on a three-point scale from 1 = 'Benefits exceed Costs' to 3 = 'Benefits less than Costs'.

research. It would be particularly fruitful to examine the relative importance of access to national culture and corporate culture for partners in terms of motivation for the alliance and the influence on correlations between objective and subjective performance measures.

## SUMMARY AND CONCLUSIONS

The first goal of this study was to consider the relationship between objective and subjective measures of alliance performance. Of the objective performance measures identified, survival was found to have the strongest and most significant set of correlations with overall subjective performance measures and perceptions of the extent to which the alliance had performed, relative to expectations across a range of individual dimensions. In comparison, the objective performance measures of duration and stability (in EJVs) were, in general, weak and non-significant. In broad terms, this supports the findings of Geringer and Hebert (1991) who reported that the survival-based measure evidenced the strongest correlations with subjective performance measures. However, Geringer and Hebert also reported a number of relatively strong and significant correlations between the objective-based measures of duration and stability and subjective performance measures, findings which data from this study were unable to confirm.

Geringer and Hebert's (1991) work is the only previous study which examines the relationship between objective and subjective performance measures in the context of alliances between partners from advanced industrial economies, with this paper representing only the second such study. The findings of this study only partly confirm those of Geringer and Hebert, with important differences in the conclusions that can be drawn from this study and that of Geringer and Hebert with respect to H1. It should be noted, however, that there are differences in the nature of the samples between this study and that of Geringer and Hebert (1991). The latter focused on manufacturing sector alliances only, whereas this study includes both manufacturing sector and tertiary sector alliances. This difference should be borne in mind when assessing the findings. Clearly, to date, too few studies have been undertaken on this topic to come to a settled view on the empirical relationship underlying H1, hence further work is necessary to develop knowledge in this area. Given that the context is different for this study in that it uses UK rather than North American data, and given the paucity of published studies on UK alliances with advanced industrial partners, this study makes a contribution in providing new findings on an under-researched area.

The second goal of this chapter was to consider the effect of national cultural and corporate cultural differences on the relationship between objective and subjective measures of alliance performance. For EJVs, the findings of this study indicate that when parent respondents believe that no difference in national culture exists, or if a difference is perceived to exist that this difference has no effect on alliance performance, then resulting correlations between the objective performance measure of survival and subjective performance measures are stronger than when a difference in national culture is perceived and such difference is believed to have an effect on performance. This result broadly supports Geringer and Hebert's (1991) finding that correlations between partners' assessments of specific aspects of alliance performance were significantly positive, as well as being stronger for partners from similar national cultures. There is an important difference, however, in that while Geringer and Hebert used a measure of cultural difference based on partner location, this study used a perceptual measure which was independent of foreign partner nationality. The inference that may be drawn from this is that in EJV studies which examine and make use of subjective performance measures, it is necessary to accommodate the respondent's perception of national cultural differences rather than assuming that partner nationality or partner location can in themselves capture the effects of national culture differences. An alternative interpretation is that as a perceptual measure of culture has provided results which are consistent with the use of objective, location-based measures, this might argue for the substitutability of measures in future research. It should be stressed, however, that this finding was not confirmed in the case of NEAs.

For EJVs (in contrast to the findings with respect to national culture) and for NEAs, this study finds that correlations between the objective performance measure of survival and subjective performance measures are stronger when a difference in corporate culture is perceived and such difference is believed to have an effect on performance. For EJVs, this finding is somewhat surprising, as it would be expected that corporate culture and national culture are not independent variables, with the latter having a strong influence on the former. To the extent that culture differences do affect subjective performance measures, the relative impact of national and corporate culture differences are clearly worthy of further examination in alliance research. In the analysis of the impact of culture, it must be recognized that the concepts of both national and corporate culture are too broad to carry the analytical content required. Parkhe (1993) notes the difficulties of including empirical variables such as trust, forbearance, reciprocity and commitment which are deemed central to the theoretical understanding of alliances by Buckley and Casson (1988).

The third goal of the study was to develop new work which examines performance measures by organizational mode of alliance, and, in particular, to consider the performance of NEAs, which has been previously neglected in the literature. A summary of the hypotheses and research findings by organizational mode is provided in Table 8.9. The organizational mode of the alliance was compared in findings which directly assessed differences in the means of subjective performance measures between contractual form as well as in the context of alliance termination, and perceptions of differences in national and corporate culture. The findings of the study indicate that the mean measure of subjective performance does not vary according to organizational mode (H2), and that there is a similar lack of support for H5 from both EJVs and NEAs. For the other hypotheses, however, there is a contrast in the findings between organizational mode. This study finds more support for H1, H3 and H4 from EJVs than from NEAs. The lack of statistical significance means that it is not possible to assert whether there is more support for H6 and H7 from NEAs than EJVs. Overall, however, the findings indicate that generalizations regarding performance

*Table* 8.9 Summary of hypotheses and research findings

| | *Equity joint ventures* | *Non-equity alliances* |
|---|---|---|
| **H1**: There will be a significant and positive correlation between objective and subjective measures of alliance performance. | Support for survival, no support for duration or stability | Weak support for survival, no support for duration |
| **H2**: The mean measure of subjective performance will not vary between organisational mode of alliance. | Support for H2 | |
| **H3**: The mean measure of overall satisfaction obtained from subjective measures of performance will be lower in those alliances which have been terminated compared to those alliances which are continuing. | Support for H3 | No support for H3 |
| **H4**: Correlations between objective and subjective measures of alliance performance will be stronger in alliances where the perception and effect of national cultural differences are not apparent to the reporting parents compared to those for whom such differences are apparent. | Support for H4 | No support for H4 |

| | | |
|---|---|---|
| **H5**: Correlations between objective and subjective measures of alliance performance will be stronger in alliances where the perception and effect of corporate cultural differences are not apparent to the reporting parents compared to those for whom such differences are apparent. | No support for H5 | No support for H5 |
| **H6**: The mean measure of overall satisfaction obtained from subjective measures of performance will be higher in those alliances where the perception and effect of national cultural differences are not apparent to the reporting parents compared to those for whom such differences are apparent. | No support for H6 | No support for H6 |
| **H7**: The mean measure of overall satisfaction obtained from subjective measures of performance will be higher in those alliances where the perception and effect of corporate cultural differences are not apparent to the reporting parents compared to those for whom such differences are apparent. | No support for H7 | No support for H7 |

outcomes of broadly defined alliances should be treated with caution. Findings in this study relating to differences in performance measures and organizational mode further indicate that future research on performance should be investigated in the context of the contingency variables that determine the choice of the organizational mode of alliance.

It should be recognized that the findings of this paper are subject to several caveats. While this study has attempted a partial replication of some of the work of Geringer and Hebert (1991), particularly with respect to H1, there are differences in the nature of the samples investigated. An obvious difference relates to the fact that this study investigates responses from UK parents, while that of Geringer and Hebert considers North American parents. As previously noted, Geringer and Hebert consider only manufacturing-sector EJVs, whereas this study includes both manufacturing-sector alliances and tertiary-sector alliances. There are also differences in the partner composition of the two studies. In Geringer and Hebert's US sample, about 38 per cent of the ventures were formed with European partners (compared with 34 per cent for this study), about 37 per cent with US partners (33 per cent in this study) and about 24 per cent with Japanese partners (21 per cent in this study). Finally, the time periods of the studies differ. For this study, the time period is 1980–91, whereas that for Geringer and Hebert's US sample is 1979–85, and that for their Canadian sample is 1981–1988. These differences should be kept in mind when comparing the results of the two studies.

Further caveats involve the nature of the research methods used in this study, which is a cross-section study relying on data from a single respondent in each UK partner firm. A number of standard caveats apply to a study of this nature, particularly the lack of information from foreign partners and (where applicable) alliance managements, and the lack of multiple perspectives from within each element of the alliance. Issues of memory decay on the part of respondents may also be a concern in studies of this type. The nature of these weaknesses can be addressed in future research by seeking multiple respondents from each of the elements of the alliance. The limitations inherent in the postal questionnaire method of securing information should also be noted A deeper understanding of the dynamics of alliance performance is only likely to come from undertaking longitudinal studies of the evolution of alliances rather than relying on cross-section data.

Evaluating alliance performance constitutes a difficult challenge. The debate over the appropriate measures to use in assessing alliance performance is clearly not settled. Such issues can only be addressed through repeated investigations using alternative data bases. Replication is an essential part of research methodology and plays a crucial role in confirming, or otherwise previously reported research. While partly performing that role, this chapter also provides additional insight into the issues examined.


## Acknowledgements

The authors would like to thank the anonymous referees for their constructive comment on earlier versions of this paper and the editor for his help and encouragement.


## References


Anderson, Erin (1990) 'Two firms, one frontier: on assessing joint venture performance', *Sloan Management Review*, 31, 2, 19–30.

—— and B. Weitz (1989) 'Determinants of continuity in conventional industrial channel dyads', *Marketing Science*, 8, 4, 310–23.

Beamish, Paul W. (1985) 'The characteristics of joint ventures in developed and developing countries', *Columbia Journal of World Business*, 20, 3, 13–19.

—— (1987) 'Joint ventures in less developed countries: partner selection and performance', *Management International Review*, 27, 1, 23–37.

—— and John C. Banks (1987) 'Equity joint ventures and the theory of the multinational enterprise', *Journal of International Business Studies*, 18, 1, 1–16.

—— and Andrew Inkpen (1995) 'Keeping international joint ventures stable and profitable', *Long Range Planning*, 28, 3, 26–36.

Blodgett, Linda L. (1992) 'Factors in the instability of international joint ventures: an event history analysis', *Strategic Management Journal*, 13, 475–81.

Buckley, Peter J. and Mark Casson (1988) 'A theory of co-operation in international business' in *Co-operative strategies in international business*, F. J. Contractor and P. Lorange (eds), 31–53. Lexington, MA: Lexington Books.

——and Mark Casson (1996) 'An economic model of international joint venture strategy', *Journal of International Business Studies*, 27, 5, 849–76.

——, Chris Pass and Kate Prescott (1988) 'Measures of international competitiveness: a critical survey', *Journal of Marketing Management*, 14, 2, 175–200.

Cameron, Kim S. (1986) 'Effectiveness as paradox: consensus and conflict in conceptions of organisational effectiveness', *Management Science*, 32, 5, 539–53.

Chakravarthy, Balaji S. (1986) 'Measuring strategic performance', *Strategic Management Journal*, 7, 437–58.

Chowdhury, Jafor (1992) 'Performance of international joint ventures and wholly owned foreign subsidiaries: a comparative perspective', *Management International Review*, 32, 115–33.

Contractor, Farok J. and Peter Lorange (1988) 'Why should firms cooperate? The strategic and economics basis for cooperative Ventures', in *Co-operative strategies in international business*, F. J. Contractor and P. Lorange (eds.), 3–30. Lexington, MA: Lexington Books.

Dussauge, Pierre, and Bernard Garrette (1995) 'Determinants of success in international strategic alliances: evidence from the global aerospace industry', *Journal of International Business Studies*, 26, 3, 505–30.

Eccles, Robert G. (1991) 'The performance measurement manifesto', *Harvard Business Review*, (Jan.–Feb.), 131–37.

Franko, Lawrence G. (1971) *Joint venture survival in multinational corporations*. New York: Praeger.

Geringer, J. Michael (1990) *Trends and traits of Canadian joint ventures*. Ottawa: Investment Canada.

——(1991) 'Strategic determinants of partner selection criteria in international joint ventures', *Journal of International Business*, 22, 1, 41–62.

——and Louis Hébert (1989) 'Control and performance of international joint ventures', *Journal of International Business*, 20, 2, 235–54.

——and Louis Hébert (1991) 'Measuring performance of international joint ventures', *Journal of International Business Studies*, 22, 2, 249–63.

——and C. Patrick Woodcock (1995) 'Agency costs and the structure and performance of international joint ventures', in *International joint ventures: economic and organisational perspectives*, K. Chatterjee and B. Gray (eds.), 75–89. Norwell, MA: Kluwer Academic.

Glaister, Keith W. and Peter J. Buckley (1994) 'UK international joint ventures: an analysis of patterns of activity and distribution', *British Journal of Management*, 5, 1, 33–51.

——and Peter J. Buckley (1996) 'Strategic motives for international alliance formation', *Journal of Management Studies*, 33, 3, 301–32.

Gomes-Casseres, Benjamin (1987) 'Joint venture instability: is it a problem?', *Columbia Journal of World Business*, 22, 2, 97–107.

——(1996) *The alliance revolution*. Cambridge, MA.: Harvard University Press.

Goodman, Paul S., and Johannes Pennings (1980) 'Critical issues in assessing organisational effectiveness', in *Organisational assessment: perspectives on the management of organisational behavior and the quality of work life*,

E. Lawler, D. Nadler and C. Cammann (eds), 185–215. New York: Wiley-Interscience.
Gulati, Ranjay (1995) 'Does familiarity breed trust? The implications of repeated ties for contractual choice in alliances', *Academy of Management Journal*, 38, 1, 85–112.
Hagedoorn, John and Rajneesh Narula (1996) 'Choosing organisational modes for strategic technology partnering: international and sectoral differences', *Journal of International Business Studies*, 27, 2, 265–84.
Hallen, Lars and Finn Wiedersheim-Paul (1979) 'Psychic distance and buyer-seller interaction', *Organisasjon, Marknad och Samhalle*, 16, 5, 308–24.
Harrigan, Kathryn R. (1985) *Strategies for joint ventures*. Lexington, MA: Lexington Books.
— (1986) *Managing for joint venture success*. Lexington, MA: Lexington Books.
Hergert, Michael and Deigan Morris (1988) 'Trends in international collaborative agreements', in *Co-operative strategies in international business*, F. J. Contractor and P. Lorange (eds), 99–109. Lexington, MA: Lexington Books.
Hofstede, Geert (1980) *Culture's consequences*. Beverly Hills, CA: Sage.
Inkpen, Andrew C. and Julian Birkinshaw (1994) 'International joint ventures and performance: an interorganisational perspective', *International Business Review*, 3, 3, 201–17.
Jacobson, Robert (1987) 'The validity of ROI as a measure of business performance', *American Economic Review*, 77, 3, 470–78.
Jacoby, Jacob and Michael S. Matell (1971) 'Three point Likert scales are good enough', *Journal of Marketing Research*, 8, 495–500.
Janger, Allen R. (1980) *Organisation of international joint ventures*. New York: Conference Board.
Killing, J. Peter (1983) *Strategies for joint venture success*. New York: Praeger.
Kogut, Bruce (1988a) 'Joint ventures: Theoretical and empirical perspectives', *Strategic Management Journal*, 9, 319–32.
——(1988b) 'A study of the life cycle of joint ventures', in *Co-operative strategies in international business*, F. J. Contractor and P. Lorange (eds), 169–86. Lexington, MA: Lexington Books.
Koh, Jeongsuk and N. Venkatraman (1991) 'Joint venture formations and stock market reactions: an assessment in the information technology sector', *Academy of Management Journal*, 34, 4, 869–92.
Lecraw, Donald J. (1983) 'Performance of transnational corporations in less developed countries', *Journal of International Business Studies*, 14, 1, 15–33.
Lewin, Arie Y. and John W. Minton (1986) 'Determining organisational effectiveness: Another look and an agenda for research', *Management Science*, 32, 5, 514–38.
Lummer, Scott L., and John J. McConnell (1990) 'Stock valuation effects of international joint ventures' in *Pacific Basin Capital Markets Research*. S. G. Rhee and R. P. Chang (eds.), 531–46. North-Holland: Elsevier.
Lyles, Marjorie A. and Inga S. Baird (1994) 'Performance of international joint ventures in two Eastern European countries: the case of Hungary and Poland', *Management International Review*, 34, 4, 313–29.

Osborn, Richard N. and C. Christopher Baughn (1990) 'Forms of interorganisational governance for multinational alliances', *Academy of Management Journal*, 33, 503–19.
Parkhe, Arvind (1993) '"Messy" research, methodological predispositions, and theory development in international joint ventures', *Academy of Management Review*, 18, 2, 227–68.
Schaan, Jean-Louis (1983) 'Parent control and joint venture success: the case of Mexico', Unpublished doctoral dissertation, University of Western Ontario, London, Ontario, Canada.
Stopford, John M. and Louis T. Wells (1972) *Managing the multinational enterprise*. New York: Basic Books.
Teece, David J. (1992) 'Competition, co-operation and innovation', *Journal of Economic Behavior and Organisation*, 18, 1–25.
Tomlinson, James W. C. (1970) *The joint venture process in international business: India and Pakistan*. Cambridge, MA: MIT Press.
Varadarajan, P. Rajan, and Vasudevan Ramanujam (1990) 'The corporate performance conundrum: a synthesis of contemporary views and an extension', *Journal of Management Studies*, 27, 5, 463–83.
Venkatraman, N. and Vasudevan Ramanujam (1986) 'The measurement of business performance in strategy research: a comparison of approaches', *Academy of Management Review*, 11, 801–14.
Yoshino, Michael and U. Srinivasa Rangan (1995) *Strategic alliances: an entrepreneurial approach to globalization*. Boston, MA: Harvard Business School Press.

# 9 Management–Performance Relationships in UK Joint Ventures*

Peter J. Buckley and Keith W. Glaister

**This chapter investigates the management – performance relationship for a sample of UK international joint ventures with partners from developed market economies. Management control is identified in terms of mechanism, extent and focus. Joint venture performance is evaluated by two subjective measures and two objective measures. The findings of the study are, first, that subjective measures of performance are not more significantly associated with the dimensions of management control than are objective measures of performance. Second, where partners dominate or have responsibility for management control they view performance more favourably than partners that do not have dominant management control. Finally, somewhat counter-intuitively the study finds that the nature of management control does not vary with the duration of joint ventures.**

## INTRODUCTION

This chapter investigates the management control–performance relationship for a sample of UK international joint ventures (JVs) with partners from developed market economies. A joint venture is created when two or more partners join forces to establish a newly incorporated company in which each has an equity position, thereby each expects a propor-

---

* First published in *International Business Review*, 7, 3 (1998).

tional share of dividend as compensation and representation on the board of directors. Harrigan (1985, p. 2) views JVs as 'separate entities with two or more active businesses as partners', where the emphasis is on the 'child', i.e. 'the entity created by partners for a specific activity' (Harrigan, 1985, p. 3). JVs thus involve two or more legally distinct organisations (the parents), each of which invests in the venture and actively participates in the decision-making activities of the jointly owned entity (Geringer, 1991). A JV is considered to be international if at least one partner has its headquarters outside the venture's country of operation or if the JV has a significant level of operation in more than one country (Geringer and Hebert, 1989).

Parkhe (1993) has identified four major dimensions of JV study in the prior literature: motives for JV formation, partner selection characteristics, control/conflict, and JV stability/performance, and in reviewing these lines of study he concludes that researchers have non-cumulatively focused on different dimensions. It is the purpose of this study to attempt to relate two of the four core dimensions of JV study identified by Parkhe, those of the management/control of JVs and JV performance. The focus of the chapter is the empirical investigation of the relationships between the dimensions of management control and the performance of a sample of JVs between UK firms and partner firms from Western Europe, the USA and Japan. The study therefore concerns JVs which have been voluntarily entered into between firms from advanced market economies and concerns a topic that has been relatively under-researched, particularly in the context of firms of European origin.

Although the incidence of JV activity has been increasing since the late 1970s (Beamish and Delios, 1997a), there is often dissatisfaction with JV performance, especially in developed countries, where prior studies indicate that reported performance has not improved substantially over the last 25 years (Beamish and Delios, 1997b, p. 105). Poor performance in JVs according to Beamish and Delios (1997b) may be attributed to lack of congruity (alignment) of objectives in performance measures at the time of JV formation. Madhok (1995, p. 117) notes that the growing incidence of JV formation combined with the poor performance outcomes is intuitively inconsistent, and indicates that although firms perceive the need for JVs they find them difficult to manage. Lee and Beamish (1995, p. 638) point out that JV performance is an important issue partly because of the costs of poor performance imposed on the parent firms, but also because of the social costs of poor performance which have to be borne by the country in which the JV activity occurs.

The rest of the chapter is set out in the following manner: the next section reviews the literature relating to the areas of JV management control and JV performance. The third section sets out the hypotheses of the study. Research methods and sample characteristics are in the fourth section. Results and discussion are in the fifth section. A summary and conclusions are in the final section.

## LITERATURE REVIEW

### The Management of JVs

In the organizational literature, management control refers to the process by which an organization influences its sub-units and members to behave in ways that lead to the attainment of organizational objectives. This conceptualization of control is more problematic in JVs because two or more parties may influence a JV's activities (Yan and Gray, 1994, p. 1481). The main purpose of control in JVs is to ensure that the benefits the parents seek are actually obtained without undue costs. However, the distinguishing characteristic of the JV as a cooperative organization means that the ability of a parent to exercise control is a function both of the influence it has over the JV managers and its influence in relation to other parent companies (Child *et al.*, 1997, p. 186). The control of the JV is thus a complex and multifaceted concept (Geringer and Hebert, 1989; Gray and Yan, 1992). In the prior literature, parent control of the JV has been suggested as a critical factor that determines performance. Yan and Gray (1994), for example, presented a model where the bargaining power of the partners is the main determinant of management control, and management control is positively related to performance. Lin *et al.* (1997) view management control as a function of the motivation and contributions of the partners, where management control in turn affects the performance of the JV. Despite the presumed relationship between management control and performance, empirical research on this relationship has produced conflicting results (Geringer and Hebert, 1989).

In their detailed consideration of the prior literature relating to JV control, Geringer and Hebert (1989) identified three dimensions of management control: the *mechanisms* or means the parents use to exercise control, the *extent* or degree of control achieved by parents over a JV, and the *focus* of control, i.e. the areas of the JV's operation in which control is exercised. It is extremely difficult to compare the results of prior studies on management control of JVs because they have tended to focus on different dimensions of control (Yan and Gray, 1994, p. 1481).

Traditionally, the main mechanism of JV control has been majority ownership or voting control (itself largely determined by majority equity share holdings). Behrman (1970), and Friedman and Beguin (1971) suggested, however, that control is not a strict and automatic consequence of ownership, but rather that a variety of mechanisms were available to firms for exercising effective control such as the right to veto the decisions of the JV managers, representation in management bodies and special agreements relating to either technology (e.g. licensing) or management (e.g. management services). Participation in the management of a JV's operations may also be obtained by a parent firm through its technical superiority and managerial skills. Managerial control can also be exercised in the nomination of one of the parent firm's managers as the JV general manager or other key positions in the JV, as well as the employment of different ownership structure arrangements (Rafii, 1978; Gullander, 1976; Schaan, 1988; Yan and Gray, 1994). Otterbeck (1981) has also pointed out that while administrative systems are introduced for coordination, performance evaluation and decision-making of certain kinds, the desire for control should lead parents to try to impose their own administrative procedures and policies upon the JV.

Most studies examining the extent of control have suggested that control is dependent upon the centralization or the locus of the decision-making process (Geringer and Hebert, 1989). Typical of this approach is the study by Killing (1983) who observed that while JVs are a difficult organizational form to manage well, some JVs were easier to manage than others and this tended to be the case where one parent was willing to play a passive role. Killing argues that the more a JV can be run as if it has only one parent, the simpler will be the management task and the better will be performance. Killing measured the extent to which a venture was dominated by either of its parents by focusing on the way in which decisions were made and, in particular, by determining how much influence each parent had on various types of decisions. The evidence on the relationship between the extent of control and JV performance is, however, mixed. Killing's (1983) research on JVs in developed countries stressed that success is associated with one partner assuming dominant control over the venture and operating it as if it were a wholly owned subsidiary. Kogut (1988a) examined a sample of domestic US JVs and found no support for the hypothesis that dominant JVs are more stable than shared-control JVs. The limitations of Killing's findings should also be noted. Killing used a convenience sample of JVs and his results were not found to be statistically significant (Beamish, 1984).

The 'extent of control' perspective has been criticized for its suggestion that parent firms seek to control the overall JV, rather than targeting specific activities or processes perceived as crucial for achievement of the JV's or the parents' strategic objectives (Geringer and Hebert, 1989). This has been emphasized particularly by Schaan (1983, p. 57) who defined control as 'the process through which a parent company ensures that the way a joint venture is managed conforms to its own interest'. Hence, a parent firm will seek to gain control over specific activities that are considered to be strategically important rather than over the whole JV. In this sense control has a focus dimension (Schaan, 1983; Geringer, 1988).

## The Performance of JVs

Partly because of the potential for conflict and disagreements between partners, JV performance is often viewed as less than satisfactory (Inkpen and Birkinshaw, 1994; Killing, 1983).

The measurement of organization performance is itself a controversial area (Goodman and Pennings, 1980; Cameron, 1986; Chakravarthy, 1986; Lewin and Minton, 1986; Venkatraman and Ramanujam, 1986; Jacobson, 1987; Varadarajan and Ramanujam, 1990; Eccles, 1991). A major issue of debate is the appropriate yardstick(s) to be used when assessing organization performance. More fundamentally, controversy surrounds the lack of clarity between indicators of performance and determinants of performance. For JVs, performance evaluation becomes even more problematic because each party in the partnership is likely to adopt idiosyncratic performance criteria (Yan and Gray, 1994, p. 1482). For these reasons it is unsurprising that the operationalization of JV performance has proved difficult, with no consensus on its appropriate definition and measure (Geringer and Hebert, 1989, 1991). Yan and Gray (1994) note that the prior literature on JV performance indicates three areas in which major inconsistencies occur. First, whose perspective is used for performance measurement – that of one parent, two parents, or the JV management? Second, variations occur in performance measures which may range from financial performance indicators to subjective perceptions of performance. Third, the appropriateness of different performance measures changes as a JV matures. Moreover, these inconsistencies make cross-study comparisons and generalizations about JV performance particularly problematic. The debate over JV performance measures is clearly a sub-set of wider concerns regarding the assessment of organization performance in general, in which the evaluation of JV performance is a particular challenge.

Most of the prior empirical studies examining JV performance relate to MNCs from developed countries forming JVs with firms from developing countries. In these studies a large number of criteria have been used to assess performance (Chowdhury, 1992). In summarizing prior empirical research, Geringer and Hebert (1991) point out that early studies relied on a variety of financial indicators, such as profitability, growth and cost position (for example Tomlinson, 1970; Lecraw, 1983). Other studies have used objective measures of performance such as: survival of the JV (Franko, 1971; Stopford and Wells, 1972; Killing, 1983; Geringer, 1990), its duration (Harrigan, 1988; Kogut, 1988a), instability of its ownership (i.e. significant changes in the equity holdings of the parents), (Franko, 1971; Gomes-Casseres, 1987), and renegotiation of the JV contract (Blodgett, 1992).

Anderson (1990) notes that JVs (as distinct from other organizational forms) may be more commonly used in highly uncertain settings with a very long-term performance horizon and no current performance baselines for comparison. In high risk/uncertain settings short-term financial measures would tend to indicate poor performance, although the venture may be making satisfactory progress towards long-term goals, or achieving current non-financial goals. In this respect, it should be recognized that JVs may not be intended to fulfil standard financial objectives such as profit generation, but are instead formed to achieve a range of objectives, for example, to enhance parent learning (Kogut, 1988b), or to improve the strategic positioning of the parent firms (Contractor and Lorange, 1988) including a presence in new markets (Glaister and Buckley, 1996a). The failure of financial and objective measures to reflect the extent to which a JV has achieved its aims is stressed by Geringer and Hebert (1991), who argue that despite poor financial results, liquidation or instability, a JV may have met or exceeded the parents' objectives and so be considered successful by one or all of the parents. Conversely, a JV may be viewed as unsuccessful despite good financial results or continued stability. Anderson (1990) argues that parents need to recognize that most JVs should be evaluated more subjectively over a longer time horizon than is typically used. Resorting to formal, financial measures of performance is likely to lead to early termination before a JV has had enough time to realize its potential. In this respect, JVs require a more balanced, often subjective, approach if their promise is to be realized.

Concern about the ability of financial and objective measures to gauge JV performance, as noted above, as well as the difficulty in obtaining such measures, led several researchers to perceptual measures of a parent's satisfaction with JV performance (Killing, 1983; Schaan, 1983; Beamish, 1985). Perceptual measures are able to provide information regarding the extent to which the JV has achieved its overall objectives. These authors, together with Janger (1980), have also made use of subjective performance measures for each of a limited number of individual dimensions of the JV. A key

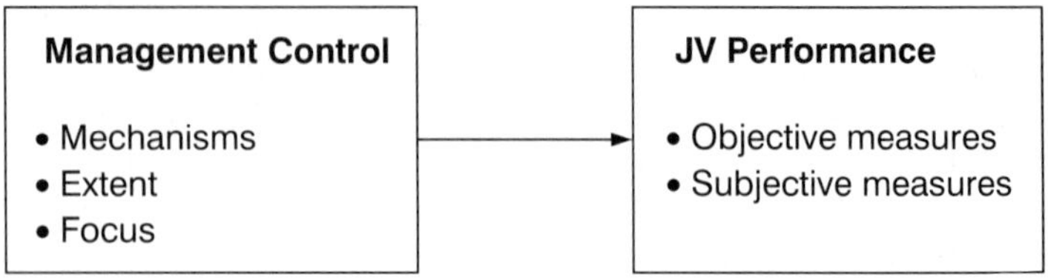


*Figure* 9.1 A model of management control and JV performance

contribution of the study by Geringer and Hebert (1991) is the comparison of objective and subjective measures of JV performance. They found that subjective satisfaction measures of JV performance and performance relative to initial objectives were significantly positively correlated to objective measures of JV performance.

Investigations of the JV control–performance relationship in the context of developed country partners has received relatively little attention in the literature, although studies by Killing (1983), Geringer (1986) and Awadzi *et al.* (1986) are exceptions. Geringer and Hebert (1989, p. 246) concluded that 'the empirical evidence regarding the control–performance relationship in IJVs (international joint ventures) is limited. The importance and direction of this relationship have yet to be established, tested and clarified.'

A basic model of the relationship between management control and JV performance is set out in Figure 9.1. The general prediction of this theoretical model is that there is a positive relationship between management control and performance. This study seeks to make a new contribution to the control–performance literature by exploring the relationship between the dimensions of management control and both subjective and objective measures of performance. The details of the expected relationship between the dimensions of management control and objective and subjective performance measures are considered in the hypotheses section which follows.

## HYPOTHESES

The considerable debate over JV performance measures clearly indicates that no single measure is entirely appropriate.

The multitude of measures used by academic researchers to assess JV performance is indicative of the way parent companies and JV managers evaluate JV performance, which in turn is a reflection of the variety of reasons for establishing JVs (Contractor and Lorange, 1988; Porter and Fuller, 1986; Glaister and Buckley, 1996a). Two of the main objective performance measures used to assess JVs between firms from advanced market economies have been survival (i.e. whether the JV has been terminated or not), and duration or longevity of the venture. Both of these measures are subject to criticism; for instance, termination of a venture may indicate successful completion of the JV task and not JV failure (Gomes-Casseres, 1987), and duration of the venture may be prolonged in the hope of 'making it work' rather than because it is operating successfully. In any event a sole indicator of performance, where many objectives may exist for the JV, cannot indicate the extent to which all of the objectives have been achieved for the JV. For instance, 'when a IJV is formed for technology transfer, measuring performance by survival or duration may inaccurately classify the IJV as a poor performer because it was dissolved, even if it first met its stated goal (which led to the dissolution)' (Beamish and Delios, 1997b, p. 107). This sort of incompatibility between performance measures and objectives encouraged the adoption of perceptual or subjective measures of performance.

Subjective performance measures are also subject to criticism, particularly with respect to respondent bias where, for various reasons, the performance of the JV may be 'talked-up'. Although Geringer and Hebert (1991) have demonstrated a significant correlation between objective and subjective JV performance measures,[1] it may be argued that, despite their shortcomings, the subjective performance measures are a better reflection of underlying JV achievement than the objective performance measures discussed here. This is because, in a sense, the subjective measures are a more direct measure of performance in that the respondents should be aware of the goals of the venture and, therefore, should be able to make an assessment of the performance of the venture in light of these goals. The performance measure Yan and Gray (1994) used, for instance, was the extent to which a JV's partners had achieved their strategic objectives in initiating the JV. 'If an objective represented a long term goal of a partner, we measured the extent to which satisfactory progress had been made. Using this measure fits well with the way that the partners actually evaluated performance' (Yan and Gray, 1994, p. 1495). To the extent that subjective performance measures are a better reflection of the success of the venture than are objective performance measures, and assuming that the way in which the JV has been managed affects venture outcomes, then it would be expected that the dimensions of management control and subjective performance measures would be more strongly associated than would the dimensions of management control and objective performance measures. This leads to the first hypothesis:

*H1: There will be stronger significant association between the dimensions of management control and the subjective measures of JV performance than between the dimensions of management control and the objective measures of JV performance.*

The subjective assessment of JV performance by a parent firm is likely to be significantly influenced by the degree to which the parent exercises management control over the JV. Yan and Gray (1994) in a case analysis of US–China JVs found that the pattern of management control was directly related to JV performance. Data showed that when the partners' control was even, each partner's performance, as assessed from its own perspective, was equal. However, when control was unevenly shared by partners, the prediction of performance was less straightforward. While in some instances finding that 'the partner who exercises a higher level of management control achieves a higher level of performance from its own point of view' (Yan and Gray, 1994, p. 1499), and 'the balance or unbalance in partners' management control is associated with a similar pattern of performance assessed in terms of the achievement of both partners' strategic objectives' (p. 1500), this was not consistent across all cases. A number of variables that might moderate the direct relationship between control and performance were identified by Yan and Gray: the level of trust between the partners, the commonality of their strategic objectives, and the level of institutionalization of these objectives, i.e., whether or not they are contractual.

Despite the influence of these potential moderating variables, it is still instructive to develop the proposition that the partner which exercises a higher level of management control will perceive a higher performance level for the JV. This perspective may be related to commitment in JVs. Cullen *et al.* (1995, p. 95) noted that commitment is an attitudinal response to the relationship. They argued that the greater the responsibility for, and investment in, running the operation (i.e. control) the greater are the psychological pressures to feel committed to the relationship. Cullen *et al.* hypothesized that commitment to the JV increases with the proportion of the ownership of the JV, the proportion of the JV directors and JV managers placed by the partner, and the larger the extent of decision-making control exercised by the partner (although they did not find support for their hypotheses).

Building on these arguments, we distinguish between 'high control parents' and 'low control parents', the former being JV parents that exercise the greater degree of authority over the dimensions of management control. We maintain that a high control parent will have a greater onus of responsibility for the performance outcomes of the JV than is the case for a low control parent. The high control parent is, therefore, more likely to associate its degree of control with JV performance and will, in consequence, be inclined to adopt a more favourable perspective on the performance outcomes of the JV. With the low control parent, and a reduced onus of responsibility for JV performance, we argue there will be a weaker perceived association between its management of the JV and JV performance, and in consequence there will be less of a tendency to view JV performance favourably. *Ceteris paribus*, the more a parent firm has responsibility for the dimensions of JV management control the greater will be the level of satisfaction with JV performance. This general argument underpins each of the particular dimensions of JV management control identified in the literature. Thus, where a parent dominates the main mechanisms of JV control it would be expected that this parent would be more likely to view favourably the performance of the JV. Conversely, where a parent company does not dominate the main mechanisms of JV control, this parent would be less likely to view the performance of the JV in favourable terms. At a more disaggregated level, where the extent of management control is measured in terms of the decision-making responsibility of the parent (Killing, 1983), the subjective measure of satisfaction would be expected to be higher where the parent had decision-making responsibility. It follows that a similar argument applies to the focus of management control. Where the focus of management control is measured in terms of the most active partner in the set of management functions of the JV, the subjective measure of satisfaction would be expected to be higher in those JVs where the partner was the most active. In other words, those JVs where the partners have focused on particular aspects of management control will be given higher subjective values of performance. This reasoning leads to the second hypothesis:

*H2: Parents who dominate or have responsibility for management control will have a higher perceived level of satisfaction of JV performance than those parents who do not dominate or have responsibility for management control.*

According to Killing where the extent of management control is dominated by one partner, this should result in better performance than where the management of the joint venture is shared. The relationship between the various dimensions of management control and performance is, however, unlikely to be as clear-cut as Killing maintains. For some ventures, autonomy of the JV in terms of management control may produce the best performance outcomes. In other instances, a joint approach to decision-making may be appropriate. A JV may start off being managed jointly and after a period of time autonomy may be given to the JV management or one of the partners may adopt a dominant management position.

Yan and Gray (1994) have noted a number of dynamic aspects of JVs which appear to prompt shifts in a partner's bargaining power and trigger structural reconfigurations in JVs over time. These factors include partners' learning, the growth of a JV's own capacity, localization of the JV's operation, environmental changes, and JV performance, each of which can have a feedback effect on the partners' relative bargaining power and existing structure of control.

In terms of Figure 9.1, there is likely to be a feedback loop from performance to management control, with the former conditioning the nature of the latter over time. More fundamentally, there are likely to be a number of moderating variables, such as those identified by Yan and Gray (1994), which will affect the direct relationship between management control and performance. Some of these moderator variables will themselves be a function of the duration of the JV, such as partners' learning and the capacity of the JV to manage itself. These moderating variables, in consequence, are likely to significantly influence the management control variables. Thus, the mechanisms of control adopted by a partner may change over time, with one partner, for example, being more prepared to allow the other partner, or a third party, to appoint the general manager of the JV or the majority of the JV's managers. The extent of JV control may be reduced over time as one partner believes that the JV management has developed the appropriate skills for running the JV. Similarly, the focus or scope of control may be reduced or expanded by a partner, depending on the development of the partners' relative combinations of competencies and the growth of the JV mangers' skills.

The nature of management control exercised by parents will be a function of the age of the JV, with different configurations of control operating across the life cycle of the venture. Accepting that management control is a function of the duration of the JV, for a cross-section of JVs it would be expected that the observed nature of management control exercised by parents would vary with the age of the ventures. This is stated in the final hypothesis:

*H3: The observed nature of management control will vary with the duration of the joint ventures.*

## RESEARCH METHODS AND SAMPLE CHARACTERISTICS

This study involves UK partners of international JVs with partner firms from Western Europe, the United States and Japan, formed since 1980. A list of qualifying JVs was obtained from press announcements in the *Financial Times*. It was assumed that this sampling frame approximated to the population of qualifying JVs and that there would be minimal selection bias. It should be noted, however, that the qualifying JVs do not include those organized through national or international government agencies, particularly European Community programmes such as ESPRIT. This ensures that the sample was derived from JVs created from the free association of firms and not those encouraged by incentives provided by external agents.

To obtain the requisite level of detail on management control and performance, the UK partners had to be approached directly. Given time and cost constraints, a postal questionnaire was used to gather the data. The specialised nature of the desired information meant that participants had to be senior managers who were knowledgeable about the management and performance of the JV. A set of semi-structured interviews with a senior manager from each of eight UK partners helped to shape the form of the final questionnaire. Results from a pre-test questionnaire confirmed the appropriateness of the data collection instrument. To enhance the quality of the data, telephone contact was made with each UK partner to ascertain the name and position of the most appropriate senior manager to whom the questionnaire was personally addressed. The questionnaire cited the JV referred to in the *Financial Times* of which the UK firm was a partner, but invited the respondent to complete the questionnaire with respect to another JV with which they were more familiar, providing the foreign partner(s) was from either Western Europe, the USA or Japan, and that this JV had been formed since 1980. The request for information on the JV with which the respondent had the most detailed knowledge was intended to improve the quality of the data.

The 520 qualifying JVs recorded from the *Financial Times* involved 277 separate UK partner firms. Several firms proved impossible to contact either because they had been taken over and restructured or had gone out of business altogether. Other firms had moved location and could not be traced. In some of the firms contacted there was no longer anyone in employment with sufficient knowledge to provide the depth of answers the study required. This left a total of 203 UK partners to whom the questionnaire was administered in the autumn of 1992. In exchange for their participation in the study and to provide motivation and accurate responses, the respondents were assured of anonymity and were promised a summary report of the findings. After one reminder, 94 questionnaires were returned, a response rate of 46.3 per cent. About 18 per cent of the returned questionnaires involved ventures with more than one foreign partner. As Geringer (1991) pointed out, there may be difficulties associated with analyzing multiple partner JVs in that two-partner ventures may demonstrate significant differences from ventures with three or more partners. Hence, this study only concerns the single foreign partner JVs. A total of 29 responses concerned non-equity joint ventures (i.e. agreements between partners to cooperate in some way but which does not involve the creation of a new firm). Given the different nature of equity joint ventures and non-equity joint ventures and consequently differences in the way they are managed, for example, non-equity joint ventures often do not have a general manager (Glaister, 1995), this class of venture was not included in this study. Also, in recognizing that performance data for very new JVs might not be meaningful, Dussauge and Garrette (1995), for example, reported that experts had difficulty in evaluating the performance of recently established alliances in the aerospace industry, it was decided to analyze only those joint ventures that had been in existence for at least one year at the time the data was collected. The time span of the study is therefore 1980 to 1991.[2]

The sample consists of 51 JVs. The majority of JVs were formed with partners from Western Europe (26) followed by the USA (14) and Japan (11). A total of 33 JVs are in the manufacturing sector and 18 are in the tertiary sector. For the sample of JVs as a whole, 33 ventures were still in existence, while 18 JVs had been terminated. The average duration was 4.8 years. The average duration of surviving (non-terminated) JVs was 5.1 years, while the average duration of terminated JVs was 4.4 years.

## Management Control Variables

The measurement of the management control variables is summarised in Table 9.1. The prior literature makes it clear

*Table* 9.1 Measurement of variables and sample characteristics

| | |
|---|---|
| **Management control variables** | |
| *Mechanisms of control*: | |
| Source of management of the JV | A trichotomous variable according to whether: (i) the general manager of the JV was originally appointed from the UK parent and the source of the JV management team was mainly from the UK parent; (ii) the general manager of the JV was originally not appointed from either parent and the source of the JV management team was either drawn equally from both partners or was mainly recruited externally; (iii) the general manager of the JV was originally appointed from the foreign parent and the source of the JV management team was mainly from the foreign parent. |
| Original equity share | UK partner's original equity stake (i.e. at the time of the venture formation) was measured as a trichotomous variable depending on whether the UK partner had less than 50 per cent, exactly 50 per cent, or more than 50 per cent of the shareholding in the JV. |
| Current equity share | UK partner's relative equity shareholding at the time of data collection was measured as a trichotomous variable depending on the UK partner's then current equity stake in the venture according to whether the UK partner had less than 50 per cent, exactly 50 per cent, or more than 50 per cent of the shareholding in the JV. |

| | |
|---|---|
| *Extent of control*: | |
| Responsibility for product pricing, product design, production process, quality standards, replacing a functional manager | A trichotomous variable according to whether the decision making responsibility was: (i) with the JV alone; (ii) dominated by the UK parent; (iii) not dominated by the UK parent. |
| *Focus of control*: | |
| Most active in production management, R&D management and marketing management | A dichotomous variable according to whether the UK partner or the foreign partner was the most active. |
| **Performance measures** | |
| Satisfaction | Ordinal scale from 1 = 'very dissatisfied' to 5 = 'very satisfied'. |
| Cost–benefit | Ordinal scale from 1 = 'benefits  costs' to 3 = 'benefits < costs'. |
| Survival | Dichotomous variable measure according to whether the JV had been terminated (T) or not terminated (NT). |
| Duration | Measured in years from JV formation to either time of data collection or to date of termination. |

that a large number of variables may be employed to control a joint venture. In order to achieve some parsimony in terms of the number of variables under study, a representative set of control variables was identified from the literature as follows.

### *Mechanisms of Control*

The mechanisms of control were considered in terms of: (i) the source of the management of the JV; (ii) the original equity shareholding of UK parent (i.e. at the time of the venture formation); the current equity shareholding of the UK parent (i.e. at the time of data collection). Where the JV has been terminated, the current equity shareholding of the UK parent will be either 0 per cent, for instance, where the foreign partner has acquired the UK partner's equity share or the JV has been liquidated, or 100 per cent if the UK partner has acquired the foreign partner's equity in the JV.

### *Extent of Control*

UK partner respondents were asked to assess the jointness of decision-making regarding five operating decisions: product pricing, product design, production process, quality standards and replacing a functional manager (this draws on Killing's (1983) measure).

### *Focus of Control*

The focus of control was measured across a set of management function – production management, R&D management and marketing management – according to whether the UK partner or the foreign partner was the most active.

## Performance Measures

The measurement of the performance variables is summarised in Table 9.1. The subjective and objective performance measures were broadly derived in the manner followed by Geringer and Hebert (1991). Two *subjective measures* were obtained: (i) the UK parent's subjective level of overall satisfaction with the JV's overall performance; (ii) at a non-sequential point in the questionnaire, the respondent was asked whether the benefits to the UK parent's overall strategy from having the JV outweighed the costs of the JV (this was not a measure used by Geringer and Hebert (1991)).

Two *objective performance measures* were obtained: (i) JV *survival* was measured using a dichotomous variable based on the survival or non-survival (i.e. termination) of the JV from the time of its formation until the data collection point in 1992; (ii) JV *duration* was measured by the number of years between the JV's formation and either its termination or the collection of performance data, whichever came first.

## Data Analysis

The appropriate form of statistical analysis is determined by the shape of the underlying distribution of the data and the level of measurement of the data. As it cannot be assumed that the sampling distribution is normally distributed, this indicates that non-parametric analysis is appropriate. The level of measurement of the management control variables is essentially nominal. With the extent of control construct, for instance, the responsibility for control is classified as follows: JV management autonomous, UK partner dominant, UK partner not dominant.[3] The appropriate measure of association chosen to test H1 is Cramér's *V*. This is a measure of association based on chi-square.[4] The performance variables are at least ordinal scaled, apart from Survival, which may be interpreted as nominal scaled. There is, however, precedent for treating this variable as ordinal in statistical analysis (for example, Geringer and Hebert, 1991), hence, we treat this variable as ordinal here. The assumption that the data is ordinal scaled also indicates that non-parametric analysis is appropriate. Accordingly, H2 was tested by considering differences in mean rank of the subjective performance measures, and H3 was tested by considering differences in mean rank of the management control variables by employing the Mann–Whitney Test or the Kruskal–Wallis Test as appropriate. These non-parametric tests appear the most relevant given the measures used and the samples' and sub-samples' sizes.

## RESULTS AND DISCUSSION

There is no support for H1, which maintains that there will be stronger significant association between the dimensions of management control and the subjective measures of JV performance than between the dimensions of management control and the objective measures of JV performance. Table 9.2 shows that for the subjective measure of overall performance, only two of the measures of association with the dimensions of management control variables are significant. In contrast, four of the measures of association between the objective performance measure of survival and the dimensions of management control variables are significant. Neither the cost–benefit based subjective measure nor the objective measure of

*Table* 9.2 Measures of association between dimensions of control and JV performance (Cramér's *V*)

| | *Performance measures* | | | |
|---|---|---|---|---|
| | *Subjective* | | *Objective* | |
| *Dimensions of control* | *Overall satisfaction* | *Cost–benefit* | *Survival* | *Duration* |
| (i) Mechanisms of control | | | | |
| Management control | 0.40** | 0.19 | 0.15 | 0.45 |
| Equity control: | | | | |
| Original equity share | 0.36 | 0.18 | 0.21 | 0.41 |
| Current equity share | 0.36 | 0.26 | 0.53*** | 0.36 |
| (ii) Extent of control | | | | |
| Product pricing | 0.31 | 0.24 | 0.36** | 0.47 |
| Product design | 0.32 | 0.27 | 0.13 | 0.41 |
| Production process | 0.29 | 0.17 | 0.24 | 0.36 |
| Quality standards | 0.23 | 0.10 | 0.21 | 0.46 |
| Replacing functional manager | 0.25 | 0.17 | 0.34** | 0.42 |
| (iii) Focus of control | | | | |
| Production | 0.38 | 0.17 | 0.56*** | 0.56 |
| R&D | 0.40 | 0.23 | 0.13 | 0.67 |
| Marketing | 0.53** | 0.27 | 0.00 | 0.58 |

Approximate significance: **$p < 0.05$; ***$p < 0.01$.

duration evidence significant measures of association with the dimensions of management control variables. Clearly, for this sample the more direct subjective measure of overall performance evidences a greater degree of significant association with the dimensions of management control than does the more indirect subjective cost–benefit measure. The highly significant moderately strong association between current equity shareholding and JV survival is unsurprising. For terminated JVs, current equity shareholding will be either 0 per cent or 100 per cent which can be expected to strengthen the association between current equity shareholding and the survival variable.

It is interesting to speculate on the extent to which the findings relating to H1 might be the result of the nature of the operationalization of the variables rather than a strong underlying association.[5] A perceptual measure (management control) might have a stronger association with another perceptual measure (subjective performance measure) because they are both perceptual measures. Similarly, this might also explain the stronger association between current equity share (which is not a perceptual measure) and Survival (which is also not a perceptual measure). The degree to which JV performance measures may be more strongly associated because they are operationalized in a particular manner (perceptual or non-perceptual), and by implication more weakly associated because they are operationalized differently (perceptual and non-perceptual) has not been widely discussed in the JV literature. This issue appears to be worthy of further investigation in order to help clarify the fundamental strengths of relationships between management control and JV performance.

Evidence relating to H2, which maintains that parents who dominate or have responsibility for management control will have a higher perceived level of satisfaction of JV performance than those parents who do not dominate or have responsibility for management control, is set out in Tables 9.3 to 9.5 for each of the identified dimensions of management control. As far as the overall satisfaction measure is concerned there is some support for H2. For the mechanisms of control (Table 9.3) the mean rank of the overall satisfaction variable is significantly higher ($p < 0.05$) where the UK partner dominates

*Table* 9.3 Mechanisms of management control and measures of JV performance

| | | Performance measures | | | | | | | | | | | |
|---|---|---|---|---|---|---|---|---|---|---|---|---|---|
| | | Subjective | | | | | | Objective | | | | | |
| | | Overall satisfaction | | | Cost–benefit | | | Survival | | | Duration | | |
| *Mechanisms of control* | *n* | *Mean rank* | *Chi-square* | *d.f.* | *Mean rank* | *Chi-square* | *d.f.* | *Mean rank* | *Chi-square* | *d.f.* | *Mean rank* | *Chi-square* | *d.f.* |
| *Management control* | | | | | | | | | | | | | |
| Dominant | 13 | 35.62 | | | 20.69 | | | 29.12 | | | 25.65 | | |
| Equal | 27 | 21.87 | | | 27.61 | | | 24.61 | | | 25.39 | | |
| Subordinant | 11 | 24.77 | 8.192** | 2 | 28.32 | 3.137 | 2 | 25.73 | 1.182 | 2 | 27.91 | 0.242 | 2 |
| *Equity control* | | | | | | | | | | | | | |
| Original equity share | | | | | | | | | | | | | |
| < 50 per cent | 12 | 22.75 | | | 28.25 | | | 25.33 | | | 29.79 | | |
| = 50 per cent | 29 | 22.66 | | | 25.19 | | | 23.36 | | | 23.66 | | |
| > 50 per cent | 8 | 36.88 | 7.104** | 2 | 19.44 | 2.156 | 2 | 30.44 | 2.27 | 2 | 22.69 | 1.871 | 2 |
| Current equity share | | | | | | | | | | | | | |
| < 50 per cent | 21 | 19.52 | | | 29.55 | | | 18.33 | | | 27.24 | | |
| = 50 per cent | 18 | 27.17 | | | 22.14 | | | 22.14 | | | 22.64 | | |
| > 50 per cent | 10 | 32.60 | 6.81** | 2 | 20.60 | 5.198* | 2 | 26.15 | 13.426*** | 2 | 24.55 | 1.04 | 2 |

*$p < 0.1$; ** $p < 0.05$; *** $p < 0.01$.

in the source of management, where the UK partner's original equity share exceeds 50 per cent, and where the current equity share exceeds 50 per cent.

For the extent of control variables (Table 9.4) the mean rank of overall satisfaction of JV performance is highest in three of the five operational decisions where the UK partner dominates and highest in the other two decisions where the JV management has autonomy, although the difference in means is significant in only two of the five decisions: product pricing ($p < 0.05$) and production process ($p < 0.1$). For the cost–benefit measure the best level of performance is achieved in four cases where the UK partners dominate (note the lower the absolute number for this measure the better the perceived performance) and in only one case where the JV management have autonomy, although the mean ranks are significantly different in only two cases: product pricing ($p < 0.1$) and product design ($p < 0.05$).

For the focus of control variables (Table 9.5), in each of the three management areas the highest mean rank of satisfaction with overall JV performance is found where UK partners focus on control, although there is a significant difference in mean ranks in only two of the three cases: production management ($p < 0.1$) and marketing management ($p < 0.01$). The cost–benefit measure shows that across the three management areas the best level of performance occurs where the UK partners have the focus of control, although the differences in mean ranks are not significant.

Evidence relating to H3, which maintains that the nature of management control will vary with the duration of the joint venture, is shown in Tables 9.3 to 9.5. There is no support for H3. For the mechanisms of control (Table 9.3) the mean rank (duration) of the JVs is lowest in those JVs where the source of management is equal for both partners. The older JVs are associated with either dominant control or subordinate control as far as the UK partner is concerned. For both the original equity shareholding and current equity shareholding variables, the highest mean rank of JV is associated with UK partner equity share below 50 per cent. For original equity shareholding the lowest mean rank is associated with UK partner equity share above 50 per cent. For current equity shareholding the lowest mean rank is associated with a 50–50

*Table* 9.4 Extent of management control and measures of JV performance

| | | *Performance measures* | | | | | | | | | | | |
|---|---|---|---|---|---|---|---|---|---|---|---|---|---|
| | | *Subjective* | | | | | | *Objective* | | | | | |
| | | *Overall satisfaction* | | | *Cost–benefit* | | | *Survival* | | | *Duration* | | |
| *Extent of control* | *n* | *Mean rank* | *Chi-square* | *d.f.* | *Mean rank* | *Chi-square* | *d.f.* | *Mean rank* | *Chi-square* | *d.f.* | *Mean rank* | *Chi-square* | *d.f.* |
| *Product pricing* | | | | | | | | | | | | | |
| JV autonomous | 18 | 25.92 | | | 27.08 | | | 26.50 | | | 27.39 | | |
| UK partner dominant | 12 | 35.29 | | | 18.63 | | | 32.88 | | | 27.29 | | |
| UK partner not dominant | 21 | 20.76 | 7.867** | 2 | 29.29 | 5.701* | 2 | 21.64 | 6.406** | 2 | 24.07 | 0.620 | 2 |
| *Product design* | | | | | | | | | | | | | |
| JV autonomous | 14 | 31.86 | | | 21.82 | | | 25.89 | | | 24.29 | | |
| UK partner dominant | 9 | 26.83 | | | 20.17 | | | 29.33 | | | 29.33 | | |
| UK partner not dominant | 28 | 22.80 | 3.770 | 2 | 29.96 | 6.272** | 2 | 24.98 | 0.853 | 2 | 25.79 | 0.665 | 2 |
| *Production process* | | | | | | | | | | | | | |
| JV | 16 | 31.88 | | | 23.00 | | | 27.03 | | | 21.16 | | |

| | | | | | | | | | | | | | |
|---|---|---|---|---|---|---|---|---|---|---|---|---|---|
| autonomous UK partner dominant | 8 | 27.75 | | | 24.13 | | | 31.81 | | | 28.06 | | |
| UK partner not dominant | 27 | 22.00 | 4.922* | 2 | 28.33 | 2.020 | 2 | 23.67 | 2.867 | 2 | 28.26 | 2.555 | 2 |
| *Quality standards* | | | | | | | | | | | | | |
| JV | 17 | 27.24 | | | 27.68 | | | 24.50 | | | 23.41 | | |
| autonomous UK partner dominant | 12 | 31.21 | | | 23.38 | | | 30.75 | | | 27.25 | | |
| UK partner not dominant | 22 | 22.20 | 3.261 | 2 | 26.14 | 0.829 | 2 | 24.75 | 2.34 | 2 | 27.32 | 0.798 | 2 |
| *Replacing functional manager* | | | | | | | | | | | | | |
| JV | 10 | 27.00 | | | 26.60 | | | 19.70 | | | 24.10 | | |
| autonomous UK partner dominant | 11 | 33.00 | | | 21.36 | | | 32.68 | | | 24.64 | | |
| UK partner not dominant | 30 | 23.10 | 3.910 | 2 | 27.50 | 1.947 | 2 | 25.65 | 5.887* | 2 | 27.13 | 0.444 | 2 |

$*p < 0.1$; $**p < 0.05$.

shareholding. However, none of the differences in means are significant.

For the extent of control variables (Table 9.4) the lowest mean rank is recorded in four of the five decision areas where the JV management has autonomy. The mean rank is highest in those JVs where either the UK partner or the foreign partner dominates the particular decision area. It should be noted, however, that the differences in mean ranks are not statistically significant.

For the focus of control variables (Table 9.5) the highest mean rank for duration is found in those JVs where the UK partner has responsibility for production management and R&D management. In contrast, the mean rank is highest in those JVs where the foreign partners focus on marketing management. However, the mean ranks are not significantly different.

Overall, the finding that there are no significant differences in the mean ranks of the JVs across the dimensions of management control clearly indicates that there is a lack of support for H3 from this study. Nevertheless, these findings are somewhat counter-intuitive, particularly with regard to the extent of control variables, as they indicate that as a JV matures, the JV managers obtain less autonomy over the identified key operating decisions, with the extent of control being vested in one or other of the partners. As the JV evolves it would be expected that its operating capacity would improve (Yan and Gray, 1994) with, *ceteris paribus*, a reconfiguring of control in favour of the JV managers. Albeit on statistically weak evidence, this does not appear to be the case in this sample, which demonstrates a counter trend – as the JV evolves, control is taken from the JV managers and rests more with the parent companies. As Yan and Gray (1994) note there may be a number of reasons for reconfiguring the management control of the JV through time, including partners' learning, environmental changes and the level of performance. The role of these variables, and others, on the configuration of management control through time and how they effect partner dominance and JV autonomy are clearly worthy of further study.

*Table 9.5* Focus of management control and measures of JV performance

| *Focus of control* | *n* | *Performance measures* | | | | | | | |
|---|---|---|---|---|---|---|---|---|---|
| | | *Subjective* | | | | *Objective* | | | |
| | | *Overall satisfaction* | | *Cost–benefit* | | *Survival* | | *Duration* | |
| | | *Mean rank* | *Mann–Whitney U* | *Mean rank* | *Mann–Whitney U* | *Mean rank* | *Mann–Whitney U* | *Mean rank* | *Mann–Whitney U* |
| *Production* | | | | | | | | | |
| UK partner | 16 | 17.00 | | 13.72 | | 17.38 | | 15.97 | |
| Foreign partner | 12 | 11.17 | 56.0* | 15.54 | 83.5 | 10.00 | 42.0** | 12.54 | 72.5 |
| *R&D* | | | | | | | | | |
| UK partner | 1[illegible] | 15.27 | | 11.36 | | 13.95 | | 14.55 | |
| Foreign partner | 14 | 11.21 | 52.0 | 14.29 | 59.0 | 12.25 | 66.5 | 11.79 | 60.0 |
| *Marketing* | | | | | | | | | |
| UK partner | 15 | 26.03 | | 17.03 | | 20.00 | | 17.60 | |
| Foreign partner | 24 | 16.23 | 89.5*** | 21.85 | 135.5 | 20.00 | 180.0 | 21.50 | 144.0 |

* $p < 0.1$; ** $p < 0.05$; *** $p < 0.01$.

## SUMMARY AND CONCLUSIONS

The objective of this chapter was to consider the JV control–performance relationship by exploring the relationship between the various dimensions of management control and both subjective and objective measures of JV performance. In presenting these findings, the paper seeks to add to the JV literature on JV management and performance. There is some support for one of the hypotheses of the study, i.e. H2, that parents who dominate or have responsibility for management control will have a higher perceived level of satisfaction of JV performance than those parents who do not dominate or have responsibility for management control. There is no support for H1, i.e. that there will be a stronger significant association between the dimensions of management control and the subjective measures of JV performance than between the dimensions of management control and the objective measures of JV performance, or H3, which maintains that the nature of management control will vary with the duration of the JV, a finding which is rather surprising. It may be noted, however, that there is likely to be a complex interaction between duration and management control. On the one hand, duration (as a measure of JV performance) is dependent on the nature of management control. Yet, the nature of management control adopted for the JV is likely to be a function of the duration of the venture, i.e. duration in this case is a moderating variable on management control, if not an independent variable (Yan and Gray, 1994). The exact specification of this relationship may, therefore, be difficult to determine.

What this chapter has not been able to demonstrate is a clear relationship between the nature of management control and performance outcomes. This remains a challenge in JV research. More fundamentally, this study (as with most of the prior research in the area) has been limited to a direct test of the JV control–performance relationship without taking account of, or controlling for, other variables (Geringer and Hebert, 1989). In particular, Geringer and Hebert (1989) have stressed the need to consider the influence of the parents' strategy and structure on the control–performance relationship in the manner pioneered by Franko (1971).

There are a number of caveats associated with the findings of this study. This study concerns JVs between partners from developed countries, hence the findings may not be generalisable to MNE-host partner JVs in developing countries. More fundamentally, managerial control is an organisationally sophisticated and complex process which has been measured in a number of rather crude ways. For instance, the study tends to focus on formal control mechanisms, partly because these are easier to measure, and thereby neglects the importance of informal control mechanisms (Yan and Gray, 1994). Examining management control over a number of dimensions obviously involves a large number of variables. Indeed, the number of variables that could be examined are more numerous than those identified in this study (see Glaister, 1995, for a more complete list). This poses a problem in terms of identifying a parsimonious set of measures of management control which remains a challenge for future research, made complicated by the fact that the overall control of the JV is a composite of all mechanisms of control and decision making control (Cullen *et al.*, 1995). It should also be noted that the performance outcomes of the joint ventures may be conditioned by factors beyond the way in which the JVs are managed, for example, they may be conditioned more by the nature of the core resources brought to the venture by each partner, and the pressing nature of the competitive environment in which the JV operates.[6]

A further caveat lies in the study's lack of control for other important variables bearing on the control–performance relationship. Future studies should move beyond direct tests of the JV control–performance relationship, as examined in this chapter and, as advocated by Geringer and Hebert (1989), seek to take account of other variables, especially the parents' strategy structure fit and the cultural process of management control.

**Acknowledgements**

The authors would like to thank the anonymous referees for their constructive comments on earlier versions of this paper.

## Notes

1. Geringer and Hebert (1991) found a significant and positive correlation between objective and subjective measures of performance: objective measures of survival, duration and stability were found to be positively correlated, although not perfectly, with parent firms' reported satisfaction with JV performance, and with perceptions of the extent to which a JV performed relative to its initial objectives. An attempt was made to replicate these findings with the data set reported here (Glaister and Buckley, 1998). Although a significant and positive correlation was obtained between subjective measures of performance and the objective measure of survival, no significant correlations were obtained between subjective performance measures and the objective performance measures of duration and stability. These findings should be borne in mind when interpreting the results of this study.
2. It is apparent that this study relies on data collected from one parent. The extent to which data collected from one element of the alliance – one parent or the alliance general manager – represents a reliable measure of alliance performance was a topic of concern in the study by Geringer and Hebert (1991). Geringer and Hebert concluded from their analysis that where it is only possible to obtain responses from one of the partners, 'use of a single respondent per JV appears to allow researchers to obtain fairly reliable and efficient data for overall JV performance' (Geringer and Hebert, 1991, p. 261). The findings of Geringer and Hebert provide some justification for the research method adopted here and confidence in the performance data so obtained.
3. With respect to the extent of control, it may be argued that the category 'JV autonomous' is actually part of the category 'UK partner not dominant'. While this is obviously the case, to conflate 'JV autonomous' and 'Foreign parent dominant' to the 'UK parent not dominant' variable, obscures the actual extent of control in many JVs, and permits less to be known about the relationship between the extent of control and performance measures.
4. Cramér's $V$ is always between 0 and 1.
5. We are grateful to one of the anonymous referees for suggesting this point.
6. A number of other variables bear on joint venture performance, which can be categorized as environmental, partner characteristics, and strategic and operational variables. While these variables have some bearing on the topic of this chapter, they are substantial enough in themselves to warrant an examination in their own right. This chapter, therefore, does not consider the effect of these variables on joint venture performance. The relationship between these variables and the satisfaction of joint venture performance is analyzed by the authors for the sample reported here in a separate paper (Glaister and Buckley, 1996b).

## References

Anderson, E. (1990) 'Two firms, one frontier: On assessing joint venture performance', *Sloan Management Review*, 31, 2, 19–30.

Awadzi, W., Kedia, B. L., and Chinta, R. (1986) 'Performance implications of locus of control and complementary resources in international joint ventures – an empirical study', Presented at Academy of International Business Conference, London.

Beamish, P. W. (1984) 'Joint venture performance in developing countries', Unpublished doctoral dissertation, Canada, University of Western Ontario, London, Ontario.

——(1985) 'The characteristics of joint ventures in developed and developing countries', *Columbia Journal of World Business*, 20, 3, 13–19.

——and Delios, A. (1997a) 'Incidence and propensity of alliance formation', in P. W. Beamish and J. P. Killing (eds), *Co-operative strategies: Asian Pacific perspectives* (chapter 4, pp. 91–114). New Lexington Press: San Francisco.

——and A. Delios (1997b) 'Improving joint venture performance through congruent measures of success', in P. W. Beamish and J. P. Killing (eds), *Co-operative strategies: European perspectives* (chapter 5, pp. 103–27). New Lexington Press: San Francisco.

Behrman, J. (1970) *National interest and the multinational enterprise*. Prentice-Hall: New York.

Blodgett, L. L. (1992) 'Factors in the instability of international joint ventures: An event history analysis', *Strategic Management Journal*, 13, 475–81.

Cameron, K. S. (1986) 'Effectiveness as paradox', *Management Science*, 32, 539–53.

Chakravarthy, B. S. (1986) 'Measuring strategic performance', *Strategic Management Journal*, 7, 437–58.

Child, J., Y. Yan and Y. Lu (1997) 'Ownership and control in sino-foreign joint ventures', in P. W. Beamish and J. P. Killing (eds), *Co-operative strategies: Asian Pacific perspectives* (chapter 8, pp. 181–225). New Lexington Press: San Francisco.

Chowdhury, J. (1992) 'Performance of international joint ventures and wholly owned foreign subsidiaries: A comparative perspective', *Management International Review*, 32, 115–33.

Contractor, F. J. and P. Lorange (1988) 'Why should firms co-operate? The strategic and economics basis for co-operative ventures', in F. J. Contractor and P. Lorange (eds), *Co-operative strategies in international business*. Lexington, MA: Lexington Books.

Cullen, J. B., J. L. Johnson and T. Sakano (1995) 'Japanese and local partner commitment to IJVs: Psychological consequences of outcomes and investments in the IJV relationship', *Journal of International Business Studies*, 26, 1, 91–115.

Dussauge, P. and B. Garrette (1995) 'Determinants of success in international strategic alliances: Evidence from the global aerospace industry', *Journal of International Business Studies*, 26, 3, 505–30.

Eccles, R. G. (1991) 'The performance measurement manifesto', *Harvard Business Review*, Jan.–Feb., 131–37.

Franko, L. G. (1971) *Joint venture survival in multinational corporations*. Praeger: New York.

Friedman, W. G. and J. P. Beguin (1971) *Joint international business ventures in developing countries*. Columbia University Press: New York.

Geringer, J. M. (1986) 'Criteria for selecting partners for joint ventures in industrialized market economices', Ph.D. dissertation, Seattle: University of Washington.

——(1988) *Joint venture partner selection: Strategies for developed countries*. Quorum Books: Westport, CT.

——(1990) *Trends and traits of Canadian joint ventures*. Investment Canada: Ottawa.

——(1991) 'Strategic determinants of partner selection criteria in International Joint Ventures', *Journal of International Business*, 22, 1, 41–62.

——and L. Hébert (1989) 'Control and performance of international joint ventures', *Journal of International Business*, 20, 2, 235–54.

——and L. Hébert (1991) 'Measuring performance of international joint ventures', *Journal of International Business Studies*, 22, 2, 249–63.

Glaister, K. W. (1995) 'Dimensions of control in UK international joint ventures', *British Journal of Management*, 6, 2, 77–96.

——and P. J. Buckley (1996a) 'Strategic motives for international alliance formation', *Journal of Management Studies*, 33, 3, 301–32.

——and P. J. Buckley (1996b) 'Success factors and performance in UK international strategic alliances', mimeo.

——and P. J. Buckley (1998) 'Measures of performance in UK international alliances', *Organization Studies*, 19, 1, 89–118.

Gomes-Casseres, B. (1987) 'Joint venture instability: Is it a problem?', *Columbia Journal of World Business*, 22, 2, 97–107.

Goodman, P. and J. Pennings (1980) 'Critical issues in assessing organisational effectiveness', in E. Lawler, D. Nadler and C. Cammann (eds), *Organisational assessment*. Wiley-Interscience: New York.

Gray, B. and A. Yan (1992) 'A negotiations model of joint venture formation, structure and performance: Implications for global management', *Advances in International Comparative Management*, 7, 41–75.

Gullander, S. (1976) 'Joint ventures and corporate strategy', *Columbia Journal of World Business, Spring*, 104–14.

Harrigan, K. R. (1985) *Strategies for joint ventures*. Lexington Books: Lexington, MA.

——(1988) 'Strategic alliances and partner asymmetries', in F. J. Contractor and P. Lorange (eds.), *Co-operative strategies in international business*. Lexington Books: Lexington, MA.

Inkpen, A. C. and J. Birkinshaw (1994) 'International joint ventures and performance: An interorganizational perspective', *International Business Review*, 3, 3, 201–17.

Jacobson, R. (1987) 'The validity of ROI as a measure of business performance', *American Economic Review*, 77, 470–78.

Janger, A. R. (1980) *Organisation of international joint ventures*. Conference Board: New York.

Killing, J. P. (1983) *Strategies for joint venture success*. Praeger: New York.

Kogut, B. (1988a) 'A study of the life cycle of joint ventures', in F. J. Contractor and P. Lorange (eds), *Co-operative strategies in international business*. Lexington Books: Lexington, MA.

——(1988) 'Joint ventures: Theoretical and empirical perspectives', *Strategic Management Journal*, 9, 319–32.

Lecraw, D. J. (1983) 'Performance of transnational corporations in less developed countries', *Journal of International Business Studies*, 14, 1, 15–33.

Lee, C. and P. W. Beamish (1995) 'The characteristics and performance of Korean joint ventures in LDCs', *Journal of International Business Studies*, 26, 3, 637–54.

Lewin, A. Y. and J. W. Minton (1986) 'Determining organisational effectiveness: Another look and an agenda for research', *Management Science*, 32, 514–38.

Lin, J. L., C.-M. J. Yu and D.-H. W. Seeto (1997) 'Motivations, partners' contributions, and control of international joint ventures', in P. W. Beamish and J. P. Killing (eds), *Co-operative strategies: Asian Pacific perspectives* (chapter 5, pp. 115–34). New Lexington Press: San Francisco.

Madhok, A. (1995) 'Revisiting multinational firms' tolerance for joint ventures: A trust-based approach', *Journal of International Business Studies*, 26, 1, 117–37.

Otterbeck, L. (1981) 'The management of joint ventures', in L. Otterbeck (ed.), *The management of headquarters subsidiary relationships in multinational corporations*. Gower: Aldershot.

Parkhe, A. (1993) '"Messy" research, methodological predispositions, and theory development in international joint ventures', *Academy of Management Review*, 18, 2, 227–68.

Porter, M. E. and M. B. Fuller (1986) 'Coalitions and global strategy', in M. E. Porter (ed), *Competition in global industries*. Boston, MA: Harvard Business School Press.

Rafii, F. (1978) 'Joint ventures and transfer of technology to Iran: The impact of foreign control', Unpublished doctoral dissertation, Harvard University.

Schaan, J.-L. (1983) 'Parent control and joint venture success: The case of Mexico', Unpublished doctoral dissertation, University of Western Ontario, London, Ontario, Canada.

——(1988) 'How to control a joint venture even as a minority partner', *Journal of General Management*, 14, 4–16.

Stopford, J. M., and L. T. Wells (1972) *Managing the multinational enterprise*. Basic Books: New York.

Tomlinson, J. W. C. (1970) *The joint venture process in international business: India and Pakistan*. Cambridge, MA: MIT Press.

Varadarajan, N. and V. Ramanujam (1990) 'The corporate performance conundrum: A synthesis of contemporary views and an extension', *Journal of Management Studies*, 27, 5, 463–83.

Venkatraman, N. and V. Ramanujam (1986) 'The measurement of business performance in strategy research: A comparison of approaches', *Academy of Management Review*, 11, 801–14.

Yan, A. and B. Gray (1994) 'Bargaining power, management control, and performance in United States–China joint ventures: A comparative case study', *Academy of Management Journal*, 37, 6, 1478–517.

# 10 The Use of Native Categories in Management Research*

Peter J. Buckley and
Malcolm Chapman

**This chapter derives from the research project 'The Management of Cooperative Strategies', currently being undertaken by the authors.[1] The authors are, respectively, a social anthropologist and an economist, who are trying to allow their different subject backgrounds to interact within the context of the research, and this chapter is one result of this interaction. 'Native categories', or at least the idea of them under various other names, are an important notion within social anthropology, and this chapter attempts to explore the usefulness, or otherwise, of the same idea within management research.**

## NATIVE CATEGORIES

By 'native' in this chapter, we mean self-generated and valid in any local context – be it the head office of a multinational or the settlement of a Native American tribe in the Amazon forest. Social anthropologists are deeply interested in 'native categories' in this broadest of senses. A social anthropologist would typically take the view that every society (however defined) had its own specific words and categories, which were, at every level, socially derived and mediated; there can, from this perspective, be no guarantee that words and categories will be congruent from one society to the next:

* First published in *British Journal of Management*, 8, 4 (1997)

'A degree of relativism must then have the status of a heuristic hypothesis' (Ardener, 1989a, p. 11). A social anthropologist would usually extend this perspective to all the categories of analysis imposed by the would-be 'objective' social analysts of the western world. In this respect, social anthropology differs markedly from economics: economics has tended to regard its own analytical categories as culturally transcendent, and not potentially subject to relativistic scepticism.

In the early decades of the development of social anthropology, within the civilizing assumptions of Empire and missionary work, European visitors to what were called primitive societies tended to travel with a conviction of their own superior civilization, and of their own superior rationality. Travellers' accounts, as well as some early ethnographic work, document this very clearly. Indeed, under the evolutionary and historicist assumptions prevailing at the time, it was given in the dominant paradigm of interpretation that primitive societies were, precisely, behind and backward in the inevitable path of social development – the lucky observer was, of course, in front.

With the appearance of professional anthropologists in the first decade or so of this century, and the institutionalization of the subject in Great Britain through the activities of Malinowski and Radcliffe-Brown, some aspects of this early evolutionary triumphalism, with its often crass ethnocentricity, became unfashionable. Analysts working within the functionalist and structural-functionalist paradigms, roughly from about 1920 until the early 1960s, perceived their task to be one of seeing reality through 'native' eyes, and giving expression to this reality. At the same time, however, they also perceived their activity as 'scientific', an exercise in the objective classification and study of other peoples; in this scientific activity, they generated a range of analytical categories which were not in any obvious sense derived from the peoples under study, but were assumed to be transcendent of cultural variation, residing rather in scientific objectivity of a universal kind. There was, then, an interesting tension between the commitment to the replication of *native* understanding, and the parallel commitment to the generation of scientific analytical categories; this tension gradually built up, and exploded in a classic series of denunciations, from the heart of anthropology, of its own practices. Confidence in the growth of the objective science, assumed in advance in the early days, and variously announced or partially realized, rather suddenly collapsed. The analytical categories which had been developed came, again rather suddenly, to look like no more than the imposition of one's own categories upon alien phenomena. This came to seem not only intellectually presumptuous, but also analytically unhelpful. Many of the major theoretical debates in social anthropology have been around these issues, such that any more lengthy discussion would involve a discussion of social anthropology in its entirety. All the major figures of post-war British anthropology have contributed importantly in this area. The result was an ever-greater commitment to the categories of analysis and understanding, the 'classifications', of the people under study, and a constant attempt to avoid the imposition of inappropriate modes of thought.

It was through the classification of people, in what came to be called 'kinship systems', that the issue was first fought through. Categories that were self-evident, to all appearances part of the natural order, in European society (like father, son, daughter, mother), turned out not to exist in all societies (see Needham, 1971); they were categories created by a particular social form, not transcendent biological realities. The kinship example developed many complexities, too much so for discussion here. What is important here is that the kinship example brought to the fore the analytical problem to which Hocart, in 1937, gave an early expression:

> how can we make progress in the understanding of cultures, ancient or modern, if we persist in dividing what the people join and in joining what they keep apart? (Hocart, 1970, p. 23)

As time went by, analysts began to notice that attempts to analyse alien societies using the categories of the observer often led to confusion; this confusion, moreover, cleared up miraculously if the native categories were taken seriously, as expressive of their own reality. In some areas of analysis, this was a simple pragmatic issue – one kind of analysis worked, another did not. Some of the most vivid examples were in the field of kinship and totemism (see for example Lévi-Strauss,

1949, 1962; Leach, 1961; Needham, 1962), but the problem has invaded all areas of cross-cultural analysis, at least as practised by social anthropologists.

The pragmatic issue – what kind of analysis *worked*? – was accompanied by some profound and disturbing philosophical issues: perhaps the categories of analysis that the western observer brought to the situation were no more objective, no more real, no more 'given in the world', than those of the 'natives'; perhaps the educated Anglophone usages were no more than native categories themselves. It is more or less from this position that the authors are approaching the problem. We are making the *assumption* that the categories of understanding used by the people under study are their own best solution. We are making the assumption that social reality is socially created, and not necessarily amenable to objective analysis, where objectivity is determined by the analyst rather than the people under study.

This throws us directly into some of the major philosophical debates of the twentieth century. A social anthropologist might want to say this: studying societies by attempting to pay attention to native categories, and showing these categories both empirical and theoretical respect, has proved to be enormously successful in the study of other cultures by social anthropologists of western European and North American origin. Purely pragmatically, many areas of difficulty were resolved. This has been increasingly demonstrated from the first attempts in this direction (whether these are attributed to Malinowski in 1921, to Hocart in 1937 or to Evans-Pritchard in 1937). The question of whether there remain *objective social realities* which are amenable to positivistic study can perhaps be left open at this stage, while the pragmatic success of attention to native categories can be accepted. Attention to native categories (where everyone everywhere is a native, including, in their different ways, Western academics and Western managers) has been social anthropology's major contribution to twentieth-century thought – disguised as functionalism, structuralism, deconstruction or however it might have been. The idea is a very powerful one: the study of forms of classification, or of native categories, has come to be almost coterminous for some practitioners with social anthropology itself (see Ardener, 1989a; Crick, 1976; Parkin, 1982; Overing, 1985). It is an idea which has been only fitfully applied, however, in mainstream business and management studies. There have been, of course, and are, hermeneutic and interpretive traditions within management studies, and these are relevant to our own discussion; these traditions have their greatest depth within the field broadly known as organization studies (for a discussion of the relevant paradigm shift in this field, see Burrell and Morgan, 1979), under the influence of more broadly sociological thought. Many areas of business and management studies are still, however, only little affected by these developments (for a discussion of this point, and for an important step forward, see Boyacigiller and Adler, 1991). In the bulk of management research, the assumption is usually made that study should be, and is, objective, with the categories of observation and analysis predetermined by the scientific observer.

## THE OBJECTIVITY OF WESTERN MANAGEMENT STUDIES

The search for objectivity, the claim to objectivity and the (often rather casual) assumption of objectivity, are very dominant features of management science. It might seem that what native categories offer is simply an alternative to this dominant orthodoxy – an alternative which could (in the language of the age) be variously called ideographic, subjective, interpretive, hermeneutic, phenomenological, symbolic, ethnomethodological, and so on.

The picture is more complicated than this, however. The case can be made that western management science has never been objective: it has, rather, consisted of an ad hoc mixture of categories generated by the observer and by the observed, where both observer and observed shared a great deal of their knowledge and understanding – shared, that is, native categories (Boyacigiller and Adler, 1991) In this light, what we have is not objectivity, but rather a spontaneously appropriate subjectivity.

A crude illustration might help. Suppose a study of people based upon a set of categories – policeman, baker, butcher, stockbroker, plumber, school teacher. Suppose that those conducting the study had defined these in advance, so that they could generate observations concerning them (prevalence, proportions and the like), and suppose that the society they were studying was their own – one in which these categories were a normal part of the daily life, perception and self-perception, of everybody concerned. The research workers had no problem going out and counting the butchers, the bakers, the candlestick-makers…

Suppose that the research workers imagined that their work was entirely objective, and that their categories of analysis were scientific, culture-free, transcendent. Suppose that they generated a set of apparently 'objective' data about the statistical prevalence and characteristics of the various categories of people that they were trying to study. These became very useful in plotting social trends, organizing policies, and so on. Suppose that the research workers attributed this success entirely to their successful objectivity, when it was in fact largely owing to their thoughtlessly shared subjectivity – the categories which they used for analysis *were* the native categories. Suppose then that the research workers decided that it was time to do some cross-cultural analysis.

They had grown used to attributing their analytical success at home to their objective, positivist and scientific stance. They went to other cultures expecting this method to work in the new context. They pursued objectivity. Remember, however, that their earlier success had in fact been based upon an unacknowledged sensitivity to local categories, not upon objectivity at all. What they needed in the new context was a new set of categories appropriate to the new culture – a new set of native categories; what they *thought* they needed was ever-tighter definition of the supposedly objective set of categories that they had brought from their indigenous culture. The true source of their original insights remained unexplored, and the cause of their problem was perceived to be its solution; the harder they pressed on the accelerator, the slower they went. They went into other cultures where there were no such simple things as policemen, bakers, school teachers, and they tried to find them. Confusion and disappointment reigned.

One of the academic subjects which underpins modern management studies is social psychology. This is an essentially monocultural subject, born and brought to strength in the

USA (Smith and Bond, 1993). It is also a (supposedly) positivist, objectivist subject. After some decades of contented study of the society from which it sprang, social psychology began to feel a need to carry out cross-cultural studies. It then began to experience all the problems already described. Social psychology, and its attempt to transform itself into cross-cultural psychology, could be taken as one model for the illustration given above. The authors take the view that it was the cultural appropriateness of social psychology to the North American context which was the source of its strength, not its objective and scientific detachment. Because, however, social psychologists attributed their strength precisely to this detachment, they attempted to replicate this in new cultural contexts, and encountered many unforeseen difficulties. The largely still-born nature of cross-cultural psychology can be attributed to this problem, experienced at all manner of conceptual and interpretive levels.

Smith and Bond (1993), social psychologists themselves, have given a thorough and detailed demonstration of the rather general *failure* of social psychology to generate cross-culturally valid procedures and concepts. Ghoshal and Westney, in a general discussion of the study of organizations, have said:

> modern organisation theory has been dominated by Americans, and ethnocentrism has characterised the theory. (Ghoshal and Westney, 1993, p. 6)

On this basis, we can argue that positivist objective study has been carried out by western management and business researchers rather less frequently than might be supposed. Research within this field has typically contained within it an unacknowledged, and untheorized, debt to native categories. Why not, however, simply carry on as we are, if this is the case? If the majority of research within our own culture already depends, whether it knows it or not, on a sophisticated apprehension of the relevant native categories, why not allow this to continue? We might recognize the need for the use of native categories in cross-cultural research, or research in alien cultures, but if we have been writing prose all our lives without knowing it, why stop now, just because we have found out?

These are good questions, and full replies are not given here.[2] The research on which the authors are engaged is predominantly a British-based project, with British researchers working on companies based in Britain (mostly British companies). It does involve, however, some degree of cross-cultural comparison, involving French case studies. In the British context, it might seem as though the native categories problem would solve itself for British researchers, and so it does to a remarkable degree. Nevertheless, the problem needs bringing to consciousness. Management research, when conducted monoculturally, has typically disguised itself as positivist objectivism; in fact, however, it has always depended upon a background of shared knowledge, of native categories. This means that discussion of problems of understanding is constantly muddied by cross-currents, by dissonance between what is actually happening in research and what is thought to be happening. When the French research is introduced, then a rather different cultural universe is opened, and the question of native categories leaps to the fore.[3]

Even remaining within the British context, however, the issue remains important. Cultures are not homogeneous (although the term culture, and its definition, sometimes seem to imply this by tautology; it depends how we use the term). If we are British, other British people are not always transparent to us – far from it. There are many fractures within our shared understanding – fractures between social classes, regions, sexes, ages, ethnicities, occupations, companies, organizations and so on. We have grown used to talking of corporate culture, of ethnic culture. The management researcher, bred on university life of a social scientific kind (say) does not necessarily share all his or her conceptual world with a middle manager with wide experience of production technologies in the pharmaceutical industry. We could say, perhaps, that the problem of native categories raises itself at the subcultural level just as importantly (if not perhaps as strongly) as at the cultural level.[4]

It is with this conviction that the two authors of this chapter are approaching their research. Most of the research on the questions that they are tackling has been objectivist and positivist. This has manifested itself in many ways, but a great deal of the research is structured according to the hypothetico-deductive paradigm (the formal dress of positivism). A problem is defined, questions are designed, hypotheses are formulated and tested, results are announced. Let us suppose that the object of research is a group of managers – there have to be enough to allow for statistical significance, as though people in themselves were not of significance, so perhaps there are 100 of them. In this form of inquiry, the only input of the managers is to answer (or, given return rates for questionnaires, *not* answer) the questions. They do not get to formulate the problem, to structure the questions, to say which questions are or are not important or to dispute the significance of the results. If their categories of understanding, their native categories, conflict with those of the researcher, this will never be exposed through this form of research in any intelligible way. And yet, there will surely be significant differences between the way the two parties to the research understand and appreciate the problems involved – the university researcher (say) with little experience of a specific industry, and the line manager (say) with vast experience of the same industry? And in the end, whose knowledge and experience is more valuable?

The answer to this last question might seem self-evident; nevertheless, there is surprisingly little attention paid within management research to the possibility that managers' own formulations of their problems might be interesting in their own right. This is partly because management studies (and so management research) has a pedagogical mission, to teach managers how to be better; a certain lack of respect for existing managerial formulations is built in to this enterprise. The hypothetico-deductive paradigm is also to blame, however. Managers often only come into the process at the data-gathering stage, by which time many avenues of expression or dissent (other than non-cooperation) are closed (perhaps this is one reason why managers do not always take a keen interest in management research).

One might argue that attention to native categories amounted to keeping an open mind. In a pre-structured questionnaire or interview schedule there is little room for a manager to express him or herself; if the managerial view of the world conflicts with that encoded in the research instrument, then this will not be recorded in any systematic way. A commitment to understanding how managers perceive their own world, by contrast, requires the researcher to forgo structures imposed by the research design, and to attempt to elicit and understand structures that emerge from managerial discourse and action. Keeping an open mind is a good English metaphor for this attitude, and one with considerable intuitive appeal. The difficulty lies in knowing how open the mind needs to be: all category systems are, in an important sense, totalizing – they all have the capacity to accommodate all phenomena, perfectly adequately in their own terms. William Brown,[5] when offered a shilling to weed his parents' garden, pulled out all the plants that he didn't know the names of, which was most of them; these were, for him, the inhabitants of the category weed. William did not get his shilling, but his concept of the category 'weed' was only slightly less sophisticated than that of most English people. There was *no* plant that William was unable to categorize; his category system, impoverished though it was, was nevertheless totalizing. All the exotic herbs of the Orient could have been there, and he would have come away with a sack of weeds. Or try another example: some languages have three colour terms, some have 20 and more: both can describe all the colours of the rainbow with perfect local accuracy. It is often relatively easy to record alien phenomena by finding comfortably familiar categories to put them in: the alien nature of the data is then lost, beyond recall. The attempt to bring to consciousness one's own categories of understanding must be constant, as must the suspicion that one is, as the researcher, imposing inappropriate categories upon the object of research. The constant process of negotiation, between one individual and another, between researcher and researched, is sometimes called intersubjectivity; like writing prose, it is something that we have all been doing all our lives; the sophistication born of this experience is available to us, if we allow it legitimacy.

## REALITY DEFINITION

Social anthropologists would usually be prepared to argue that reality is socially defined. This glib formulation conceals a host of problems, but for brevity it will serve. Against this is the positivist ethic, which regards reality as something independent of social definition, something which endures independently of (say) what people think about it. There is a very great difference in perspective, then, between the two approaches. The formulation that reality is socially defined is one in which attention to native categories is fundamental to research; there can be *no* research which does not make this a central issue. The positivist formulation, by contrast, is one in which native categories might enter as a fringe issue, one concerning rather minor matters of perception at the edges of reality. The same opposition might indeed be phrased as one concerning perception; if reality is socially defined, then *all* reality is perceived reality, and structures of perception and cognition become central to research. If reality exists independently of social definition, then questions of perception turn into peripheral matters, where objective reality as perceived by the researcher might be contrasted with strange or quirky perceptions held by misguided natives (the similarity of this to the approach of early ethnocentric social anthropologists is no accident, of course).

The question of objectivity needs to be re-examined in the light of this. Social anthropology, in its earlier objectivist phase, held the ambition of being objective. The abandonment of this in its naïve early forms was not, in principle, an abandonment of the pursuit of rigour or truth. It was rather, a recognition of the fact that studying native categories seemed to be the best way of *being* objective in social enquiry. The old forms of observer-defined ethnocentric objectivism began to look, by contrast, like a form of unrecognized subjectivism, disguised in pseudo-scientific self-importance (and it is in this phase that a great deal of management research is still trapped). If what matters is what people do, how they generate and understand and interpret their own activity, then an objective study of the people can have no option but to take native categories into account. Behaviourist rhetoric provides another defence against this, since it allows researchers to cherish the illusion that action can be objectively recorded, even in the absence of any understanding of the cognition and symbolism that winds it around and makes sense of it; there is no space here to dispel this illusion, although it readily yields to arguments similar to those already presented; see Ardener (1989b); Chapman (1992).

Many of the quasi-theoretical oppositions which form the substance of argument in this area are rendered problematic by this kind of perspective. The opposition objective/subjective, in particular, begins to look unhelpful and misleading, at least in its most commonly used forms. The existence of a category of people called managing directors, for example, is objectively real within the subjective vision of the modern capitalist world; there are real people within this category, recognized by all around them. Nevertheless, for most of history, and for many people still, no such category exists. The typical implications of the objective/subjective opposition cut across the nature of a native category of this kind. The category is subjective, in that it only exists because people believe that it does (what would Alaric the Goth have done with somebody who said 'you can't do this to me; I'm a managing director!'?), but it is objectively real within the society that makes sense of it; you can touch managing directors and count them. It might seem, from the tenor of the presentation so far, that what is being advocated is an abandonment of objectivity, and its replacement by subjectivity; that would be to leave objectivity inviolate, however, as a position to which one could later return. The message is stronger than that: attention to native categories requires that objectivity itself be reconstructed (and deconstructed, if we must) in every new social environment.

## HOW DO YOU STUDY NATIVE CATEGORIES?

There is no simple answer to this question, perhaps predictably. Anthropologists have typically tried to achieve this by long-term fieldwork, long-term exposure to the people under study and many conversations in many different contexts with as many people as possible, repeated as often as possible. The process can never be regarded as complete, nothing arises which can be fed into SPSS and there are no tests of significance.

### Context and Opposition

The contextual aspect is important. Our modern ideas of the contextual nature of ideas, words and concepts derive in many ways from the work of the linguist Ferdinand de Saussure (1916). Saussure gave rigorous form to the long-standing truism that a thing could only be defined in relation to what it was not. The need for contextual study sprang directly from this, in both linguistics and anthropology. In social terms, there were no objective realities, tied to the world; there were, rather, categories that derived their shape from their relationship to the other categories around them. In many areas of study, within anthropology and linguistics, this insight has generated important developments over the last 40 or 50 years.[6] It is an insight which has been appropriated as their own novelty by the post-modernists (and bowdlerized in the process; see Ellis, 1989; Ardener, 1989a; Brown, 1995, pp. 82–83, p. 185, note 5).

It is also important to stress that native categories are not just words; they are part of a lexicon, certainly, but they are also a living part of action and understanding. It is often the case that a category contains many important features which are rarely overtly realized in speech; they are realized, rather, through repeated and intelligible actions.

This raises some difficult and long-standing anthropological problems. In brief, we might say that anthropologists are prepared to allow meaning to inhere as much in the non-linguistic as in the linguistic aspects of human action and expression (which is why they find behaviourism so crude and misguided). Language is an important aspect of this meaning, but it is not imperial; action inhabits a field of meaning which is to some degree autonomous of language, although it usually intersects with language to a greater or lesser degree (for sophisticated discussions of this, see Ardener, 1989a; Bourdieu, 1977; Jenkins, 1994). Important clues to the non-linguistic aspects of native categories, in this sense, can arise when mistakes are made, when a taboo is broken or an anomaly appears. You might, for example, as an imaginary visiting anthropologist from Korea, live for years among the people of Yorkshire, and dine off roast pork in their houses many times. You might decide to treat some of them to a meal of your own cooking. Until you put roast dog on the plate before them, you would not necessarily have any idea that roast dog was not a perfectly satisfactory categorical substitute for roast pork. You would quickly find out, however, and the medium of your discovery would not necessarily be linguistic.

Because a great deal of social activity is not realized in language, carrying meaning in other media, we impose a great burden upon language in asking it to convey, *post hoc*, our descriptions. This problem is perhaps particularly obvious in cross-cultural understanding, but it is no less acute in familiar settings. Action, events, materialities, are, in social terms, to some degree autonomous of language, and in describing them after the event all that we can hope to provide, in language, are what Ardener called 'language shadows' (1989a, ch. 5).

## Fieldwork

The need for context, and the need for an appreciation of non-linguistic aspects of meaning, both demand considerable investment in research time. This is one reason why anthropologists typically view their research as measured in months and years (of participant observation, using the native languages), rather than in hours or minutes (as in the time taken to conduct an interview or fill out a questionnaire).

## Measurement and Definition

This point requires another paper, but it arises from the importance that we give here to native categories. If society is the sovereign defining power of reality, then it is clear that some phenomena to which we have brought a positivist mensurational approach, need to be treated rather more carefully. For an act of definition is, by *fiat*, often an act of measurement also. A positivist researcher would readily accede to the view that you needed to define something before counting it; so much is simple. But in the world of native categories the definition is out of the hands of the research worker; it is in the hands of the society and the people under study, and their acts of definition and attempts at enumeration are always in interaction. Any attempt at measurement, however naïve, must finally resolve itself in definition (where do we stop?); and any attempt at definition necessarily has implications for the count. Ardener has written of 'the collapse of measurement into definition', as a common sequence not only in positivist social science but in social life more generally

(1989a; p. 149). If there are too many or too few (for whatever purpose), we can change the definition; if when the definition is applied, there are too many or too few, we can make more or destroy some, imagine or ignore. We make often only part-conscious decisions of this kind all the time. Because of the primacy given to enumeration in positivist social science, it is perhaps salutary, in the context of a discussion of native categories, to stress the importance attached to social definition *by societies themselves* (and the large literature on classification and category anomaly is immediately relevant here; see for example, Douglas, 1966; Davis, 1976; Durkheim and Mauss, 1963; Parkin, 1982; Ellen and Reason, 1979). In the interplay of definition and measurement, it is often *definition* which is the driving force. Measurement always requires definition. Definition does not require measurement, but it often implies it, or affects it: if we change the definition of the category, we thereby change the number of things within it. For observer-constructed categories of an obviously arbitrary kind (small and medium sized enterprises, for example, defined as having a turnover of $< x$), this is obvious and banal. For socially defined categories which people live within, the issues rapidly get serious. These arguments have well-established force in social anthropology.

## THE MANAGEMENT OF COOPERATIVE STRATEGIES AND NATIVE CATEGORIES

What good does the idea of 'native categories' do us in our own immediate research?

First, we can revisit some of the issues already raised. Because both researchers involved are English, English-speaking, male, white, middle-class (at least by adoption), and well-educated (at least by some measures), they share many of their native categories with those British managers whom they are studying. This should never be taken for granted; it needs to be thought about, and brought to the surface as a problem; the boundary where shared understanding stops and starts is unreliable, fluctuating, difficult to see; and so on – a host of problems. Nevertheless, this shared knowledge is in many ways a precondition of the kind of research they are doing. They are working using long unstructured interviews, and they can rely on a fair degree of shared understanding between themselves and those whom they are interviewing. If this were not so, they would be obliged to work like anthropologists, and spend years learning the language and carrying out participant observation. As it is, they are relying on long unstructured interviews, repeated as often as possible.

It is important to stress another reason for being careful about the nature and degree of shared knowledge in a context like this. Management research has tended to operate as if there were only one object of study – western capitalism and its variants, and only one audience for the research – Euro-Americans (other threads are slowly being woven in, but historically this has surely been the case, and the bias is still very marked). For these, a common degree of shared knowledge can perhaps be assumed (although this is arguable and certainly often wrong). Outside this, however, even the most elementary aspects of management may need explication. If management research is going to develop into a truly international and global activity (involving all manner of people in all the nations of the world), then a multiple audience needs to be assumed, an audience for whom nothing can be taken for granted, an audience with whom no knowledge is necessarily shared.

We might say that there were two apparently separate ways of handling the problem of native categories, one more radical than the other:

1. We might regard attention to native categories as a necessary, indeed vital, step towards adequate positivist research. If we want to count the number of policemen in a society, then it makes good sense to find out what the native category of policemen is, otherwise we make basic ethnocentric errors. *Good* positivism, in this light, would simply be good anthropology; and good anthropology, too, would be good positivism. This is a respectable position, although ethnocentrism is very deeply tied into positivist behaviourism, and extreme statements of the native category issue may well be needed to remedy this.

2. Alternatively, we can regard the native category approach as one which simply invalidates positivism, always and everywhere. Many social anthropologists in the 1970s and 1980s came to occupy a position rather like this, not always with easy minds (for those who had not encountered the problems in a previous generation, the work of Clifford and Marcus came to be emblematic (see Clifford and Marcus, 1987)).

Both of these are defensible positions, although both present problems. The first suffers from the defect that it does not fully take into account the argument that all of the categories that the researcher brings to the problem are themselves native categories (including, for example, the notion that objective knowledge is available and desirable). It also does not fully take into account the previously discussed reality-defining power of societies; if we adhere to an alien native category, and perform our positivist count in its terms, what are we to do with the fact that the society may change its mind about the definition while we are analysing our results?

The second position suffers from the obvious defect that it seems, to many, to render organized research of any kind impossible. Since we know that organized research has produced many interesting and plausible results, this would seem to be *prima facie* evidence against this position. It is true, also, that some who have espoused what they perceived to be positions of extreme relativism have ended up by writing poems about themselves, rather than accounts of other people (see Kuper, 1994, p. 542).

For immediate purposes, it is probably best to say that our attention to native categories comes under the first of these positions. However, the opposition between the two possibilities, 1 and 2 as given above, is itself in some ways philosophically flawed, and once the issue of native categories is broached, positivism holds no peace. Ardener says:

> There was a time when the relativity of cultural categories was raised to a philosophical bogey as 'relativism'. Anthropology was then discovering a mismatch between the categories of the observer and those generated by the purported object – other people. When the differences

> are more subtle, the gap is narrower between these two; the mismatch is virtually simultaneous. Since mismatch *is* our experience of relativity, then the reduction of 'transmission time' (between the observer and the purported object) and the narrowing of the mismatch (between the categories of the observer and the other), demonstrates that the process that we first called relativization is *not* a form of anti-objectivity, but (as its application to 'familiar' experience more clearly shows) is on the contrary our only mode of objectivization. (1989, pp. 212–13)

Under position 1, however, as described above, we can go on to suggest a few delimited conceptual areas where the idea of native categories seems to be of immediate relevance in relation to the data that we have collected (or, say, the partial knowledge that we have acquired). These are raised under three headings, the transaction, the company and core business. None of these is fully developed here; they are used, rather, as examples, to make some points relevant to our discussion so far in this chapter.

## The Transaction

Williamson (1975) tends to treat the transaction as a given. Martin, discussing Williamson's approach, says that 'relatively little attention is paid to defining the concept of transaction; it is regarded as unproblematic' (1993, p. 1088). In *Markets and Hierarchies* Williamson perhaps has enough on his plate, and can be forgiven for this. There is one stage of his argument, however, where the transaction itself is relativized, at least in potential. Williamson, while discussing blood donors in the USA, says:

> The standard economic model... assumes that individuals regard transactions in a strictly neutral, instrumental manner. However, it may be more accurate, and sometimes even essential, to regard the exchange process itself as an object of value. Concern for atmosphere tends to raise such systems issues; supplying a *satisfying exchange relation* is made part of the economic problem, broadly construed. (1975, p. 38)

Buckley and Casson (1988) suggest this change of relationship as a possible development of cooperative dealings within a joint venture. This is introduced by the notion of commitment:

> It is also possible... to encourage cooperation by changing an agent's preference so that the successful completion of the venture receives a higher priority than it did before. One way of doing this is to encourage the agent to perceive cooperation not as a means but as an end in itself. Cooperation then ceases to be based on strategic considerations... and becomes based on commitment to cooperation in its own right. (1988, p. 39)

> From the standpoint of economic theory, these propositions are equivalent to a postulate that an agent's preferences depend not only upon material consumption (or profit) but also upon the characteristics of the ventures in which it is involved. These characteristics relate both to the nature of the venture itself and to the extent of mutual commitment shown by the parties concerned. (1988, p. 40)

For most social anthropologists, the work of Marcel Mauss on exchange is part of their most familiar mental furniture (see Mauss, 1954); as such, they would typically have no difficulty in agreeing with Williamson's formulation, or with the propositions of Buckley and Casson. Concern with such issues is nevertheless rare in main-stream management research. Williamson pursued the matter no further in the work cited, and in an article published in 1993 returns briefly to the problem, and says 'not having made more headway, however, I had little to add' (1993, p. 480).[7] Williamson introduces atmosphere in order to argue for a calculative approach to virtually everything, not to allow in ideas from social anthropology. It could be argued, however, that by introducing the idea of atmosphere Williamson was, wittingly or not, potentially opening transaction-cost economics to the anthropological issues raised by the general discussion above – native categories, context, reciprocity and so on. If the idea of atmosphere was fully explored, rather than thrown in as a passing metaphor, then Williamson's argument would need to be revised to take this into account. Williamson's work in various different (and often only half-visible) ways threatens to become, or wish to become, a theory of the universe: Williamson cites, with approval, Karl Llewellyn's view of 'contract as framework', 'a framework for well-nigh every type of group organization and for well-nigh every type of passing or permanent relation between individuals and groups' (Williamson, 1993, p. 461). This does not leave much out; we might expect that a research agenda such as this must necessarily, at some stage, encounter the native category problem, and there is as yet little evidence that this has happened. (Yamin, 1993, has recently criticized the overweening ambition, as he sees it, of the transaction cost approach.) Williamson considers 'that a science of organization is in progress' (1993, p. 484), and is pursuing Simon's ambition of developing:

> adequate linguistic and conceptual tools for realistically and significantly describing . . . administrative organization – describing it, that is, in a way that will provide the basis for scientific analysis of the effectiveness of its structure and operation. (Williamson, 1993, p. 484, citing Simon, 1957, p. xlv)

This is a scientific ambition; the linguistic tools in question are unambiguously defined by the research worker, not by the society or people under study; native categories (or the idea under any terminology) are given short shrift; trust, for example, which is a term that many people use to understand the kind of phenomena to which Williamson draws attention, is, in his 1993 paper, magisterially defined away.

We can pause, however, to remember the trajectory of social anthropology. Radcliffe-Brown and Malinowski both, in their different ways, imagined that they were constructing a science of society from within social anthropology (see Radcliffe-Brown, 1952; Malinowski, 1944). This ambition foundered, when rigorously confronted with the native category problem, through a continuous series of intellectual assaults that began in the 1960s, and is still ongoing (Leach, 1961; Needham, 1962; Ardener, 1971). Will this happen to Williamson's version of transaction-cost economics? Simon began the chase for science in 1945, and speculated that within a couple of decades his work would seem out of date (1957, p. ix). He is still cited as relevant, however (see Williamson, 1993, quoted above), even though the science can scarcely be said to have appeared. Williamson, for ten years, had 'nothing further to add'. Perhaps some kind of upheaval is pending, by analogy with the example of social anthropology.[8]

The idea that there might be separate *types* of transactions, in native definition, is an old one in anthropology, and some of the most important classics of the subject have been about this problem (see Malinowski, 1922; Mauss, 1954, Lévi-Strauss, 1949). The phenomenon of spheres of exchange, where a society sets clear limits on different areas of exchange activity, which are not allowed to interconnect, is widespread; it has generated a large literature, which is relevant in many ways to some important taken-for-granted aspects of our own society (Bohannan, and Bohannan, 1968; Douglas, 1963, 1967; Barth, 1967).

The existence of different categories of transaction has recently been explicitly treated from an anthropological viewpoint by John Davis (1992). Although Davis is not an economist (and freely admits that he is 'not learned in economics', 1992, p. 88), he has long held the view that economic phenomena cannot be ignored in the analysis of other apparently non-economic social activity (for example, Davis, 1976). His (1992) book, *Exchange*, performs the valuable task of bringing an anthropological approach to our own collective representations, in this case in relation to our conceptualization, as a society, of different *kinds* of exchange activity. The notion that there exist different kinds of exchange relationship is expressed, in a somewhat different way, by Buckley and Casson (1988), in their analysis of joint ventures, where they show in particular that the concepts of forbearance, commitment and trust may exist differentially according to transaction types. There is a potentially fruitful link to be made between the anthropological literature, and these emerging economic considerations.

Economists tend to think of the world as made up of morally homogeneous and mutually commensurable transactions (for an expansion on this criticism, see Martin, 1993, pp. 1088–91). Another way of expressing this is to suggest that economists tend to treat *all* transactions as if they were capable of expression in monetary terms, where all exchanges had a movement of a mensurable amount of money in at least one direction: money is intrinsically mensurable, at least in note and coin, and it does have a capacity to flow into many spheres that were previously ignorant of it (it is, so to speak, meaningless value, and as such has the potential to serve as a metaphor for all other forms of value). Mary Douglas (1967) has pointed out that we make many mundane attempts to stop the flow of money, and have a repertoire of metaphors to express this flow capacity – 'liquidity', for example, among economists, and 'money that just goes like water' in the vernacular. There are many transactions, nevertheless, where money is not an appropriate exchange item (Davis, 1992). This varies from culture to culture, however, and the range of limitations is an empirical matter, needing to be explored in each cultural context.

One issue which recurs in current debate about the efficiency of companies, of groups of companies, even of whole economies, is that of trust (see Casson, 1991). In this, as in other areas, business research tends to assume that a concept like trust is generally applicable across the cultural universe: we need to be very careful, however, of assumptions of this kind (Davis, 1992, p. 29). One might say that trust-like phenomena are culturally universal, but nevertheless argue that the local range of possibilities needs in every case to be investigated, and accorded its proper ethnographic due – semantic, structural, moral, lexical and so on. Transaction cost economics throws up the idea that trust is a good thing in an economy – the higher is trust, the lower the transaction costs arising from fear of opportunistic behaviour, and so the greater the efficiency. It is often implied that trust is unambiguous in its definition, and that cultures vary simply in having more or less of it (usually, Japan more, England less, or some such comparison). The problem is more complicated than this however, since the changing context as we pass from one culture to another, implies that trust (however hard we might seek for legitimate translation) varies from culture to culture, not just in quantity, but in quality (from a Saussurean point of view, this is virtually a truism). It must surely be the case that trust, as it is expressed and understood in (say)

Japan, is so deeply embedded in a specific cultural web that it can not be transfused, as it were by the pint, into another culture, however beneficial this might be from a transaction-cost perspective. If England (say) wants more trust, then it must find more of its own *kind* of trust.

Transaction-cost economics regards the threat of opportunism as something that needs to be bought off, and trust as something that comes free – hence the efficiency gain that arises when opportunism is replaced by trust. It might be interesting, however, to look at this in a different light, and regard opportunism as what you get for free, and trust as something that you need to pay for: not necessarily, however, in coin. You pay for it, more likely, in long-term constraints on your own action, in forgoing short-term material gain by forbearing to pursue self-interest to the full, in the need for sustained reciprocity, possibly in the fear of forfeit, in the tedium of certain connections, in the moral and mental effort of deciding where relations need to be maintained and where not, in the persistent need for long-running calculation of incommensurable gains and losses – whole social systems exist, without money, where these kinds of moral and mental activities make up much of the fabric of daily life (Malinowski, 1922; Evans-Pritchard, 1956). These notions parallel the development of the concept of mutual forbearance within joint ventures, leading to a commitment to cooperate. Agents with such a commitment gain welfare directly from the constructive role in such exchanges (Buckley, Casson, 1988).

The interviews that we have conducted have so far brought out some rich examples of the intersection of economic considerations with other issues that might come under headings such as trust, friendship, corruption, influence, bribery and so on.

One production manager, for example (let us call him A), told a story of his relationship with a good friend (B), who lived in the same village as A, and drank in the same pub. B was a manager in a firm which supplied components to A. In A's recital of this (which was in the general context of a discussion of the role of friendship in determining the direction of subcontracting, where there was a large choice of potential subcontractors), A insisted that the fact that B was his *friend*, made A more scrupulous than he normally would have been, in ensuring that the contract between them was economically sound, competitively priced, rigorously monitored, and so on. By contrast, A told of a different manager (C) from a firm to whom he gave subcontracting work, who offered A a large Christmas bribe (a fistful of banknotes delivered in the course of a handshake), along with the *sotto voce* spoken message 'you look after me, and I'll look after you'. C was someone with whom A's relations had always been amicable, but he was not prepared to be bought in this way; the bribe had been proffered at the start of a Christmas party (a sort of stand-up buffet), and A, finding the notes in his hand, dropped them on the floor and pointed at them, at the same time asking C, in loud public tones 'What the hell is that, C? What the hell is that?' He thus made public the bribe, his refusal of the bribe, and the humiliation of C. C got no more business out of A.

This story was one of many from the same manager about the moral difficulties of managing inter-company relationships. It is of course morally quite familiar; it allows us, however, to begin to look at those transactions which can be mediated by money, and those which cannot. In A's understanding, friendship was to be kept categorically separate from economic dealing (as in his relationship with B), and was not to be bought with money (as in his relationship with C). We might note, however, that B gets the contracts and remains a friend, while C does neither; friendship was construed as categorically separate from contracting, but at the same time the sharing of this sense of propriety was a basis for friendship.

Williamson's approach in a recent paper (1993) is to redefine the conceptual universe of analysis until the concept of trust is rendered virtually redundant, being incorporated (by the analyst) into various forms of calculativeness. There is a radical difference between this approach and, for example, the approach of the anthropologist John Davis to similar problems (1992). Williamson, confronted with an ambiguous set of vernacular categories, redefines them for his own purposes (whether successfully or not is not at issue here). Davis, confronted with vernacular categories, treats them as irreducible data, arguing, as anthropologists have already done in other areas, that ignoring native categories can only lead to confusion. Our informant, reported above, used the word trust frequently. In order best to understand what this informant is doing, should we define away his understanding and replace it with our own, or respect his forms of expression and meaning? This issue is not resolved here; in the meeting of transaction-cost economics and social anthropology, however, we have a particularly stark version of the question, of the clash of paradigms that has riven the social sciences.

We might also pause to remember (from a social anthropological perspective) the polluting aspects of anomaly (Douglas, 1966); A found 'matter out of place' in his hand, and dropped it on the floor, where dirt belongs. Money and friendship, at least in that configuration, do not mix. We might also pause to think about the cultural specificity of this definition of the problem. There are many business cultures in the world (including most of Mediterranean Europe), where friendship between two people would define in, rather than define out, the giving of contracts and the exchange of sums of money (if we call them bribes, we perhaps cast an inappropriate moral light upon them). If we think that trust in economic relationships is a good thing, then we might need to concede that in some cultures trust involves being able to trust your friends to send contracts your way, being able to trust your colleagues to accept offered *douceurs*.

## The Company

Transaction-cost economics is in part an attempt to theorize the boundaries of the firm, the boundaries between market and hierarchy (Williamson, 1975). The project which we are undertaking is in large part an attempt to put empirical flesh upon the economic theory of the boundaries of the firm. Most of the data so far gathered relates directly to this question, and there is a great deal that could be said. What follows is only suggestive.

In Coase's original formulation, and as developed by Williamson, the transaction-cost explanation for the existence of companies is open to the charge of tautology (see Coase, 1991, p. 48; Williamson, 1979). If everything works according to the theory, then high transaction costs are avoided and low transaction costs sought; every outcome is transaction-cost minimizing: and, if it is not, there is no way of ever knowing, since the alternative outcome never comes to be. In an ideally measurable world, transaction costs could be measured in advance and compared, just as can production costs or interest-rate costs. In fact, transaction costs are made up of components which are exceptionally difficult to put figures to; it would perhaps not be an exaggeration to say that in many respects they are outside the domain of quantification altogether. Certainly, the managers that we have talked to often raise issues which could be regarded as imposing transaction costs – fear of opportunism, the costs of overcoming uncertainty, problems of asset specificity, the costs of building and maintaining relationships and so on. In almost all cases, however, decisions in these areas are resolved by appeal to what the managers in question call by such names as judgement, intuition, gut feeling, and the like. Where there *are* available numerical studies, then these may be consulted, but the general trend of comment is that, when numbers come up against judgement, and they conflict, then judgement has it every time (if necessary some new numbers are commissioned). In such an environment, it is rather idle to continue to pretend that all the relevant transaction costs are really there to be measured, if only someone took the trouble. The transaction costs that are *really there*, in the sense that they determine the outcome, are those transaction costs *that are perceived by the manager (or managers) who make the decisions*. If a manager perceives the future costs of buying the small supplier to be less than the future costs of continued cooperation with this supplier, then (assuming he is in a position to do so) he will decide to buy the supplier; the outcome is transaction-cost minimizing, in this very important sense – that transaction costs as perceived by the decision-makers are minimized. We are clearly and totally in the perceptual realm here, and it is not a realm that positivist management and business studies are accustomed to visiting.

One aspect of this perceptual realm is that it is very difficult to split into separate functional or social domains; the revolution in anthropology which led to the collapse of the functional specialisms is entirely relevant here: put very crudely, social anthropology, under the influence of structuralism and subsequent developments, moved the location of structure from the material world to the intellect. Within the intellect, structures and concepts can often move rather freely through the fabric of thought: symbolic oppositions that make sense in the family home, can be expected to carry their weight into the company; structures of relationship that might be considered political, prove to have considerable influence in economic matters, and so on. The realm of causation becomes primarily cognitive – not a world of material billiard balls on a two-dimensional surface, but a multi-dimensional non-material space. We generate, then, an appeal for rich contextual understanding of management activity, of the kind that anthropologists have already provided in other areas.

All transaction costs are, in an important sense, perceptual matters. That is what we have said. The positivist will not let go of the bone so easily, however. It might at the very least be objected that the issue of whether the transaction costs have *really or objectively* been minimized will be decided by the longer-term outcome, according, that is, to whether or not the company survives, and that perceptual issues are neither here nor there if the company goes bust or gets bought out; but all companies are faced with a highly complex perceptual environment, and their shape is not the result of one decision about such issues, but hundreds, all overlapping and interacting; sorting out the effects of one decision as against others is usually impossible: when a company fails, it is difficult, even in retrospect, to be precise about exactly *which* transaction-cost estimation, which decision, was at fault. Again, the appeal to *real* mensuration is meretricious.

The question of how managers conceive of their companies, therefore, and conceive of the boundaries of their companies, is of the first importance. We need to look carefully at the vocabulary employed, and at the relative weight given, in managerial account, to different kinds of information. We could even begin the construction of a semantic field (from a linguistic tradition that is far from obsolete; see Trier, 1931; Ulmann, 1962), within which the various elements of vocabulary could be given their status in the context of all the rest. We are dealing with terms like alliance, partnership, relationship, trust, joint venture, understanding and so on, not as these might be defined in advance by an ambitious strategic management consultancy, but as they are actually understood by the people who speak of them.

The company is a native category; it is also a category which is much discussed and documented by would-be objective observers. These observers, in the legal professions, in academia and in the City, all form part of the flow of definition which feeds back into the native category; this is the modern condition – there are no longer (if ever there were) native categories which are exempt from the roundabout of external commentary, internalization of that commentary, subsequent modification of the category itself and off round again.

The company, as a native category, is an important aspect of the way we all live. It is a difficult and complex category. Long-established manual workers regard it in a very different way from, say, asset strippers, or business process re-engineers. Nevertheless, everybody that works in a company has a working knowledge of what that company is in particular, and what a company is in general. Working to that knowledge, they create the reality that they understand.

In the seminal works on classification produced by the *Année Sociologique* school (for example Durkheim and Mauss, 1963), and in modern works which developed the themes (for example Lévi-Strauss, 1962; Douglas, 1966), we see emerging the idea that each society classifies the world in its own way; we also see that societies attach urgent moral importance to the integrity of their own particular classification. Things that do not fit the classifications are perceived as dangerous, filthy, revolting, laughable. In our own view of ourselves, we inhabit a society where companies exist as discrete social entities. They buy and sell between them. The verbs buy and sell are perceived to be opposites of one another. Companies compete. Within a company, authority prevails. Between companies, the market prevails. We could make this more complex, but it is a bald summary of the common experience and understanding of most people who work for, and interact with, companies. It is interesting, therefore, to note the fascination that we exhibit (as academics, management consultants, businessmen) for the dangerous and classification-threatening *demi-monde* where company boundaries are broached, dissolved or over-stepped – the world of joint ventures, strategic alliances, partnerships, networks and so on. It is not fanciful to turn the tools of classificatory analysis, which have produced such interesting results in the sphere of primitive classification, onto these quintessentially modern (even, perhaps, postmodern) phenomena. Classificatory anomalies are both an excitement and a moral threat, now as always.

**Core Business**

Another area of definitional interest that has appeared is the idea of the core business. Almost all of the managers that we have talked to have expressed some notion that what their firm is concentrating on is its core business (or business). This has arisen in discussion of alliances, acquisitions, divestments, and of subcontracting in and out. It is clear, however, that the idea is definitionally very pliable. All companies are engaged in a constant search for their own ideal configuration. For various reasons, there is no rest in this process, and while one company is going one way (for what seem to it to be good reasons), another company is running counter (again, for its own good reasons). There is no way, either of recognizing the ideal configuration (in a transaction-cost minimizing sense) even when you stumble across it: the counterfactuals which could make comparative sense of such an ideal have never come into being, and the only way to try them out is to make them happen, which entails further change. The flux of other companies around you means that the test environment, the control experiment, can never be considered stable.

And yet, all the companies are concentrating on their core businesses. One could regard this as a marvel of strategic insight. Or one could regard it as definitional sleight of hand – what we do is core business: core business is what we do: measurement, so to speak, collapses into definition.

## CONCLUSION

The use of native categories has proved to be of great value in social anthropological work. The notion is one which, once appreciated, subverts many of the more naïve securities of traditional positivist research. We have tried to introduce the idea, using general examples. Using examples from our ongoing research, we have discussed some key areas where the ideas can be applied (areas which will receive full empirical elaboration in subsequent papers). The chapter is set in the context of the general debate around theoretical paradigms within business and management studies; in particular, positivism and interpretivist approaches are contrasted. Transaction-cost economics has proved to be of great importance in the understanding and analysis of organizations; it has been, however, to date, a solidly positivist enterprise. Social anthropology, by contrast, has long occupied a non-positivist position. The theoretical meeting of social anthropology and transaction-cost economics provides an exemplar, therefore, of the larger debate. We have tried to bring this issue to the foreground, and suggested (no more) some empirical areas where it can be argued.

## Notes

1. An earlier version of this paper was presented at the BAM 1994 Conference at Lancaster University. The authors are grateful for comments given during the conference, and for the insightful and thorough comments and criticism of two anonymous referees.
2. The questions raised relate to the general problem of the stance of the ethnographer in relation to the people under study, both morally and intellectually. This problem (perhaps we could say 'exploring the nature of otherness') has generated a large literature over the last decade or so. See, for some discussion, Jackson, 1987; Narayan, 1993; Kim, 1990; Messerschmidt, 1981; Kuper, 1994.
3. This paper is not about the Anglo-French comparison, although many points could be made. Some of the differences between English and French business culture are discussed by, for example, Barsoux and Lawrence, 1990, and there is of course a literature, deriving from centuries of mutual fascination and disdain, on the Anglo-French divide (see, for example, Zeldin, 1977; Gerbod, 1991). Hofstede's contribution to this topic demands consideration (see Hofstede, 1984; 1991); more important, perhaps, in the present context, is the anthropologically sophisticated and fine-grained work of Philippe d'Iribarne (1989).
4. Expressing the problem as one of cultures and subcultures is conceptually tidy, and again we probably know what we mean. It is worth stressing, however, that the tidiness is largely spurious. There are not two different things – cultures and subcultures; there are, by contrast, multidimensional clines of difference, with greater and lesser discontinuities of all kinds woven into them – what looks subcultural from one perspective, might look cultural from another (England as a subculture of European culture, Basingstoke as a sub-culture of English culture).

5. William Brown is the fictional creation of Richmal Crompton: his doings have been staple reading for two or three generations of English (perhaps British?) children; see the many titles, from 1922 onwards, published by George Newnes.
6. There are various areas of anthropology and linguistics which are linked together in the idea of native categories. Saussure's work found one prominent expression in the semantic field work of Trier in the 1930s (Ulmann, 1962), and linguistics was tied back into anthropology (after a long estrangement) through the structuralism of Lévi-Strauss (1963; Ardener, 1971). Semantic field theory was an attempt to render, in an empirical way, the Saussurean insight that the meaning of an element in a system (a word, say) depended upon its relation to all the other elements. Versions of this idea have developed into important areas of linguistics, and have developed into anthropological specializations with names like ethnoclassification. There is a large and interesting literature to draw upon here, which management research has virtually ignored.
7. The full text needs to be cited to do justice to the quotation:

> A colleague noted that the economics of atmosphere plays a larger role in *Markets and Hierarchies* than in *The Economic Institutions of Capitalism* and asked about the de-emphasis. I replied that I thought atmosphere at least as important to an understanding of economic organization in 1985 as I had in 1975. Not having made more headway, however, I had little to add. (Williamson, 1993, p. 480)

8. The revolution of thought in social anthropology, now rather ancient history, was unquestionably experienced as an upheaval, and dramatic and sometimes violent language was what practitioners seemed to need to describe it, both to make it happen, and to understand and criticize it. To those steeped in positivism, suggestions of relativism often seem redolent of chaos, violence or pollution; Ardener, in an essay first published in 1971, said:

> A degree of relativism must then have the status of a heuristic hypothesis. There seems no pressing need to fear it, although a social anthropologist cannot avoid the comment that, in all societies, any tampering with the boundaries of categories does awaken the fear of anomaly – generating pollution beliefs, inversion phenomena, and taboo. It is the thought categories of our own tradition that are tampered with in such studies. 'Relativism' may then sometimes appear as a fundamental philosophical danger. (Ardener, 1989a, p. 11, citing Douglas, 1966)

To suggest that an upheaval of this kind might be pending within the sphere of transaction cost economics is not to suggest that the upheaval has not already begun in other related areas. These things take a while to reverberate through the intellectual fabric. Organization studies, in one of its guises, is well advanced in this direction (see

Burrell and Morgan, 1979); aspects of marketing have followed (e.g. Brown, 1995). Transaction costs economics has so far resisted any accommodation with these trends. The point of bringing together economics and social anthropology is that they are, in their dominant guises, far apart in these matters; the junction is high voltage. It is not our intention to suggest that other subjects, other academic discourses, have not made advances in these areas, or have no claim upon them. The relationship of these issues to postmodernism, although raised in some of the texts cited, is too complex for discussion here.

## References


Ardener, E. W. (ed.) (1971) *Social Anthropology and Language*. Tavistock, London.

—— (1989a) *The Voice of Prophecy and Other Essays by E. W. Ardener*. Blackwell, Oxford.

—— (1989b) 'Behaviour – a Social Anthropological Criticism', in M. Chapman (ed.), *The Voice of Prophecy and Other Essays by E. W. Ardener*. Blackwell, Oxford.

Barsoux, J.-L. and P. Lawrence (1990) *Management in France*. Cassell, London.

Barth, F. (1967) 'Economic Spheres in Darfur', in R. Firth (ed.), *Themes in Economic Anthropology*. Tavistock, London.

Bohannan, P. and L. Bohannan (1968) *Tiv Economy*. Longmans, Green and Co., London.

Bourdieu, P. (1977) *Outline of a Theory of Practice*. Cambridge University Press, Cambridge.

Boyacigiller, N. and N. Adler (1991) 'The Parochial Dinosaur: Organisational Science in a Global Context', *Academy of Management Review*, 16, 2, pp. 262–90.

Brown, S. (1995) *Postmodern Marketing*. Routledge, London.

Buckley, P. and M. Casson (1988) 'A Theory of Cooperation in International Business', in F. Contractor and P. Lorange (eds), *Cooperative Strategies in International Business*. Lexington Books, Lexington, KY.

Burrell, G. and G. Morgan (1979) *Sociological Paradigms and Organisational Analysis, Elements of the Sociology of Corporate Life*. Heinemann, London.

Casson, M. (1991) *The Economics of Business Culture*. Clarendon Press, Oxford.

Chapman, M. (1992) 'Defining Culture – a Social Anthropological Perspective', paper delivered to the annual conference of the UK Academy of International Business, Brighton Polytechnic, March 1992.

Clifford, J. and G. Marcus (1987) *Writing Culture: the Poetics and Politics of Ethnography*. University of California Press, California.

Coase, R. (1991) 'The Nature of the Firm: Meaning', in O. Williamson and S. Winter (eds), *The Nature of the Firm: Origins, Evolution and Development*. Oxford, Oxford University Press, Oxford.

Crick, M. (1976) *Explorations in Language and Meaning – Towards a Semantic Anthropology*. Dent, London.

Davis, J. (1976) *The Peoples of the Mediterranean*. Routledge and Kegan Paul, London.

—— (1992) *Exchange*. Open University Press, Buckingham.

d'Iribarne, P. (1989) *La Logique de l'Honneur*. Seuil, Paris.
Douglas, M. (1963) *The Lele of the Kasai*. Oxford University Press, London.
—— (1966) *Purity and Danger*. Penguin, Harmondsworth.
—— (1967) 'Primitive Rationing', in R. Firth (ed.), *Themes in Economic Anthropology*. Tavistock, London.
Durkheim, E. and M. Mauss (1963) *Primitive Classification* (trans. and intro. R. Needham). Cohen and West, London.
Ellen, R. and D. Reason (1979) *Classifications in their Social Context*. Academic Press, London.
Ellis, J. (1989) *Against Deconstruction*. Princeton University Press, Princeton.
Evans-Pritchard, E. (1937) *Witchcraft, Oracles and Magic among the Azande*. Clarendon Press, Oxford.
—— (1956) *Nuer Religion*. Clarendon Press, Oxford.
Gerbod, P. (1991) *Voyages au Pays des Mangeurs de Grenouilles*. Albin Michel, Paris.
Ghoshal, S. and D. E. Westney (1993) 'Introduction and Overview', in S. Ghoshal and D. E. Westney (eds), *Organization Theory and the Multinational Corporation*. Macmillan, London.
Hocart, M. (1937) 'Kinship Systems', *Anthropos*, 22, 345–51.
—— (1970) *The Life-giving Myth*, 2nd edn, R. Needham (ed.). Methuen, London.
Hofstede, G. (1984) *Culture's Consequences*. Sage, Beverly Hills.
—— (1991) *Cultures and Organisations*. McGraw-Hill, London.
Jackson, A. (ed.) (1987) *Anthropology at Home*. Routledge, London.
Jenkins, T. (1994) 'Fieldwork and the Perception of Everyday Life', *Man*, 29, 2, 433–56.
Kim, C. (1990) 'The Role of the Non-western Anthropologist Reconsidered: Illusion Versus Reality', *Current Anthropology*, 31, 196–201.
Kuper, A. (1994) 'Culture, Identity and the Project of a Cosmopolitan Anthropology', *Man*, 29, 3, 537–54.
Leach, E. (1961) *Rethinking Anthropology*. Athlone Press, London.
Lévi-Strauss, C. (1949) *Les Structures Elémentaires de la Parenté*. Presses Universitaires Françaises (PUF), Paris.
—— (1962) *Le Totémisme Aujourd'hui* (trans. as Totemism. Merlin, London, 1964).
—— (1963) *Structural Anthropology*. Allen Lane, London.
Malinowski, B. (1922) *Argonauts of the Western Pacific*, Routledge and Kegan Paul, London.
—— (1944) *A Scientific Theory of Culture and Other Essays*. University of North Carolina Press, Chapel Hill.
Martin, R. (1993) 'The New Behaviorism: a Critique of Economics and Organization', *Human Relations*, 46, 9, 1085–101.
Mauss, M. (1954) *The Gift*. (trans. I. Cunnison). Cohen and West, London.
Messerschmidt, D. (ed.) (1981). *Anthropologists at Home in North America*, Cambridge University Press, Cambridge.
Narayan, K. (1993) 'How Native is a "Native" Anthropologist?', *American Anthropologist*, 95, 671–86.
Needham, R. (1962) *Structure and Sentiment*. Chicago University Press, Chicago.

Needham. R. (ed.) (1971) *Rethinking Kinship*. Tavistock, London.
Overing, J. (ed.) (1985) *Reason and Morality*. Tavistock, London.
Parkin, D. (ed.) (1982) *Semantic Anthropology*. Academic Press, London.
Radcliffe-Brown, A. R. (1952) *Structure and Function in Primitive Society*. Cohen and West, London.
Saussure, F. de (1916) *Cours de Linguistique Générale*. Payot, Paris.
Simon, H. (1957) *Administrative Behavior*. 2nd edn. Macmillan, New York.
Smith, P. and M. Bond (1993) *Social Psychology across Cultures*. Harvester Wheatsheaf, New York.
Trier, J. (1931) *Der Deutsche Wortschatz im Sinnbezirk des Verstandes: Die Geschichte eines sprachlichen Feldes I*. Carl Winter, Heidelberg.
Ullmann, S. (1962) *Semantics*. Basil Blackwell, Oxford.
Williamson, O. (1975) *Markets and Hierarchies*. Free Press, New York.
——(1979) 'Transaction-cost Economics: the Governance of Contractual Relations', *The Journal of Law and Economics*, 22, 233–61.
——(1993) 'Calculativeness, Trust, and Economic Organization', *Journal of Law and Economics*, xxxvi, 453–86.
Yamin, M. (1993) 'Alliances as Learning Strategies: the Limits of Transaction Cost Analysis', Conference Proceedings, 19th Annual Conference of the European International Business Association, Lisbon, December 1993.
Zeldin, T. (1977) *France 1848–1945: Intellect, Taste and Anxiety*. Clarendon Press, Oxford.

# 11 The Management of Cooperative Strategies in R&D and Innovation Programmes*

Peter J. Buckley and
Malcolm Chapman

**This chapter reports on an ESRC-funded project investigating 'the management of cooperative strategies', testing hypotheses drawn largely from (transaction cost) economics using data derived from the investigative methods of social anthropology. Cooperative strategies in a sample of British and French companies were investigated, with a wide range of their contact firms and related institutions being interviewed. The project was part of the ESRC's 'Contracts & Competition' Programme, and the results of the empirical material gathered during the study indicated clearly that the opposition cooperation/competition cannot, in any simple way, be regarded as descriptive of the public/private opposition. The study demonstrated, and the chapter argues, that the private business sector involves a broad spectrum of collaborative agreements between one company and another, and that a complex range of intermediate possibilities exist between the two notional extremes of markets and hierarchies.**

The project 'The Management of Cooperative Strategies: A Comparative and Longitudinal Study' is an attempt to test hypotheses largely drawn from (transaction cost) economics

* First published in *International Journal of the Economics of Business*, 5, 3 (1998).

using data derived from the investigative methods of social anthropology. The philosophies of economics and anthropology and their use of 'empirical data' are so different that a great deal of effort was necessary to attempt to reconcile what each regards as legitimate knowledge (Buckley and Chapman, 1996a, 1997, 1998; Chapman and Buckley, 1997). However, the subject matter of international business provides an excellent meeting ground for fruitful cross-fertilization (Buckley and Chapman, 1996b).

The subject matter of the project concerned the investigation of cooperative strategies in a small sample of British and French pharmaceutical companies and British instrument engineering companies. (The sample consisted of 12 British pharmaceutical companies, four French pharmaceutical companies and three British instrument engineering companies.) In addition a wide range of their contact firms and related institutions were interviewed – suppliers, customers, banks, retailers, consultants and regulatory and industry bodies.

The key research instrument was long, repeated, open ended interviews of managers focusing on their cooperative relationships outside the firm, over a three-year period. These interviews were supplemented by participant observation where possible. Anonymity was guaranteed to the participating managers and companies so false company names are used here. This method enables decisions to be observed in prospect, in concurrent real time and in retrospect. It provides an in-built check on veracity, as the managers know that future interviews will revisit current issues and it builds a deep relationship between interviewer and interviewee. As far as possible, the interviews were conducted using the categories of the manager rather than the interviewers (see Buckley and Chapman, 1998). Problems of disclosure, access and the scope of the enquiry occurred (Buckley and Chapman, 1996b) but in general the method was appropriate and allowed considerable insight into cooperative decisions.

The particular cooperative strategies which were discussed typically covered:

1. agency/distribution agreements;
2. joint ventures and alliances;

3. contract manufacturing (in and out);
4. joint research projects.

All of these activities involve cooperation across the boundaries of the firm and raise key issues of management. This chapter concentrates solely on the sub-class of joint research projects, but draws insights from the other types of cooperative strategy.

## THE MEANING OF COOPERATION IN R&D AND INNOVATION AND ITS ANALYSIS

Buckley and Casson (1988) define cooperation as 'coordination effected through mutual forbearance' and defined alliances [and joint ventures – a subset of alliances cemented by an exchange of equity ownership (Buckley, 1992)] as vehicles within which cooperation might occur. Conditions conducive to building such alliances (in R&D as elsewhere) are: (1) the possession of complementary assets, (2) similarity or congruence of goals (which may include a desire to reduce competition) and (3) barriers to full integration: economic, financial, legal or political. The choice of a joint venture in technical or research cooperation usually involves a complex of factors; moreover, recent analysis has shown that extreme values of variables do not explain joint ventures, which are often chosen as intermediate choices in positions of uncertainty: 'moderation in all things' may be a good description of the policy choice behind joint ventures (Buckley and Casson, 1996). Much has been made of the role of trust in joint ventures (Casson, 1991b, 1995; Buckley and Michie, 1996). In general 'obligational relational contracting', where informal relationships, including goodwill, mediate self-interested bargaining seems to prevail over a wide area of business behaviour and to provide the social underpinning (or glue) which keeps the business world together (Dore, 1996; Sako, 1992; Macaulay, 1996).

Joint ventures may also be considered as a device to organise inter-firm collusion (Buckley and Casson, 1988). Collusion can apply to the establishment of inter-firm specialization in R&D which avoids the duplication of effort and reduces the risk of patenting and innovation races (Casson, 1991a). Joint ventures in R&D, cemented by an exchange of shares, or contractual research alliance arrangements, provide a greater incentive against cheating than does a cartel because each firm is to some extent a hostage to the other.

Research lends itself to a team approach and the skills in coordinating a research team may well be similar to the skills necessary in coordinating a cross company team of different functions. It is therefore possible that companies with successful research teams will be capable of organizing successful joint ventures – in R&D as elsewhere.

There is enormous competitive pressure for a successful R&D innovation process within companies. As Casson (1991a) points out, 'the increasing length of the post-patent development process threatens monopoly rents', but the potential for harnessing scientific advances (e.g. in genetic engineering) remains enormous. Inter-company specialisation agreements in R&D and innovation are one means of facing this dual challenge. The management of R&D is a key determinant of corporate performance.

One key issue underlying both R&D management and corporate performance is company culture (Kreps, 1986; Casson, 1991b; (1995)). Openness to influences outside the firm, skills in recognizing opportunities for collaboration and in managing across the boundaries of the firm will be crucial determinants of successful collaboration. Whilst it is true that these skills reside in individuals, it is companies which encourage or discourage collaboration by their formal and informal incentive systems. The 'not invented here' syndrome is a recipe for isolationism which can be damaging where competencies are dispersed among firms.

## COSTING AND COOPERATION

A key part of the internalization decision (make or buy) is the cost of producing in-house. Quantification depends upon cost accounting. It can be expected that the quality (and quantity) of this information varies considerably from firm to firm and depends upon the resources put into the construction of a cost accounting system. Given an external price for a product, a cost accounting formula should be able to compute at what cost the firm can produce an equivalent product.

It is essential to confront the issue of the subjectivity of costs. Ideally, costs should be equivalent to opportunity costs, the costs of the best alternative foregone. This has a subjective element because as a counterfactual comparator, opportunity costs require evaluation by the decision maker. Management accounting techniques attempt (among other things) to provide decision rules in order to make costings consistent, but they often ignore the issue of cost subjectivity.

In evaluating costing decision, the issue of comparability arises. It is possible to compare extant costing systems with (a) a theoretical ideal (a perfect system) or (b) the norms of the industry – best practice techniques. It is also essential to distinguish what a firm should do from what it actually does do! For example, in an interview with a manager whose primary responsibility was contracting in, the costing issue was raised (Newdrug). The Manager was assured by the Finance Director of the company when he was interviewed for his current job that the firm possessed an excellent cost accounting system. After securing the job, the manager found that no such system existed and that it was almost pure guesswork to come to a judgement about costs of production.

> In an exaggerated sense, the cost accountant's main mission might have been depicted as the pursuit of absolute truth, where truth was defined in terms of getting as accurate or precise costs as possible ... [While in management accounting] the theme of 'different costs of different purposes' was stressed – a preoccupation with finding condition truth. (Horngren, 1975, pp. 9–10, quoted by Scapens, 1991, p. 8)

It seems that the phrase 'different costs for different purposes' is associated with J. Maurice Clark (1923).

In a recent interview with a senior project manager, the following discourse took place. The manager was asked by a director of the company how much a particular venture cost. His reply was 'How much do you want it to cost? One million, two million, three million ...'. Warming to his theme, the project manager said 'Costs mean different things in different situations'. A recent cooperative project between his company and a European collaborator was costed at one million for his company's board (because they were paying for it) and at three million for the collaborator (so more fees could be taken from them). The manager twice used the phrase 'Costs aren't important to me'. Perhaps they are to others who monitor his decisions. The manager's clear view was that he could undertake a project at a price. If his firm were not willing to commission the project at that price, then it wouldn't be done. This is disturbing but need not be surprising or destructive of formal approaches.

Even if costs can be calculated today, their variation over time presents problems. Neither external price nor internal costs are invariant over time. Projected costs and revenues from internalization can be discounted to a present value and this can be compared to the projected external price. In *reducto ad absurdum* form, if discounted revenues are less than the external price – produce internally. This abstracts from the fact that costs are dependent on the quantities produced, which implies accurate projections of demand and knowledge of returns to scale over the appropriate quantities. Significant discontinuities arise. These projections will be very different in situations where the facilities already exist in-house *vs*. the situation where a significant investment needs to be undertaken in order to make the product. Flexible budgets can be produced which project costs forward, even if the basis for this is crude. An example might be (projected costs + Retail Price Index). For novel projects, further careful investigation may be required. Distortions of information may arise. It is arguable that, in the British context, financial accounting for the owners of the business (shareholders in public companies) has dominated cost accounting for managers (see, for example, Johnson and Kaplan, 1987).

Johnson and Kaplan argue that the nature of management accounting information is actually counterproductive as an aid to decision making.

> Today's management accounting information, driven by the procedures and cycle of the organisation's financial reporting system, is too late, too aggregated and too distorted to be relevant for manager's planning and control decisions. (1987, p. 1)

A major plank in the arguments that accounting systems are obsolescent is given by Johnson and Kaplan as its inability to give managers information about the efficiency and profitability of internal process.

> Contemporary cost accounting and management control systems, ... are no longer providing accurate signals about the efficiency and profitability of internally managed transactions. Consequently, managers are not getting information to help them compare the desirability of internal *vs.* external transactions. (1987, p. 205)

## COMPARING EXTERNAL PRICE AND IN-HOUSE COSTS

Given the difficulties of calculating with any exactitude *ex ante* prices and internal costs, how are internalization or externalization decisions made? Guesswork (hunches) rules of thumb, traditional behaviour and imperfect calculation are possible ways of proceeding. An example from a recent interview follows 'So the decision whether to go out is a cost decision, based on the costs of hiring out. I like to keep 75 per cent of the work in-house, and contract out 25 per cent, so that if the amount of work declines, I do not have to lay people off. Having to lay people off is difficult and unpleasant and building up again afterwards is hard; so I keep our in-house capacity to about 75 per cent of the workload.' Further, 'The contract laboratories will do virtually anything we want – they are eager to establish a relationship with a big pharmaceutical company – they see it as a long-term relationship. They do compete, but we don't let contracts out to bid it is not costs that are important but whether we can work with them, their quality, do we trust their scientists? We don't want to miss deadlines, in fact, we can set the contract labs tighter deadlines than we impose in-house.'

On specific assets: 'If a contract lab needs specific equipment to do a job for us, then they do. We might pay them to get it. Several contract labs bought expensive equipment to do work for us, they took a risk and gambled that they would ensure future business from us by doing this. Does this give us power over them? Well, we certainly intend to carry on working with them, but what if we have to drop it for reasons outside my department? There are no guarantees to keep the contract going – the contract labs take the risk in investing. One contract lab has set aside people and equipment which is kept waiting on us – they kept a slot open for us, because they knew how important speed was to us for commercial reasons.'

A paraphrase of a manager's comment follows: 'Most of what our company does is made from bought-in components. These are bought in to stock – we can cost them at the price we bought them or the average for the year or we can mark them up by a 10 per cent overhead. On labour, the problem is even more complicated – do we try to cost it every day? How do you put a cost on the daily work of a design engineer? These are arbitrary decisions made by accountants, which produce apparent answers, which are then used to inform what we do. In our other plant, we mark up by two people to stop people buying things in. You run a number for a couple of years, you get a profit maybe, businessmen make an arbitrary judgement and then get on with it.'

It is arguable that the existence of widespread cooperation within an economy actually changes the nature of costs. As Fruin points out, cooperation (in Japan) 'included a wide range of behaviours where costs were not exactly calculated or catalogued: for example, sharing physical equipment and facilities, providing market and technical information, or supply giving that extra consideration when needed. Organizational learning or the organizational capacity to change and evolve intelligently was the basis for effective cooperation' (Fruin, 1992, p. 7). 'This ethos is also related to wider issues of competition and collaboration in business systems. In Japan, cooperation makes good sense because acquiring another firm's assets is generally not an alternative – shares are closely held and thinly traded' (Fruin, 1992, p. 8). Networks of cooperation thus enable firms to become highly specialised and focused.

## INNOVATION IN CONTRACT MANUFACTURING

Innovation processes in the pharmaceutical industry have altered dramatically over the past decade. As one manager said, 'No one expects to make anything from earth, fire and water any more.' As the chemistry has become more sophisticated, pharmaceutical companies start from more developed material now – companies have become more specialized and the development of fine chemical service companies means that 'late intermediate' products are available. Consequently, a company can be vertically integrated through some long stages of production from basic materials *vs.* buying 'late intermediate' products. Essentially, the creation of a new compound requires a completely new factory.

This increased specialization and complexity means that the distinction between R&D/innovation and production is becoming increasingly blurred and that test production is a key stage in innovation. Consequently, partnerships involving early contract manufacture involve a complex interchange between principal (the owner of the compound) and agent (the contract manufacturing company producing a test batch or early production). Genuine contract manufacturing needs to be distinguished from contract packing – simply filling bottles with capsules, etc. although the two may go together.

From the point of view of the contract manufacturer two types of production are on offer from the principals. (1) Products at the beginning of the life cycle where the big companies do not know whether the product will be profitable and are uncertain whether to invest in the product. (2) Products at the end of life 'tail end products' which are 'under the manager's feet' taking away margins and blocking the principal's factory.

Given the highly regulated nature of pharmaceutical production both the product and the production site have to be licensed (and therefore inspected) by the regulatory authorities. The product licencee must register (in the UK with the Medicine Control Inspectorate) where the production is carried out. An international standard has emerged under the US FDA requirement. The FDA do not approve the entire factory, but each product has to be approved separately. This regulation extends all the way down the supply chain. Contract manufacturers can be registered as a production site by the principal without knowing it because of their quality and good manufacturing practice. For the principal, what is important is 'the comfort factor' – knowing that a good quality job will be done. Quotation for contract manufacturing is not usually price sensitive ('finger in the air' pricing, as one manager described it). From the principal's point of view, it is quite difficult to alter the licensee and it can take 3–4 months to change this. Clients do not want to change their contract suppliers regularly.

The arrangements between clients and contract manufacturers are complex. Initially, clients 'come down and talk', have a tour of the factory and a first familiarization visit. Then the contractor is audited by the Quality Assurance team of the principal who examine the systems and control procedures. There may well be an open agreement by which the principal can visit at any time. The important factors in the relationship are quality, staff and infrastructure, the 'kit' (capital equipment) is not crucial ('it's only money') although where contract specific investments are involved, the cost issue becomes important.

An example from Newdrug was that a controlled drugs manufacturing contract involved 'spending a fortune on videos and other security devices for a small number of products – these costs were passed on to the principal'. Newdrug made a large investment in a sterile products department and needed to maintain its client base in order to service this investment.

In new product areas a standard supply agreement 'the contentious part', basically the commercial agreement ('very few of our clients do we have a written agreement with – mostly we deal on normal terms and conditions') is supplemented by a technical agreement (an EU legal requirement) ('not usually a legal document – we can agree this in an afternoon'). The technical agreement is a working document which fixes the boundaries of each person's authority. It has to be reviewed on a regular basis and these changes have to be put into the document ('These are in English not jargonese'). There are 'little or no disagreements about these' and the Medicine Control Inspectorate likes these documents because it avoids loopholes when the principal or agent misses things. Again this has implications for the cooperative relationship – 'You get three questions in order – (1) can you do it? (2) how much? and (3) when? But once that is over, it is highly unusual for somebody to come back querying the price.' 'In situations of real uncertainty, you can say "we don't know what this is going to cost" and you can quote a price for the first lot, on the understanding that this will be renegotiated in the light of experience.'

The views of managers at Ingelby Pharmaceutical on contract manufacture are reinforcing. 'The key question from contract manufacture enquiries is "can you do this molecule?". The best thing is to contract on a repeated basis (i.e. establish a relationship). The hardest thing is to get a foot in the door, the easiest thing is to do a bad job and lose the contract. What we (IP) want is to get in on a development from scratch – to build a relationship and a get a long-term partner. Because of FDA requirements, the principal cannot switch sites.' Outsourcing has increased and many principals have gone out for early quantities of a drug – for the first one or two years. 'The "out of laboratory or pilot plant" drug was developed a lot by the people who did the early production.' Although increasing cost pressure is now on the pharmaceutical majors, as the active ingredient is typically less than 10 per cent of the selling price, there are larger areas of cost to focus on.

## JOINT PRODUCT DEVELOPMENT

Geraint plc was happy to have co-development (of new compounds) with other companies, according to their head of project management. Relying on their own products was 'very risky because we can't do the whole lot ourselves'. In collaborate ventures, they are 'used to working interactively with other companies'. One particular development concept needed to be developed cooperatively because of the skills needed being dispersed in different companies, who each held patents. However, 'Geraint's senior management was paranoid about working with a company which was bigger or stronger because of the danger of take-over'. A great deal of internal negotiation and politicking was necessary in order to get collaboration off the ground. Eventually, it was with a similar-sized German company rather than with a larger British rival (with any one of whom our interviewee said that he would be happy working). One of Geraint's general managers used to work for the German company and was a close friend of one of their key board members. He persuaded the CEO to go ahead with the joint development. Even then, the development only went ahead when the regional market director for Europe lobbied for the development to go ahead – it was aimed almost exclusively at the German market for which he was responsible. A similar joint venture with a Japanese company failed, because of the side-effects of the drug. The project manager said that to 'clearly define the project objective and to keep the blinkers on is the principal factor' in the success of development projects.

In fact, the German project did not run smoothly. Four times the project manager was told (by the R&D and commercial directors) to stop the project, but four times it called in the German partner to persuade the company to continue. This was a truly joint development programme and 'I stuck my neck out as to its scientific success'. There were many cross-national team meetings and the project is now a commercial success as well as being one of the fastest on record into commercial development.

The key factors, in working across company boundaries, were identified as the attitudes and interpersonal skills of the individuals and a high level of trust. (The two companies began later cooperative projects.) It was essential that both companies wanted success and that a 'foundation for the resolution of conflict' be found. There was a clear joint objective of getting the development to market. This was helped by Geraint 'giving help even on products which the development wasn't directly concerned with'. Technical issues 'need to be debated in full and frank discussions' as do issues on the commercial agreement side, such as transfer prices.

On a second, ongoing collaboration with a US company where Geraint licensed in some technology for development, the manager felt that 'the right people and a kindred spirit of objectives is necessary [in collaborative ventures], . . . there are hurdles when you don't choose the right people to be interfaces'.

In a more general discussion, the manager was asked if it was more difficult to work within the company rather than with outside collaboration. He felt that it was not necessarily the case that outside collaboration was more difficult. 'If there is the right mind set, then there's no problem.' Information disclosure is not a problem if you have a focused objective, such as product development and getting the product to market, 'because nothing then interferes with this'. Once there are firm agreements and commitment and a working understanding, 'If push comes to shove then a written agreement is important because if one partner was obstructive then we could use it. There is "No harm" in reviewing it to know the options.'

The company wants more products than its own R&D organisation can produce at one time. Even after bringing in non-R&D people into development projects (which has proved very successful) external collaboration is necessary. The importance lies in picking teams; 'I can turn out a team from Geraint (hand-picked individuals) who can collaborate with *anybody*.' 'Virtue belongs to *people* not companies.' Everyone on the team knows that he (as project manager) will come to them and ask if they have done the prescribed tasks.

One aside – this manager felt resentful of a particular project being put out to a US University, because he felt that Geraint's own in-house team could do the job if they were given the resources. 'We know more about these compounds than anyone else in the world.' His boss replied that he wanted to see if the University *did* know any more than them – 'If not, then we are the best in the world and we have nothing to learn from outside, if they do, then we can capture it.' A risk-free strategy?

A director of the same company gave the following thoughts on alliances. Alliances have to be clearly set down on paper – they need a *preamble* (what was in the minds of the people when they set the alliance up). It is better to arrange the terms of the divorce before you get married but, hopefully, if it works well, the parties can put the contract in the drawer and forget about it: 'culture takes over'.

A French company (Pharmco) having a joint-venture agreement with a large American pharmaceutical company (Bigcorp) reached agreement on how to share research and development, such that research remained particular to each company, but that results were shared so that the companies could decide whether to co-develop or not. This arrangement was superseded before it was tested by the offer for sale of Bigcorp by its US owner. Having shared its intellectual property with Bigcorp, Pharmco was virtually obliged to buy it.

Pharmco established a large in-house research centre, to internalize R&D, and to internalize *discovery*. The research scientists found this centre 'created by financiers', 'inflexible', '*le fonctionnariat*' (and so slow-moving in a rapidly changing research environment). The head of research said, 'Yes, in a society like this, the idea is to keep it closed, to do everything within. But I am a researcher, we find many things in research that are not directly related to our main research objectives at any one time but which are *fortement interessant*, often much more interesting than the thing we are concentrating on. For me, the important thing as a researcher is "does the thing get researched or not?" (*ca se recherche ou pas?*); so I put things out all around me to other researchers ('*je les seme autour de moi*') outside the organization. The organization is *rigide, la bureaucracie, ils n'aiment pas se detourner* – i.e. when it has got a project going it doesn't like turning to outside allies, but often these are the most important – in a small society you can be flexible, in a big bureaucracy like this you can't.'

## DEVELOPMENT BY CUSTOMER CONTACT

British Developments plc (BD) is a specialist chemical company which claims that its business is customer relations where the chemicals are simply the reason for going into the company to solve their problems. The real business is customer relations and problem solving in which personal relationships are vital. A (much) earlier strategy was simply to sell the chemicals through agents ('just bunged it out') but selling to industry with high technology products with increasing competition meant that BD had to improve the technical specification and to develop direct contacts and to develop tailored products ('we don't sell chemicals, we sell solutions to customers' industrial problems') and related consultancy services. This depends on BD having an intimate knowledge of individual customers in order to sort out their problems in industrial uses where downtime is expensive. The company is now moving towards expanding its technical services and research orientation towards customer needs. These 'special effect chemicals rather than speciality chemicals' are developed with significant customer input. This involves understanding the customer's technology and devoting a large amount to research and technical services (5 per cent of turnover). 'These sales are built on trust, that someone from BD knows what he is doing. One sales manager said "I don't have customers, I have friends that I sell to".'

## DEVELOPMENT IN COOPERATION WITH SUBCONTRACTOR

SmartTec's managers talked about its relationships to subcontractors in technologically vital areas. The prevailing ethos of the corporate group was to contract out *all* manufacturing where this did not threaten the knowledge base of the company. The problems of opportunism and loss of capability were to the fore in this particular example. A senior manager in SmartTec elaborates as follows. 'Within a year, probably a bit less, we'll be a final assembly or test house. All the bits, pc's, washers, will be bought in from outside. We have a small team who make the cables, electro-mechanical manufacture, which I can't see us getting away from, partly because the specification of these comes rather late. I need to have a small flexibility for rapid response in first time orders. So I will retain a small skilled staff to do this. Also, testing is an issue. We will never be a piece part manufacturer, this is highly specialised – the machining of tantalum is done by the two brothers – they spark corrode it. We use them an awful lot, to develop new parts. They work for other people. I would never – I would be very careful about placing work with people for whom we were the only customers. If we have a downturn we put them in difficulty, or in an upturn they can't respond. So we are about 25 per cent of their business, probably; they share information about their load; we take a deliberate decision to take work away from them, with their agreement, the less sophisticated stuff – they don't want to be . . .'

> [*Question: Is there any fear of them holding you to ransom on price, since they are the only supplier*?] They don't do it. For example doubling their prices; it would be part of a conversation; we keep in touch with them; they have a problem – we talk about it. One company effectively did that to us, so we took

all the work away from them. They said O.K., and two months later were out of business. It can happen, so we try to have not a sole source, but a second also gets a small amount of work so that we can turn the tap on with them, and you can be open with them up to a point, and the ones we deal with understand that this is their position, they have work coming in from elsewhere, and they know that if we have capacity problems we will go to them. That's on the machine parts side of things.

## COOPERATION VS. IN-HOUSE R&D

Agipharm regarded itself as too small (in its subsidiary form) to undertake R&D itself. It was (is) part of a large continental European conglomerate with diverse pharmaceutical interests, grown in part out of previous industrial activity in bulk chemicals, but largely based on acquisitions (international, and only very partially integrated). The company regarded licensing-in as 'R&D on the cheap'. Their cooperations with other companies included cooperation with small research-intensive companies, themselves spin-offs from university research led by researcher-entrepreneurs. Their licensing-in agreements with one such company were talked of as 'absolute lunacy' on the part of the licensor, but it is 'easier to let out a short lead than pull in a long one', and the agreement of lunacy was not insisted upon; 'we've increased the percentage of price for them in kindness to the dog'.

Agipharm, when licensing-in, suffered constant problems of the 'not invented here' variety – 'we had to get on the phone and decide to bang heads together'. There were also problems of corporate culture and functional culture ('marketing guys, white socks and tie button undone, with ghetto blasters – the head of the other company said "God, what's this? I only listen to Radio 3" . . .'). One manager interviewed was experienced at licensing; 'the contract is, in my view, a way of solving the balls-up amicably: if things are going well, you don't bother to read them'.

'Not invented here' was regarded as a major problem 'every time'. 'Much worse if you're buying a molecule in the pre-clinical phase, they're much more sensitive, you supplant one of their babies.'

## LESSONS FOR THE PUBLIC SECTOR AND BUSINESS SECTOR

The distinction between the public sector and the business sector has, in recent years, been phrased thus:

*Public Sector*:
No competition
Cosy arrangements
Vested interests
Uncompetitive
Cooperation
Inefficiency
Waste

*Private Sector*:
Arm's length contracting
Ruthless
Competition
Efficiency
Competitive

The 'lessons for the public sector' which might most readily emerge from the above, would be the following: 'the public sector needs more (or some element of) arm's length contracting, ruthlessness and competition, in order to achieve greater efficiency and to become competitive'.

Our study of the private sector has shown that the simplistic dichotomies invoked here are of only limited value. For example, the empirical material shows that the opposition cooperation/competition cannot, in any simple way, be regarded as descriptive of the public/private opposition. It is clear from our study of the business sector that the spectrum of collaborative agreements between one company and another is a broad one, and that a complex range of intermediate possibilities exists between the two notional extremes – markets and hierarchies. Various economic theories can be invoked to make sense of these intermediate forms and this has become the stock-in-trade of transaction cost economics. From this point of view, any attempt to reform the public sector by introducing a crude notion of 'business sector competition' has to be misconceived. There are, in the business sector, long-term collaborative agreements, and trust-based inter-corporate arrangements; these are not antithetical to the 'market', but are part of the way in which real markets work.

It is, perhaps, important to stress that if the 'public' sector cannot be attacked in (simple) terms of the oppositions invoked above, neither can it be defended in the same terms. For example, take the oppositions:

Competition: Cooperation
Profit: Non-profit

The public sector, and particularly the health sector, has frequently argued (or had argued on its behalf) that competition was inappropriate in its sphere. In the health sector, it has often been said that competition, leading to profit, was morally inappropriate to the health arena ('the commodification of health', 'making money out of people's misfortune'). If the competition/cooperation opposition, however, is complex and heterogeneous *within* the business sector, then so must we expect it to be within the public sector. The moral advantage has often seemed to be with those who defend *cooperation*, within the public sector, and oppose it to *competition* within the business sector: cooperation is, again, within the terms invoked above, a more morally elevated condition – non-profit as opposed to profit, selfless as opposed to selfish, and so on. Once the opposition cooperation/competition breaks down, however, then so too do the easy moral securities at issue here. It would then be quite possible, and has surely happened, that inefficiency, waste and vested interests within the public sector, could be defended (or at least morally concealed) through the assertion that competition was morally selfish. In the public sector, as in the business sector, the conceptual oppositions that we use need to be more subtly rendered.

## CONCLUSION

In cooperative strategies in R&D and innovation as in other decisions involving transactions costs, three dimensions appear to be critical: (i) frequency of transacting, (ii) uncertainty and (iii) the degree to which the transaction is supported by specific investments (asset specificity) (Williamson, 1975).

It is virtually impossible to exaggerate the importance of repeated transactions, particularly in situations of uncertain outcomes, such as research cooperations. Words such as trust, commitment and 'comfort zone' were frequently used by managers in setting up R&D contracts and contacts. The existence of specific assets is not a clear obstacle, given the recognition of the two (or more) parties to the arrangement. Rarely, if ever, did we find that potential R&D cooperations were aborted because of 'up-front' asset costs.

## References


Buckley, P. J. (1992) in *Studies in International Business*. London: Macmillan.

——and Casson, M. (1988) 'A Theory of Cooperation in International Business', in F. J. Contractor and P. Lorange (eds), *Cooperative Strategies in International Business*. Lexington, MA: Lexington Books.

——and Casson, M. (1996) 'An Economic Model of International Joint Ventures', *Journal of International Business Studies*, 27, 5, 849–76.

——and Chapman, M. (1996a) 'Economics and Social Anthropology – Reconciling Differences', *Human Relations*, 49, 9, 1123–50.

——and Chapman, M. (1996b) 'Theory and Method in International Business Research', *International Business Review*, 5, 3, 233–45.

——and Chapman, M. (1997) 'The Perception and Measurement of Transaction Cost', *Cambridge Journal of Economics*, March, 21, 2, 127–45.

——and Chapman, M. (1998) 'The Use of "Native Categories" in Management Research', *British Journal of Management*, 8, 4, 283–99.

——and Michie, J. (eds) (1996) *Firms, Organizations and Contracts*. Oxford: Oxford University Press.

Casson, M. (ed.) (1991a) *Global Research Strategy and International Competitiveness*. Oxford: Basil Blackwell.

——(1991b) *The Economics of Business Culture*. Oxford: Oxford University Press.

——(1995) *The Organisation of International Business*. Cheltenham: Edward Elgar.

Chapman, M. and Buckley, P. J. (1997) 'Markets, Transaction Costs, Economists and Social Anthropologists', in J. Carrier (ed.), *Meanings of the Market: The Free Market in Western Culture*. Oxford: Berg.

Clark, J. M. (1923) *Studies in the Economics of Overhead Costs*. Chicago: University of Chicago Press.
Dore, R. (1996) 'Goodwill and the Spirit of Market Capitalism', *British Journal of Sociology*, 34, 4, 459–82 (reprinted in Buckley, P. J. and Michie, J., eds, *Firms Organization and Contracts*. Oxford: Oxford University Press).
Fruin, W. M. (1992) *The Japanese Enterprise System*. Oxford: Clarendon Press.
Horngren, C. T. (1975) 'Management Accounting: Where are We?', in *Management Accounting and Control*. Madison: University of Wisconsin Press.
Johnson, H. T. and Kaplan, R. S. (1987) *Relevance Lost – The Rise and Fall of Management Accounting*. Cambridge, MA: Harvard Business School Press.
Kreps, D. M. (1986) 'Corporate Culture and Economic Theory', in M. Tsuchiya (ed.), *Technological Innovation and Business Strategy*. Tokyo: Nikon Keizai Shimbun, 1986 (reprinted in Buckley, P. J. and Michie, J., eds, *Firms, Organizations and Contracts*. Oxford: Oxford University Press, 1996).
Macaulay, S. (1996) 'Non-Contractual Relations in Business: A Preliminary Study', in P. J. Buckley and J. Michie (eds), *Firms, Organizations and Contracts*. Oxford: Oxford University Press.
Sako, M. (1992) *Prices, Quality and Trust*. Oxford: Oxford University Press.
Scapens, R. W. (1991) *Management Accounting: A Review of Recent Developments*, 2nd edn. London: Macmillan.
Williamson, O. (1975) *Markets and Hierarchies*, New York: Free Press.

# 12 Cross-Border Governance in Multinational Enterprises*

Peter J. Buckley

## INTRODUCTION

The primary meaning of governance in the literature and in common parlance is that decision-takers (in the firm) must be accountable to someone for their actions. The problem arises from the separation of ownership from control in the modern (multinational) company. The structures which constrain managers' pursuit of self-interest at the expense of the true owners' (shareholders') interests are nowadays termed the 'governance structure' of the company. The accountability of managers to shareholders can be accomplished by a number of such means and the choices between these means are grist to the mill of those who study corporate governance.

Structures of governance are largely national. There are immense differences in the structures of governance between countries – even within economic blocs such as the European Union. Multinational firms, by definition, operate across these national governance structures and are, therefore, faced with problems of cross-border governance as a major consequence of international expansion.

This chapter analyses cross-border governance by examining the two meanings which analysts have given the term. The first meaning of governance is the conventional one outlined above, which concerns the control of managers by owners and

* First published as Chapter 9 in Kevin Keasey, Steve Thompson and Mike Wright (eds), *Corporate Governance: Economic, Management and Financial Issues* (Oxford University Press, 1997).

which has been analysed by variants of principal–agent theory (following Jensen and Meckling, 1976). The second meaning, more often utilized by international business theory, concerns the governance of economic transactions. This mode of analysis follows Williamson (1975, 1979, 1985) and Teece (1983) and relates closely to the internalization approach to the explanation of multinational enterprise (Buckley and Casson, 1976, 1985; Buckley, 1983, 1988, 1990) which builds on the pioneering work of Ronald Coase (1937) (see Blaine, 1994 for an exposition). This chapter attempts to combine these approaches, and to point out the complementarities between them in a fuller explanation of cross-border governance.

There are, of course, many extra dimensions of governance when we consider cross-border issues. Overlapping regimes is only one additional issue. Multinational firms straddle all forms of system but also have internal governance issues – in particular the relationship between subsidiary managers and parent companies.

## GOVERNANCE COSTS

If we begin with the notion of the firm as a set of relationships or a portfolio of contracts, it is easy to see that the particular configuration of contracts (the architecture of the firm, as Kay, 1994 puts it) will be a major determinant of its success and of the nature of the firm (to echo the key sentiment of Coase's seminal 1937 article). The boundary of the firm is set by the point at which further internal relationship is more expensive than an external market-based relationship (Buckley and Casson, 1976), thus the 'make or buy' decision is the determinant of the boundary of the firm. This feature, the internalization decision, has been well analysed in the analysis of the growth of the (multinational) firm. What has not been so well analysed is the precise configuration of the internal architecture of the firm, i.e. its governance structure (Buckley and Carter, 1996a, b).

An attempt to show the power of these ideas was made by Teece (1983), who investigated technological and organizational factors as determining the scope of the firm through production costs. Teece's analysis of horizontal integration envisages governance costs and production costs as both being a function of an 'index of the complexity of know how' in the firm. Governance costs of different forms of doing business abroad (licensing versus foreign direct investment, FDI), are a function of the complexity of technology. The FDI mode is invariant to increasing complexity of knowledge because of the ease with which tacit knowledge can be transferred by internal markets. But the governance costs of licensing increase with the complexity of knowledge because of increasing costs of firm-to-firm transfer. A similar evaluation is made of the production costs in each mode, and then production costs and governance costs are summed to give total costs of the modes of doing business abroad so that an optimal scope of horizontal integration is given for each level of complexity of know-how. A similar exercise is conducted for vertical integration. Market based relations are contrasted with vertically integrated relations by making their governance costs of market relations and vertical integration functions of an index of asset specificity where vertical integration has both a set-up cost (higher than setting up market relationships) and a lower variable cost of operation. As asset specificity increases, so does the possibility of integration.

In Teece's model (which has much in common with Buckley and Casson, 1981), governance costs are a function of complexity of knowledge and asset specificity. There is also a (minor) international determinant of governance costs of integration – the risk of expropriation. The greater these risks, the more international governance costs will rise, favouring arm's length relationships (licensing, purchasing) rather than internal ones (FDI, integration).

Teece's analysis is interesting from our point of view in attempting to put governance costs centre-stage in the analysis of multinationals, but it does so only as an intermediate variable (the real drivers are complexity of (tacit) knowledge and asset specificity) and it has a weak international dimension. That governance costs and production costs are separable and additive also requires justification, at the least.

If we step back from Teece's exposition to Williamson's basic framework, we can first agree with Williamson's most recent work that markets and hierarchies are not a simple opposition, but may be more like extreme points on a continuum. Richardson (1972) made this point most cogently, arguing that firms are surrounded by a sea of cooperative relationships.

Williamson himself argues that 'governance structures – the institutional matrix within which transactions are negotiated and executed – vary with the nature of the transaction' (1979, p. 103). All transactions are not equal. Some may be endowed with social characteristics which others lack. Moreover, repeated transactions may take on a different character than one-off deals. This opens the possibilities for a more rounded discussion of governance costs.

## GOVERNANCE AND INTERNAL TRANSACTION COSTS

Theoretical arguments on the internal organization of the firm suggest two polar extremes: the purist view of internalization expounded by Buckley and Casson (1976, 1985), in which the firm functions as an approximation to a perfect market, which can be contrasted with the 'markets and hierarchies' approach of Williamson (1975, 1979), which considers that integration (internalization) is accompanied by suspension of the price mechanism and the allocation of internal resources by management fiat.

In the first of these approaches, the firm's internal organization is designed so as to transmit shadow prices to managers between decentralized cost centres and profit centres, so that the overall profits are maximized (Buckley, 1983). Hennart (1986) has drawn parallels between this view and approaches to economic planning (Heal, 1973). Each decision-maker within the firm maximizes profits, given the internal prices; in effect the firm includes in these prices an optimal tax, leaving members with an income which is just enough to keep them in their present employment (Hirshleifer, 1986).

In contrast, the markets and hierarchies approach takes the view that 'bounded rationality' and 'opportunism' mean either that it is impossible to find the 'correct' prices, even in an internalized market, or that individuals' response to price would result in damaging externalities for the rest of the organization. Hierarchy overcomes these problems by constraining actions through management directive rather than price signals, replacing the market by another mechanism and not merely internalizing it.

In practice, internal organization often lies between these two extremes. The actual internal organization of the firm is a response to three problems of organizational design: the *motivation problem* arising from decentralized information, the *coordination problem* arising from the complementarity between the actions of separate individuals, and the *maturation problem* arising from the pursuit of individual rather than shared goals. Buckley and Carter (1996a, b) use these problems to construct a classification of internal transaction costs.

These internal transaction costs are the result of derogation from the optimal set of actions, which only arise if:

1. all participants have access to the best decision-relevant knowledge (*perfect information*),
2. all complementary actions are chosen jointly (*perfect coordination*), and
3. all members of the firm share the firm's objective function (*perfect motivation*).

The following cost measures arise from departures from the optimal pay-off for the firm:

| | |
|---|---|
| Information loss: | the reduction in pay-off to the firm caused by members (managers) not having the best available information |
| Information cost: | the cost of acquiring and transmitting information |
| Coordination loss: | the reduction in pay-off to the firm arising when complementary actions are not chosen jointly |
| Coordination cost: | the cost of communication about complementary actions or of providing for them to be combined |
| Motivation loss: | the reduction in pay-off to the firm caused by members pursuing their own objectives |
| Motivation cost: | the cost of incentive measures taken by the firm. |

Motivation costs might include the cost of incentive schemes to align the actions of managers with the objectives of the firm, i.e. eliminating 'agency costs' through shadow pricing (Jensen and Meckling, 1976), or the cost of supervision and monitoring of employees' actions or the cost of training and socializing designed to induce employees to adopt the firm's goods.

Information, coordination, and motivation losses are, in effect, internal 'externalities' arising from the division of managerial labour within the firm, and the associated costs measure the resources deployed in correcting the externalities. The goal of the firm's governance structure is to minimize the sum of these internal transaction costs.

## GOVERNANCE AND INTERNAL TRANSACTION COSTS IN MULTINATIONAL FIRMS

There are grounds for believing that organizational externalities and costs (information, coordination, and motivation), and therefore problems of governance, will be more severe in multinational firms than in uninational ones (Buckley and Carter, 1996a, b). The simplest set of factors which increase the costs of communication and the exchange of ideas and knowledge is the spatial separation of individuals who hold complementary knowledge and who could gain from coordinating the actions. In a multinational firm, it is likely that spatially separated individuals have different first languages. Advances in technology and in education have played a large part in reducing these costs in recent years. The growth of electronic mail and video conferencing, together with the adoption of English as the world's business language, make it likely that international intra-office communications costs will converge with local costs. For example, English is the official language of the ABB group, even though only a third of its employees speak it as their mother language (*Economist*, 1996).

Language may, however, be obscuring more fundamental differences between national outlooks and routines, which fundamentally influence communication and coordination. Hedlund and Nonaka (1993) examine the way in which information and knowledge are constructed in different cultures. They summarize common perceptions about the differences between Japanese and Western firms in terms of differences in the extent to which the firm's knowledge is 'tacit' or 'articulated' and the degree to which knowledge is held by individuals or groups. Western firms are characterized by individually held, articulated knowledge and Japanese firms by tacit knowledge held at the level of the group. More generally, there are numerous differences in the everyday assumptions (norms) which individuals make about the actions of others in a given situation, about the standards of acceptable behaviour and the interpretation of tacit signals, such as body language, which play a major part in the successful coordination of the actions of groups. These differences in routines may in themselves imply differences in performance of some kinds of task (cf. Buckley and Casson, 1992, pp. 228–31), but where related tasks are to be carried out by individuals who hold different social and cultural assumptions, the dangers of misunderstanding and misinformation may detract significantly from the joint effectiveness of the collaboration, unless considerable time is spent in developing mutual understanding.

It may be particularly difficult to motivate individuals in different countries diligently to pursue the interests of the organization as a whole. In the conventional economic arguments on moral hazard and adverse selection in organizations, the monitoring problem is exacerbated by the geographic and cultural distance involved in multinational operations. The risks of opportunism may therefore be higher and the costs of counter-measures may be higher, too. In cultures which do not conform to the individualist stereotype, individuals may identify with a group or community, within which they behave altruistically, or with the shared interest of the community in mind. Thus, it may be expected (or suspected) that individuals will favour the perceived interests of their national subsidiary rather than the overall interests of the firm.

## GOVERNANCE IN INTERNATIONAL BUSINESS THEORY

A large part of micro- (firm-) level international business theory has concerned the foreign market servicing decisions of multinational firms. Crudely put, this concerns the choices which firms make between exporting, foreign licensing of technology (or rights), and foreign direct investment. The key elements determining this decision can be resolved into two: the location decision and the internalization (or externalization) decision. Thus exporting is foreign-located, internally controlled, licensing is foreign-located, market-determined (externally controlled), and FDI is foreign-located, internally controlled. The governance decision (represented crudely by internal versus market transfer) is a key element in this analysis.

However, this crude picture becomes more complex – and more interesting – when we move to a consideration of intermediate forms: alliances and joint ventures. It is in the analysis of alliances and joint ventures where issues of governance are central. Alliances (usually meaning an alliance between two established multinational firms to do business globally, in third countries or within one 'trading bloc') and joint ventures (most often used to denote a venture between a foreign multinational and a host country entity to do business, initially at least, in the host country or in its trading bloc) involve some notion of shared governance. Shared internationally; moreover, key issues then become the nature of cooperation and the cultural influences on governance.

Buckley and Casson (1988) define cooperation as 'coordination effected through mutual forbearance' (p. 32). This leads to the notion that the operation of a joint venture is a repeated game in which the partners move towards a *modus operandi* where each forbears from damaging the interests of the other. Over time, mutual goals can be achieved by the operation of this mechanism and a second-order condition comes into being where cooperation becomes an end in itself. The partners can then begin to build a reputation for cooperative behaviour and, as with any other asset, this reputation can yield returns of its own.

Mutual forbearance generates trust between the partners and trust has an economic value in that it substitutes for monitoring costs making governance less expensive. Thus a link is established between the social concept of trust and the economic concept transaction costs. Governance costs in the presence of trust will be lower. Thus we have an alternative scenario to the principal–agent model. Rather than engineering incentives to engender action in accord with the wishes of the principal, trust between the two can be a (less costly) substitute.

## THE CULTURAL DIMENSION

Hofstede's studies (1980) have shown that even in a multinational with a strong company culture (IBM was the key example), national differences between (workers and) managers can have strong manifestations. This can potentially give an extra dimension to the principal–agent problems where the principal (the headquarters company) and the agent (the subsidiary management) have a very different cultural orientation. This can entail extra costs of global governance.

As well as this internal dimension, the external societal and institutional structures which multinational firms encounter differ greatly across nations and continents. These two issues are not additive, however. The use of local subsidiary management can help to offset 'costs of foreignness' because of their understanding of local institutions and markets.

Of particular importance in this context are lesser forms of association between companies (and other local institutions) including networks such as keiretsu structures in Japan and throughout Asia in different guises. Such associations have a social as well as an economic dimension. They may be regarded as alternative forms of governance (Blaine, 1994; Johanson and Mattson, 1987; Hakansson and Johanson, 1993) or as major variations on the theme of cooperative relationships between companies.

The legal system reflects and supports the institutional culture at national level This has ramifications from determining the mode of entry of multinationals (preventing wholly owned subsidiaries in favour of joint ventures, excluding imports (except of technology), etc.) through to setting standards of corporate behaviour which may differ from those of the host country. Codes of corporate governance, such as those set by the Cadbury Committee in the UK, are invariably national codes, even within the European Union, and awareness and compliance with these codes have non-trivial costs.

Wider notions than legal regulations need to be invoked. Norms of behaviour – expectation, public opinion, unwritten rules – need to be respected by multinational firms even more so than local ones that do not have the stigma of foreignness. An important example of this issue can be seen in the contrasting attitudes to exchanges of personnel between government (political) service and business. In Britain, a set of rules is being enacted, following the Nolan Committee's recommendations, to inhibit (if not prevent) the transfer of recently retired government ministers to private sector boardrooms. In Japan, the transfer of expoliticians and particularly civil servants to the private sector is known as *amukadari* (descent from heaven) and is often held by commentators to account, at least in part, for the unity of view and of purpose between government policy and business strategy.

Many commentators have divided systems of corporate governance between market-based systems and bank-based systems (e.g. numerous chapters in Dimsdale and Prevezer 1994). The market-based systems of Britain and the USA are often contrasted with the bank-based systems of Germany and Japan. Frequently, the bank-based system is held to be superior because of the superior recent economic performance of its representative country cases. In a market-dominated system, titles can be traded without the ownership right being exercised. It is argued that the bank-based system enforces the accountability of managers to shareholders on a long-term basis because of the closer cooperation between the suppliers of capital (the banks) and the users of capital. This caricature has been clouded recently by recent Japanese bank crises, which have caused doubts to emerge about the efficacy of the system. In theory at least, stock markets allow managerial failure to be corrected through markets for corporate control.

Multinational firms straddle both 'systems'. To some degree this is an opportunity because it enables them to access a wide variety of (local) financing. It also imposes adjustment costs. In a sense, multinational firms operate both systems as a matter of course.

## GOVERNANCE IN MULTINATIONAL FIRMS

Adam Smith felt that there was serious doubt about the ability of managers of joint stock companies to behave efficiently and reliably . . . particularly managing foreign ventures! Smith puts the principal–agent problems firmly at the forefront of the difficulties of managing a joint-stock company.

> The trade of a joint stock company is always managed by a court of directors. This court, indeed, is frequently subject, in many respects, to the control of a general count of proprietors. But the greater part of those proprietors seldom pretend to understand anything of the business of the company, and when the spirit of faction happens not to prevail among them, give themselves contentedly such half yearly or yearly dividend, as the directors think proper to make to them. This total exemption from trouble and from risk, beyond a limited sum, encourages many people to become adventurers in joint stock companies, who would, upon no account, hazard their fortunes in any private copartnery! (Smith, 1776/1976, pp. ii. 264).

This problem is compounded when large joint-stock companies venture into foreign lands.

> The directors of such companies, however, being the managers rather of other people's money than of their own, it cannot well be expected, that they should watch over it with the same anxious vigilance with which the partners in a private copartnery frequently watch over their own. Like the stewards of a rich man, they are apt to consider attention to small matters as not for their master's honour, and very easily give themselves a dispensation from having it. Negligence and profusion, therefore, must always prevail, more or less, in the management of the affairs of such a company. It is upon this account that joint stock companies for foreign trade have seldom been able to maintain the competition against private adventurers. They have, accordingly, very seldom succeeded without an exclusive privilege, and frequently have not succeeded with one. Without an exclusive privilege they have commonly

> mismanaged the trade. With an exclusive privilege they have both mismanaged and confined it. (Smith 1776/1976, pp. ii. 264–5)[1]

Far from regarding multinationality as a problem for the governance of firms, many modern commentators see it as an advantage. Kogut (1983) sees sequential internationalization as conferring dynamic benefits on multinational firms. Whilst it is true that experience in international operations lowers governance costs relative to an inexperienced foreign investor, it is not self-evident that governance costs will be lower than a purely local (or uninational) firm. Indeed, this is in opposition to the Hymer postulate (1976) that the costs of doing business abroad are positive and that firms require a compensating advantage in order to be able to compete with locals. It seems reasonable to conclude that the extra costs of cross-border governance will be positive but will be a declining function of time and geographical spread. There will be exceptions to this, however, particularly for idiosyncratic markets, unusually large foreign markets, and ones with large cultural entry and operational barriers.

## ORGANIZATIONAL RESPONSES OF MULTINATIONAL FIRMS TO PROBLEMS OF GOVERNANCE

There has been no shortage of organizational prescriptions for solving the problems of governance in multinational firms. Buckley and Casson (1992) discuss several responses: divisionalization, matrix structures, and strategic business units and joint ventures.

The divisional (M-form) organization makes use of local information in decision-making by devolving operating decisions to specialist divisions, coordinates the application of shared assets via the head office, and motivates divisional managers through their profit contributions in the firm's internal capital market (see Williamson, 1975, ch. 8). The process of internationalization often results either in national divisions, where divisions duplicate marketing and sometimes production, or in product division, where several divisions operate within the same territory. Both forms of divisionalization leave residual opportunities for sharing common resources and knowledge, and the matrix approach is an attempt to provide cross-cutting channels of information exchange and coordination of activities. However, these channels are often a cumbersome way of dealing with information, for they can be bureaucratic and excessively hierarchical in character, and they complicate managerial motivation, for 'no man can serve two masters'. Divided loyalties can result in losses of motivation, and the cost of information and coordination can result in the heavy overheads of a large head office.

The strategic business unit can be seen as a development of the full matrix structure and it has been termed the 'weak matrix' (Lorange, 1993). Selected linkages (e.g. country and product) are combined into identified 'business element' teams charged with achieving specified targets where an opportunity has been identified for capitalizing or improving the combination of knowledge and coordinating action. Team performance targets can provide clear motivation for team members. However, competition between groups can reduce the beneficial sharing of complementary knowledge and resources, particularly as the business unit leaders are often engaged on a 'managerial' promotion track which encourages them to focus on group performance rather than the fullest possible exploitation of technology (Buckley and Casson, 1988).

Networks of joint ventures and alliances are often claimed to have advantages of increased flexibility and decentralization of authority, but these are not always evident in practice. A key advantage of joint venture networks is that individual elements of the firm can be free to choose appropriate collaborations and can, if they wish, participate in several joint ventures (Buckley and Casson, 1995). Knowledge can be exploited in the way that its holders choose, and the motivation for success comes from the holders' returns on their portfolio of joint ventures. However, the value of joint ventures is contingent upon the circumstances of the partners, and the risk that they will prove short-lived has often resulted in reduced trust between the partners and less than complete disclosure of the information that the venture is established to share (Buckley and Casson, 1988, 1992).

## CONCLUSION

The problems of cross-border governance are the analogue of the costs of internalizing a market across national boundaries. There are four categories of such costs: the resource costs of managing internal markets, the extra communication costs involved, the higher management costs, and the specifically international element stemming from (potential) discrimination against foreign owned firms (Buckley and Casson, 1976). Although only the final cost is specifically international, differences in culture and language and problems of distance are likely to mean that the internalization of markets across international boundaries (costs of cross-border governance) are likely to be greater than purely domestic internalization.

There are undoubtedly learning effects which reduce the cost of cross-border governance both over time and in repeated international ventures. It is not, however, possible to claim that cross-border governance costs ever fall to zero (or below zero).

## Note

1. Part of this section is quoted by Leslie Hannah (1976, pp. 19–20), whose book on the rise of the corporate economy can be read as a business history of corporate governance.

## References

Blaine, Michael (1994) *Cooperation in International Business: The Use of Limited Equity Arrangements*. Aldershot: Avebury.

Buckley, Peter J. (1983) 'New Theories of International Business: Some Unresolved Issues', in Mark Casein (ed.), *The Growth of International Business*. London: George Allen & Unwin.

——(1988) 'The Limits of Explanation: Testing the Internalisation Theory of the Multinational Enterprise', *Journal of International Business Studies*, 19, 181–93.

——(1990) 'Problems and Developments in the Core Theory of International Business', *Journal of International Business Studies*, 21, 657–65.

——and Martin J. Carter (1996a) 'The Economics of Business Process Design: Maturation, Information and Co-ordination within the Firm', *International Journal of the Economics of Business* (forthcoming).

——(1996b) 'The Economics of Business Process Design in Multinational Firms', in Ram Mudambi and Martin Ricketts (eds.), *The Organisation of the Firm: International Business Perspectives*. London: Routledge, forthcoming.

——and Mark Casson (1976) *The Future of the Multinational Enterprise*. London: Macmillan.

——(1981) 'The Optimal Timing of a Foreign Direct Investment', *Economic Journal*, 92, 75–87.

——(1985) *The Economic Theory of the Multinational Enterprise*. London: Macmillan.

——(1988) 'A Theory of Cooperation in International Business', in Farok J. Contractos and Peter Lorange (eds.), *Cooperative Strategies in International Business*. Lexington, Mass: Lexington Books.

——(1992) 'Organising for Innovation: The Multinational Enterprise in the Twenty-First Century', in Peter J. Buckley and Mark Casson (eds.), *The Multinational Enterprise in the World Economy: Essays in Honour of John H. Dunning*. Cheltenham: Edward Elgar.

——(1995) 'An Economic Model of International Joint Ventures', Centre for International Business, University of Leeds (CIBUL), mimeo.

Chandler, Alfred D., Jr. (1962) *Strategy and Structure: Chapters in the History of the American Industrial Enterprise*. Cambridge, Mass.: MIT Press.

——(1977) *The Visible Hand: The Managerial Revolution in American Business*. Cambridge, Mass.: Belknap Press.

——and Herman Daems (eds.) (1980) *Managerial Hierarchies: Comparative Perspectives on the Rise of the Modern Industrial Enterprise*. Cambridge, Mass.: Harvard University Press.

Coase, Ronald H. (1937) 'The Nature of the Firm', *Economica*, 4: 386–405.

Dimsdale, Nicholas and Martha Prevezer (eds.) (1994), *Capital Markets and Corporate Governance*. Oxford: Oxford University Press.

*Economist* (1996), 'The ABB of Management', 6 Jan. 1996, 64.

Hakanson, Hakan and Jan Johanson (1993), 'The Network as a Governance Structure: Interform Cooperation beyond Markets and Hierarchies', in G. Brabher (ed.), *The Embedded Firm: On the Socioeconomics of Industrial Networks*. London: Routledge.

Hannah, Leslie (1976) *The Rise of the Corporate Economy*. London: Methuen.

Heal, Geoffrey M. (1973), *The Theory of Economic Planning*. Amsterdam: North-Holland.

Hedlund, Gunnar and Ikujiro Nonaka (1993) 'Models of Knowledge Management in the West and Japan', in Peter Lorange, Bela Chakravarthy, Johan Roos, and Andrew Van der Ven (eds.), *Implementing Strategic Processes: Change Learning and Cooperation*. Oxford: Blackwell.

Hennart, Jean-François (1986) 'What is Internalisation?', *Weltwirtschaftliches Archiv*, 122, 791–804.

Hirshleifer, Jack (1986) 'On the Economics of Transfer Pricing', *Journal of Business*, 29, 172–84.

Hofstede, Geert (1980) *Culture's Consequences: International Differences in Work Related Values*. London: Sage.

Hymer, Stephen H. (1976) *The International Operations of National Firms*. Cambridge, Mass.: MIT Press.

Jensen, Michael and William Meckling (1976) 'Theory of the Firm, Managerial Behavior, Agency Costs, and Ownership Structure', *Journal of Financial Economics*, 3, 305–60.

Johanson, Jan and Lars-Gunnar Mattson (1987) 'Interorganizational Relations in Industrial Systems: A Network Approach Compared with the Transactions-Cost Approach', *International Studies of Management and Organization*, 17, 34–48.

Kay, John (1994) 'Corporate Strategy and Corporate Accountability', in Dimsdale and Prevezer (1994).

Kogut, Bruce (1983) 'Foreign Direct Investment as a Sequential Process', in C. P. Kindleberger and D. Audretsch (eds.), *The Multinational Cooperation in the 1980s*. Cambridge, Mass.: MIT Press.

Lorange, Peter (1993) *Strategic Planning and Control: Issues in the Strategy Process*. Oxford: Blackwell.

Richardson, G. B. (1972) 'The Organisation of Industry', *Economic Journal* (Sept.), 883–96.

Smith, Adam (1776) *An Inquiry into the Nature and Causes of the Wealth of Nations*, ed. Edwin Cannan. Chicago: University of Chicago Press, 1976.

Teece, David (1983) 'Technological and Organisational Factors in the Theory of the Multinational Enterprise', in Mark Casson (ed.), *The Growth of International Business*. London: George Allen & Unwin.

Williamson, Oliver E. (1975) *Markets and Hierarchies*. New York: Free Press.

—— (1979), 'Transaction Cost Economics: The Governance of Contractual Relations', *Journal of Law and Economics*, 22: 223–61.

—— (1985), *The Economic Institution of Capitalism*. New York: Free Press.

# People Index

Adler, N. 239
Agarwal, Sanjeev 64
Allen, Linda 31
Anderson, Erin M. 64, 157, 161, 162, 163, 165, 173, 207
Ardener, E. W. 236, 238, 245, 248, 251, 254, 265
Arpan, Jeffrey S. 40
Awadzi, W. 208

Baird, Inga S. 164
Bakema, Harry G. 66
Banks, John C. 65, 162
Bartlett, Christopher A. 29
Baughn, C. Christopher 158
Beamish, Paul W. 65, 160, 162, 164, 202, 203, 205, 207, 209
Beguin, J. P. 204
Behrman, J. 204
Bell, John H. J. 66
Benito, Gabriel R. G. 66
Best, Michael H. 26
Birkinshaw, Julian 65, 164, 205
Blaine, Michael 290, 297
Blodgett, Linda L. 65, 164, 207
Bohannan, L. 255
Bohannan, P. 255
Bond, M. 241
Bourdieu, P. 247
Boyacigiller, N. 239
Brown, S. 247, 266
Buckley, Peter J. 5, 13, 15, 20, 21, 26, 34, 37, 45, 63, 64, 65, 66, 67, 94, 95, 96, 97, 104, 118–19, 125–6, 127, 128, 129, 144, 145, 146, 157, 158, 161, 163, 207, 209, 230, 252, 255, 257, 270, 271, 290, 291, 292, 293, 294, 295, 296, 300, 301, 302
Burrell, G. 239, 266

Cameron, Kim S. 161, 206
Campa, Jose Manuel 34
Cantwell, John 27
Capel, Jeanette 30
Carr, C. 128
Carter, Martin J. 290, 294
Casson, Mark C. 5, 13, 15, 16, 18, 19, 21, 23, 25, 26, 29, 34, 36, 37, 45, 63, 64, 65, 66, 67, 95, 96, 118–19, 144, 158, 161, 252, 255, 256, 257, 271, 272, 290, 291, 292, 293, 295, 296, 300, 301, 302
Caves, Richard, E. 9, 63
Chakravarthy, Balaji S. 161, 206
Chapman, Malcolm 13, 254, 270
Chi, Tailan 36
Child, J. 203
Chinta, R. 208
Chowdhury, Jafor 164, 206
Clark, J. M. 273
Clegg, J. 109
Clifford, J. 251
Coase, Ronald, H. 145, 259, 290
Cole, R. E. 125
Contractor, Farok J. 64, 65, 158, 159, 163, 209
Coughlan, A. T. 64
Cravens, K. S. 126, 128
Crick, M. 238
Cullen, J. B. 211, 229

Davidson, William H. 64
Davis, J. 249, 255, 256, 258
D'Cruz, Joseph R. 26
Delios, A. 202, 209
DeMeza, David 30
Dempster, Michael A. H. 33
Dimsdale, Nicholas 298
d'Iribarne, P. 264

Dixit, Avrinash 33
Dore, R. 271
Douglas, M. 249, 255, 256, 259, 262, 265
Drucker, P. F. 125
Dubin, Michael 65
Dunning, John H. 15, 18, 44–6, 48–9, 52, 53, 55, 56, 62, 98, 118, 119
Durkheim, E. 249, 262
Dussauge, Pierre 164, 215

Eccles, Robert G. 161
Ellen, R. 249
Elliott, J. 124
Ellis, J. 247
Ergas, Henry 18
Evans-Pritchard, E. 238, 257

Flowers, E. B. 66, 98
Franko, Lawrence G. 66, 98
Fransman, Martin 16
Frecknall Hughes, J. 125–6, 127, 128, 129
Friedman. W. G. 204
Fruin, W. M. 275
Fukuyama, Francis 30
Fuller, M. B. 209

Garrette, Bernard 164, 215
Gatignon, Hubert 64
Gerbod, P. 264
Geringer, J. Michael 13, 65, 159, 160, 162–6, 169–75, 177, 180, 187, 189, 191, 192, 196, 202, 203, 204, 205, 206, 207, 208, 209, 215, 219, 228, 229, 230
Ghauri, Pervez N. 63, 97, 146
Ghoshal, Sumantra 29, 241
Glaister, Keith 96, 97, 157, 163, 207, 209, 215, 229, 230
Gomes-Casseres, Benjamin 65, 158, 164, 207, 209
Goodman, Paul S. 161, 206
Gorg, Holger 89
Graham, Edward M. 66, 98, 147
Gray, B. 203, 204, 206, 209, 210, 226, 228, 229
Gripsrud, Geir 66

Gulati, Ranjay 65, 165
Gullander, S. 204

Hagedoorn, John 158
Hakanson, Hakan 297
Hallen, Lars 64, 97, 145, 160
Hamada, K. 128
Hamel, Gary 63
Hannah, Leslie 302
Harrigan, Kathryn R. 65, 159, 164, 202, 206
Hayes, R. H. 125
Heal, Geoffrey M. 292
Hebert, Louis 13, 65, 159, 160, 162–6, 169–75, 177, 180, 187, 189, 191, 192, 196, 202, 203, 204, 205, 206, 207, 208, 209, 219, 228, 229, 230
Hedlund, Gunnar 29, 294
Hennart, Jean-François 65, 69, 97, 292
Hergert, Michael 157
Higson, C. 124
Hill, C. W. L. 64
Hirsh, Seev 63
Hirshleifer, Jack 33, 292
Hocart, M. 237, 238
Hofstede, Geert 65, 66, 160, 264, 297
Hood, Neil 10
Horngren, C. T. 273
Horst, T. D. 63
Hwang, Peter 64
Hymer, Stephen H. 61, 63, 98, 300

Inkpen, Andrew C. 65, 164, 205
Innes, J. 128, 139
Ito, Kiyotaki 66

Jackson, A. 264
Jacobson, Robert 161
Jacoby, Jacob 172
Janger, Allen R. 164, 207
Jenkins, T. 247
Jensen, Michael 290, 294
Johanson, Jan 35, 64, 297
Johnson, H. T. 274, 275
Johnson, J. L. 211

Kaplan, R. S. 274, 275
Kato, M. 128
Kay, John 290
Kay, Neil M. 97
Kedia, B. L. 208
Kharbanda, O. P. 125
Killing, J. Peter 65, 164, 205, 206, 207, 208, 212
Kim, C. W. 264
Kim, W. Chan 64
Kindleberger, C. P. 61, 63
Knickerbocker, Frederick T. 66, 98, 147
Kogut, Bruce 30, 35, 37, 64, 65, 66, 163, 164, 205, 206, 207, 300
Koh, Jeongsuk 164
Kotter, John 30
Kreps, David M. 36, 272
Krugman, Paul 14–15, 20
Kulatilaka, Nalin 30
Kuper, A. 251, 264

Lall, Sanjaya 14
Leach, E. 238, 254
Lecraw, Donald J. 164, 206
Lee, C. 203
Lévi-Strauss, C. 237, 255, 262, 265
Lewin, Arie Y. 161, 206
Lin, J. L. 203
Llewellyn, Karl 254
Loasby, Brian J. 32
Lorange, Peter 65, 158, 159, 163, 209, 301
Lu, Y. 203
Lummer, Scott L. 164
Lyles, Marjorie A. 164

Macaulay, S. 271
Madhok, A. 202
Makino, Shige 65
Malinowski, B. 236, 238, 254, 255, 257
Marcus, G. 251
Marglin, Stephen A. 11
Marris, Robin L. 17
Marschak, Jacob 34
Marshall, Alfred 26
Martin, R. 255
Matell, Michael S. 172
Mattson, Lars-Gunnar 294
Mauss, M. 249, 252, 255, 262
McConnell, John J. 164
McFetridge, D. G. 64
McGuire, Donald J. 36
McMann, P. J. 125
Meckling, William 290, 294
Mello, Antonio S. 33
Messerschmidt, D. 264
Meyer, K. E. E. 65
Michie, J. 271
Minton, John W. 161, 206
Mirza, Hafiz 17
Mitchell, F. 128, 139
Monden, Y. 125, 128
Morgan, G. 125
Morgan, M. J. 157

Nanni, A. J. 125
Narayan, K. 264
Narula, Rajneesh 45–6, 47, 48–9, 52, 53, 55, 158
Needham, R. 237, 238, 254
Nelson, Richard 32
Ng, J. 128
Nitsch, Deklev 65
Nonaka, Ikujiro 294

Osborn, Richard N. 158
Otterbeck, L. 204
Overing, J. 238

Pantzalis, Christos 31
Park, Young-Ryeoul 65
Parkhe, Arvind 193
Parkin, D. 238, 249
Parsons, John E. 33
Pass, Chris L. 20, 97, 104, 161
Pearce, Robert D. 19, 23, 64, 119
Pennings, Johannes M. 66, 161, 206
Penrose, Edith 63
Pentelow, L. 124–5
Pindyck, Robert S. 33
Pliska, Stanley R. 33
Porter, Michael E. 14–15, 26, 36, 209
Prahalad, C. K. 63

Prescottt, Kate 20, 97, 104, 161
Prevezer, Martha 298

Radcliffe-Brown, A. R. 236, 254
Radner, Roy 34
Rafii, F. 204
Ramanujam, Vasudevan 161, 206
Ramaswani, Srindhar N. 64
Ramsay, Harvie 97
Rangan, U. Srinivasan 160
Reason, D. 249
Reich, Robert B. 23
Richardson, George B. 32, 292
Riley, John G. 33
Rivoli, Pietra 34
Roberts, Brian R. 95
Root, Franklin R. 63
Rugman, Alan M. 26, 63, 97

Sakano, T. 211
Sako, M. 271
Sakurai, A. 125, 127
Salgado de Matos, Luís 47, 52, 56
Salorio, Eugene 34
Saussure, F. de 247, 265
Scapens, R. W. 273
Schaan, Jean-Louis 162, 164, 204, 205, 207
Schor, Juliet B. 11
Shane, Scott 66
Simon, H. 254
Singh, Harbir 65, 66
Singh, Satwinder 19, 23
Smith, Adam 299–300
Smith, P. 241
Sparkes, John R. 132, 134
Stopford, John M. 64, 164, 206
Streeten, Paul 14
Svensson, Roger 65

Tanaka, M. 142
Taveira, Eliza Ferreira 47, 52, 56
Teece, David J. 158, 290, 291
Thurow, Lester C. 21
Tirole, Jean 63
Tolentino, Paz Estrella E. 45, 46, 48
Tomlinson, James W. C. 164, 206
Triantis, Alexander J. 33
Trier, J. 261, 265
Trigeorgis, Lenos 27, 34

Ullman, S. 261, 265

Vahlne, Jan-Erik 35, 64
Van der Ploeg, Frederick 30
Varadarajan, N. 161
Venkatraman, N. 161, 164, 206
Verbeke, Alain 26
Vernon, Raymond 61, 63

Weerakoon, P. S. H. 125
Weitz, B. 173
Wells, Louis T. 64, 164, 206
Westney, D. E. 241
Wiedersheim-Paul, Finn 64, 97, 145, 160
Williamson, Oliver 252, 253, 254, 255, 258, 259, 265, 287, 290, 291, 292, 300
Wilson, Brent 65
Winter, Sydney G. 32
Woodcock, Charles Patrick 65, 164
Wu, Shi-yen 32

Yan, A. 203, 204, 206, 209–10, 212, 213, 226, 228, 229
Yan, Y. 203
Yip, George 65
Yoshikawa, T. 128, 139
Yoshimoto, Masoru 147
Yoshino, Michael 160
Young, Stephen 10, 63
Yu, Chow-Ming 66

Zander, Udo 35, 64
Zejan, Mario C. 65
Zeldin, T. 264

# Subject Index

*Note*: references in **bold** refer to tabular and/or illustrative material.


*Accountancy Age* 124, 125
Africa 17–18
alliances, international
  definitions of 95, 159
  as flexible form of organization 158
  measurement of performance in 161–3, 170–2; assessment of actual 171; cultural differences in 172–3; data analysis for 173; parent's level of satisfaction with 171; results on 174–91; subjective measures of 171
  organizational modes of 158–63, 193–6, **194–5**
  performance of: empirical research on 163–8; national culture and 166, 167, 183–91, **184–5**, **186**, **188**, **190**, 172–3; objective and subjective measures of 165, 176–80, **178–9**, 191; subjective measures and mode of alliance 165–6, 180–1, **181**; subjective measures and termination 166–7, 181–3, **182**; summary and conclusions on 191–7, **194–5**
  performance measures for, in UK 157–97
  research hypotheses for 161–3
  research methods in measurement of performance of 168–73; data collection method 168–70
  technological volatility and types of 158
  termination of 165
analysis of MNEs
  new techniques of 33–6
  *see also* models
Asia
  motor vehicle manufacturers from, in UK 24
  productivity growth in 12
  South-East 16, 33
Atlantic foreign direct investment 94–120
  alliances in 97
  cultural similarity of flows in 97
  empirical analysis of 98–116
  FDI theory and 97–8
  integration among participants in 97
  intra-industry flow in 97
  levels of economic development in 97
  resource endowments of participants in 97
  *see also* Canada; foreign direct investment: theory; United Kingdom; United States
Austria **110**

Banco de Portugal 47–8, **48**, **53**, 54, 56
banking industry, US outward FDI into 104, **105**, 106, **112**, **113**
Belgium **100**
brand names acquisition in FDI 96
Bretton Woods agreement 19
bribery 258
Britain *see* United Kingdom

business
  education in 23
  links with universities 23
business networks 11, 26
business people in public life 23

Cadbury Committee (UK) 297
Canada 97, 98
  EJVs in 160
  inward FDI from Europe 109, **110**, **111**, **112**, **114**
  outward FDI to Europe 98–100, **99**, 100–4, **102–3**
  statistical service of **99**, **110**
categories *see* classificatory analysis; native categories; vernacular categories
Central Europe 10, 54, 62
change
  corporate response to 15
  forecasting 27
  recognizing 28
chemicals industry
  FDI into **102**, 104, **112**, **113**, 115, 116, 117
  US outward FDI into 104, **105**, 106
China 62, 88, 210
choice under uncertainty, theories of 33
classificatory analysis 262–3
Cold War 17
collective bargaining 17
communications industry, FDI into 101, **103**
communist system *see* Soviet bloc
communitarians 30
company
  culture 272
  and native categories 259
comparative advantage 20
  loss by West of 22
  nation-specific 21–2
competition, cost of 83
competitive advantage 10
  firm-specific 21–2; and flexibility 31–2
competitive individualism 23
competitiveness
  GNP as indicator of 46
  national 20–4
  restoring 22
  of the West 12
  *see also* comparative advantage
construction industry, FDI into 101, **102**
consumer demand 16
consumer goods industry, FDI into 101, **102**
containerization 33
contract as a framework 254
control, corporate, definition of 94–5
cooperative strategies in R&D, management of (research project) 269–87; capacity to change and 276; costing and 272–5; definitions of cooperation 271; joint venture in 271; meaning of cooperation 271–2; research methods 270; types of strategy 270–1; *see also* costs; pharmaceutical industry
corporate culture 11
'corporate economy' (Marris) 17
corruption 18
costs
  adjustment 39
  comparability of 273
  different, for different purposes 273
  exit, from foreign market 37
  fall in 11
  information on, counter-productive to decision-making 274–5
  in-house, and external prices 274–6
  subjectivity of 273
  suppliers', controlling 128
  target 128
  variation over time of 274
cost tables in FCA 139–40
cross-border governance in MNEs 289–301
  coordination problems in 293

costs of 290–1
cultural dimension of 297–8
governance definitions 289–90
governance structures 292
and internal transaction costs 292–5
in international business theory 295–7
maturation problem in 293
motivation problem in 293
organizational responses to 300–1
vertical integration and 291
*see also* multinational enterprises
cultural categories, relativity of 251–2
cultural engineering 36
cultural homogeneity 36, 118
cultural specificity of anomalies 259
customs unions 33

de-industrialization 20
Denmark **110**
development level 44
distribution networks acquisition in FDI 96
domestic market, protection of 17

Eastern Europe 10, 54, 62, 88
economic functions analysis 139–47
economies of scale 17, 25, 68, 86
EEC *see* European Economic Community
efficiency 256
EFTA *see* European Free Trade Agreement
electrical and electronics industry
FDI into 101, **102**
US outward FDI into 104, **105**, 106
energy industry, FDI into **102**, 104
entrepreneurship 11, 23
managerial 28
equilibrium (Buckley and Casson) 15
equity joint ventures (EJVs) 158–60, 162, 164
EU *see* European Union
Europe 168
FDI into North America 109–14, **110**, **111**, 115–16
European Economic Community (EEC) 16, 24, 55
European Free Trade Agreement (EFTA) 16, 55
European Union (EU) 53, 97, 106, 160, 168
Arbitration Convention 124
definition of 100
exchange controls 124
exchange rate
fluctuations in 19
risk 126
shocks and locational flexibility 30
expert systems 14

FDI *see* foreign direct investment
finance and insurance industry
FDI into 101, **103**
US outward FDI into 104, **105**, 106, **112**, **113**, 115, 116, 117
*Financial Times* 168, 169, 214
firm
boundaries of 10, 290
fuzzy boundaries to 20
'network' 20
as portfolio of contracts 290
scope of firm 290–1
'virtual' 20
flexibility
corporate 10, 11, 18–20; definition of 11, 27
costs of 29–30
of firm and location, interaction of 30–1
and firm-specific competitive advantage 31–2
in foreign market entry 39
and privatization 23
in production 31
in R&D 26–7
and transaction costs 29
of working hours 22

food, beverages and tobacco industry
FDI into 101, **102**, **112**, **113**, 115
US outward FDI into 104, **105**
foreign affiliate 119
foreign direct investment
acquisition in 96
into Central and Eastern Europe 10
cost-oriented 96, 146, 148
definition of 94, 119
flexibility in terms of market growth 37
foreign joint ventures 95
and foreign portfolio investment 94
greenfield entry into 96
as high-risk strategy 37
information capture in 37
input-oriented 96
internalizing approach to 61, 144–5
and international strategic alliances 95
in Japan 144–53
joint ventures in 96
and location theory 145, 146
market-oriented 96, 146, 148
and MNEs 95
motives for 146
net stock of 44, 49
ownership strategy in 96
portfolio, definition of 119
resource-seeking 146, 148
stock statistics for 98
theory of 94–6
*see also* Atlantic; Japan; Portugal
foreign joint ventures *see* international joint ventures
foreign market entry
adaptation costs in 73, 78, 83–6, **84**, **85**, 86
cultural factors in 66
distribution in 62, 67, 69, 71, 74, **74**, **75**, 82, 83, 87
economies of scale in 68, 86
internal information flow in 68
internalization in 63–4, 86
joint ventures versus wholly-owned subsidiaries in 65–6, 89
learning costs in 73, 86, 87
location effects in 86
marketing activity in 68
market structure and entry strategy in 66, 87
mergers and acquisitions versus greenfield ventures in 64–5, 70, 74, **74**, **75**, 78, 87
model of 67–86; assumptions for 67–73; defining strategy set for 73–6; deriving profit equations for 77–9, **78**; dominance relations in 79–82; flexibility of 88; propensity to adopt given strategy in 83–6, **84**, **85**; properties of solution to 82–3; results discussion 86–8; implications for future research of 88–9
model assumptions for: the entrant 67–70; host country rival 70–2; international joint ventures 72–3
non-production activities in 64
ownership in 74, **74**, **75**
political risk in 88
production in 62, 67, 70–2, 74, **74**, **75**, 82, 83–6, **84**, **85**
profitability in 73, 77, 83–6, **84**, **85**
research and development in 68
stages models of entry in 64
strategies for 73–6, **74**, **75–6**
subcontracting in 87
tariffs in 68, 86
tax incentives in 88
technology: licensing in 83–6, **84**, **85**; transfer in 68, 69, 87
theory of 61–89; historical development of 63–7
transaction costs in 69, 70, 78, 83–6, **84**, **85**, 86

transport costs in 68, 86
trust-building costs in 73, 83–6, **84**, **85**, 86, 87
foreign portfolio investment 94
frameworks, definition of 14
*see also* models
France 97, 100, 106, **107–8**
outward FDI into Canada and US 109, **110**, **113**, 114, **114**, 117
pharmaceutical companies in 270
friendship and economic dealing 258
functional cost analysis (FCA) 139

games, theory of non-cooperative 36
GATT *see* General Agreement on Trade and Tariffs
General Agreement on Trade and Tariffs (GATT) 16
Germany 100, 106, **107–8**
outward FDI into Canada and US 109, **110**, **113**, 114, **114**, 117
globalization
IJVs in 62
of markets 38
mergers and acquisitions in 62
'golden age' 13
end of 16–18
government policy, *laissez faire* 31
'Great Society' 17
Greece **110**
greenfield investment 87
by MNEs 146
Gross Domestic Product 48, 49

Hong Kong 21
Hymer–Kindleberger theory of FDI 61
hypothetico-deductive paradigm in management research 242–3

industrialization *see* pre industrialization
inflation of wages 17
information
capture of 37, 38
collection of 27
cost of, and adjustment cost 28
efficient search for 33–4
sharing of, within organization 36
for strategic decision-making 28
information processing 10
information technology (IT) 28
infrastructure 17, 45
insurance industry, US FDI into **112**, **113**, 115, 116, 117
insurance, national 22
interest rate 83
intermediate inputs 17
internalization 37
approach to FDI 61, 144–5
theory of 95–6
international alliances *see* alliances, international
international business environment, volatility in 10
internationalization effects
in foreign market entry 86
Scandinavian model of 35
international joint ventures (IJVs) 13
conflict potential in 205–6
control/conflict in 202
definitions of 201–2
and FDI 95
flexibility of 37–8
globalization 62
growth of 15
incidence of 202
information capture in 38
management control of: centralization of 204–5; definition of 203; dimensions of 204; and duration of IJV 213, 214, 219, **222**, 223–6, **224–5**, **227**; literature review 203–5; mechanism of 221–3, **222**; parent control in 203, 211–13; and performance 204; purpose of 203; voting in 204

international joint ventures (IJVs) – *continued*
management–performance relationships in UK 201–30; control variables in 215–18, **217**, 223, **224–5**, **227**; data analysis for 219; model of, 208, **208**; performance measures for **217**, 218–19; questionnaire design 214; research methods and sample characteristics 213–15; results and discussion of analysis 220–1, **220**; summary and conclusions 228–9
motives for formation of 202
partner selection in 202
performance, literature review 205–8
performance measures of 206; hypotheses on 208–13; objective and subjective 207–12
stability/performance in 202
trust in 38
and wholly owned investment 38
International Monetary Fund (IMF) 119
investment
inward direct 45; *see also* foreign direct investment
resource-seeking 15–16
infrastructure 17
irreversibility of 34
outward direct investment 45–6; *see also* foreign direct investment
and volatile environment 34–5
investment development path (IDP) 44–55
conclusions on testing of 55
five stages of development (Dunning) in 45
as prediction mechanism 55
*see also* Portugal
investment position, international (net FDI stock) 44
Ireland
inflow of FDI from Canada into 100
outflow of FDI to Canada and US from **110**
Italy, outflow of FDI to Canada and US from **110**, **114**

Japan 16, 21, 106, 123–41, 168, 213, 276
business success of 125
commitment to, by foreign investors 149
competition in 150–1
consumer goods market access in 148
control of partner in 150
EJVs in 160
as FDI host 149–52
foreign direct investment in 144–53; barriers to 151, 152–3; internalization factors in 147–9; by mergers and acquisitions 149
hypothetical group of companies for transfer pricing analysis 129–39, **130**, **138**; cross-holding of shares in **130**, 133; finance company in 136; loan for expansion in 136–9, **138**
internalization factors in FDI in 147–9
joint ventures in 149–50
keiretsu structures in 148, 297
longtermism in 151
markets sought in 148
MNEs in, as one entity 128–9
multinationals in 123–4
process issues in FDI in 151–2
product servicing and aftercare in 150–1
'psychic distance' between investors and 148–9
subsidiaries and profit in 129
tariff barriers in 149

tax advantages in 124
transfer pricing paradigm of 123
trust in 256–7
vertical purchasing structure in 150
*see also* transfer pricing

Japanese Value Engineering, Society of 139

joint ventures (JVs) 11, 16, 24–7, 83, 271–2
in distribution 87
in inter-firm collusion 271–2
by MNEs 146
mutual forbearance within 257
*see also* international joint ventures

Korea, Republic of 21, 106

labour force
from agriculture to industry 21
female 16
from manufacturing to services 21
temporary 22
versatile 31

labour market flexibility 21
internal 24
restoration through legislation 22

'language shadows' (Ardener) 248

Latin America 17

leadership, charismatic 32

learning costs 86, 87

'learning organization' 32

licensing agreements 16, 37, 86

Lille 31

location
advantages of 45, 86; *see also* Portugal
flexibility of 30
theory of 96, 145–6

Luxembourg **110**

machinery and equipment industry
FDI into 101, **102**, **112**, **113**
US outward FDI into 104, **105**, 106

management
buyout by 26
competence of 11, 32
consultative 32
entrepreneurship 29
equity in business activities 29–30
horizontal communication in 28–9
retraining of 32
strategic 14

management studies
cultural homogeneity in 242–3
managers' formulation of own problems in 243
native categories in 239
objectivity of 239–44
*see also* native categories; social psychology

manufacturing industries
FDI into 101, **102**, **112**, **113**, 115
flexibility in 24
high-technology, predominance of US MNEs in 13
MNEs in 104
US outward FDI into 104, **105**

market entry, modelling of 36–40

market volatility 11, 38

markets and hierarchies 291–2

mass production 16, 17

matrix approach to management 301

Medicine Control Inspectorate (UK) 277, 278

mergers and acquisitions
in foreign market entry 87
in globalization 62
in MNEs 146

metallic minerals industry, FDI into 101, **102**

metals industry, US outward FDI into 104, **105**, 106, **112**, **113**

Mexico 97, 110–14, **114**

military expenditure 17

mining industry, FDI into **112**, **113**, 115

MNE *see* multinational enterprise

models, economic
  nature of 13–14
  versus frameworks 12–16
money, flow of 256
monopoly power 19, 87
  within MNEs 19, 25
moral values 30, 36
multinational enterprise (MNE)
  control in 145
  decentralization of R&D within 23
  definition of 95–6
  federal structure of 19
  governance structures in 289
  growth of, as path-dependent process 35
  internalization in 145
  models of 9–40
  ownership and control in 289
  and pricing control over intermediate products 145
  reasons for existence of 144–5
  strategy of 147
  in utilities 23
  *see also* cross-border governance in MNEs; firm; internalization; Japan

NAFTA *see* North Atlantic Free Trade Association
nation state and regional government 19
native categories in management research 235–66
  in action and understanding 247
  authors' research: background of subjects and researchers 249–50; unstructured interviews 250
  company and 259–63
  context for 247
  core business and 263
  economics analytical categories 236
  fieldwork and 248
  invalidating positivism 251
  literature review 235–9
  and management of cooperative strategies 249–63
  measurement and definition of 248–9
  and objectivity 245
  in positivist research 250–1
  study of 246–9
  the transaction and 252–9
  *see also* management studies; social anthropology; transaction
Netherlands 106, **107–8**
  FDI inflow from US 100
  outward FDI into Canada and US 109, **110**, **113**, 114, **114**, 117
newly industrializing countries (NICs) 16–17
NICs *see* newly industrializing countries
Nolan Committee (UK) 298
non-equity alliances (NEAs) 158–9, 163
North Atlantic Free Trade Association (NAFTA) 97
Norway **110**

objectivity
  in management studies 239–44
  and native categories 245
  observer-defined ethnocentric 245
  and reality definition 244–6
  in social anthropology 244–5
  and subjectivity opposition 246
  *see also* management studies; native categories; social anthropology
OECD *see* Organization for Economic Cooperation and Development
oil price shock (1973–74) 11, 16
optimization (Buckley and Casson) 15
organization, science of 254–5
Organization for Economic Cooperation and Development (OECD) 119, 124, 127, 134, 136

overheads 134–5
ownership advantages 45–6

patent protection 17
petroleum industry
FDI into **112**, **113**, 115
US outward FDI into 104, **105**, **107**
pharmaceutical industry, cooperative R&D in 269–87
customer relations in 282–3
development with subcontractor in 283–4
innovation in contract manufacturing in 276–9
joint product development in 279–82; advantages of 281; trust and interpersonal skills in 280
lessons for public sector and business sector 285–6
licensing of 284
specialization and complexity in 277
supply agreements in 278
takeover danger in co-working with other companies 279
types of production in 277
versus in-house R&D 284–5
vertical integration in 277
Portugal
comments on estimation of IDP for 52–4, **53**
conclusions on testing of IDP in 54–5
data for testing of IDP in 47–8
EEC membership of 53
estimation of IDP of 50–1, **50**, **51**
FDI flows in 47, 52, **53**
function for test of IDP in 48–9
investment development path (IDP) in 44–55
investment in Central and Eastern Europe 54
inward direct investment into 53, 54
location advantages in 49
outward investment from 53, **110**
testing IDP in 46–55, **48**, **50**, **51**, **53**
pre-industrialization 45
prices
alignment of internal and external 25–6
arm's length 127, 129, 132
'limit' 72
privatization
of heavy industries 23
of public transport 23
of utilities 23
probability theory 33
product cycle theory (Vernon) of FDI 61, 63
product innovation, profits from 23
production
flexibility in 31
location of 10
*see also* mass production
products, intermediate 26
profit
maximization hypothesis 13
measurement 25–6
protectionist policies 18
public sector and business sector, distinction between 285–6

R&D *see* research and development
recruitment, skill in 31–2
regional government 19
regional hub and IJV 38–9
research, collaborative 17
research and development
cooperative management in (research project) 269–287; *see also* cooperative strategies
cost of 27, 135
decentralization of, in MNEs 23
in foreign market entry 68
research facilities 19
acquisition in FDI 96
'reverse engineering' 17

SEM *see* Single European Market
services sector
  Canadian FDI into 101, **104**
  MNEs in 104
  strength of Western economies in 20
  US outward FDI into 104, **105**, **112**, **113**
shocks 19
  exogenous and endogenous 33
  *see also* oil shocks
Singapore 31
Single European Market (SEM) 97, 168
social anthropology 260–1
  'atmosphere' (Williamson) in 253
  categories of 236–9
  kinship systems of 237
  native categories in 238, 263
  and non-linguistic aspects of action 247
  as objective science 236–7
  and reality definition 244–6
  science of society within 254
  taboo in 247
  *see also* management studies; native categories; social psychology; transaction
social mobility 16
social psychology 240–1
  cross-cultural studies in 241
Soviet bloc, demise of 19, 33
Spain 97, 110
subcontracting 22, 25, 30, 87
supplier networks 31
supply responsiveness 11
Sweden **110**, **114**
switching costs 37
Switzerland 100, 106, **107–8**
  outward FDI into Canada and US 109, **110**, **113**, 114, **114**, 117

takeovers *see* mergers and acquisitions
tariffs 86
tax
  avoidance 126
  base 124
  on profits, calculation of 127
  reduction of rates of 23, 124
technological convergence 27
technology transfer 16, 17, 18, 68, 86
Thailand 33
tourism 20
trade barriers 124
  *see also* tariffs
trade liberalization 16
trades unions 17, 22
training 68
transaction
  commitment in 253
  cooperative dealings within 253
  economist's view of 255–6
  and native categories 252–9
  repeated, importance of 287
  *see also* contracts
transaction cost economics
  positivist 264
  and social anthropology 269–70
transaction costs 69, 70, 86, 253–4, 256
  and boundaries of firm 259
  explanation for existence of firms 259–60
  internal, and governance 292–4
  as perceptual matters 260–1
  theory of *see* internalization
transfer payments to the poor 17
transfer pricing
  current context 127–39
  development costs in 135
  and economic functions analysis 123–41
  overheads allocation in 134–5
  for profit manipulation 125–6
  research and development costs in 135
  transaction-based calculation of 127–9, 133, 141
  *see also* Japan
transport 17
  costs of 31, 68, 86

transportation equipment industry
FDI into 101, **102**
US outward FDI into 104, **105**, 106
trust 25, 29–30, 296
in acquisitions 70
in foreign market entry 73, 86, 87
in IJV 38
and opportunism 257
in supplier networks 31
universality of 256

uncertainty 11
and information-gathering 33
unemployment benefit 22
United Kingdom 24, 97, 100, 106, **107–8**
cultural affinities with Canada and US in AFDI 100
cultural differences
inflow of Canadian and US FDI 99–100, **107–8**
Inland Revenue of 125
outward FDI into Canada and US 109, **110**, **111**, **113**, **114**, 116, 117
pharmaceutical companies in 270
Social Chapter opt-out 100
tax administration of 125
tax rates in 124
trust in 256
*see also* alliances
United States 97, 98, 168, 210, 213
Department of Commerce **99**, **110**
Food and Drugs Administration (FDA) 277
inward FDI from Europe 109, **110**, **112**, **113**, 115–17
outward FDI into Europe 89–100, **99**, 104–9, **105**, **107–8**

vernacular categories 258
vertical integration, flexibility discouraging 24–5
Vietnam 62
volatility, market
in foreign market entry 39
and globalization of markets 38
and investment 34–5
modelling of 33
reasons for 18–19
timing of decisions in 34

wages
inflation of 17
minimum 22
welfare state 17
Western Europe 213
wholesale industry, US outward FDI into 104, **105**, 106, **112**, **113**
women 16
wood and paper industry, FDI into 101, **102**